DATE DUE

MAR 30 1992		
NOV 11 1992		
MAY 10 1994		
MAY 12 1994		
FEB 13 1996		
DEC 12 1996		
MAR 24 1999		
NOV 19 1999		
FEB 09 2000		
NOV 15 2002		
OCT 24 2008		

DEMCO 38-297

AIDS
in the
Workplace

———

AIDS
in the
Workplace

Legal Questions and
Practical Answers

William F. Banta

Kullman, Inman, Bee & Downing
New Orleans

Lexington Books

D.C. Heath and Company/Lexington, Massachusetts/Toronto

Library of Congress Cataloging-in-Publication Data

Banta, William F.
AIDS in the workplace.

Includes index.
1. Industrial hygiene—Law and legislation—United States. 2. Labor laws
and legislation—United States. 3. AIDS (Disease)—Law and legislation—
United States. I. Title.
KF3570.B36 1987   344.73′0321969792   86–46309
                     347.304321969792
        ISBN 0–669–15334–6 (alk. paper)

Published simultaneously in Canada
Printed in the United States of America
Casebound International Standard Book Number: 0–669–15334–6
Library of Congress Catalog Card Number: 86–46309

The paper used in this publication meets the minimum requirements of
American National Standard for Information Sciences—Permanence
of Paper for Printed Library Materials, ANSI Z39.48–1984.
⊗™

88 89 90 91 92 8 7 6 5 4 3 2

Everybody knows that pestilences have a way of recurring in the world; yet somehow we find it hard to believe in ones that crash down on our heads from a blue sky.

—Albert Camus, *The Plague*

In terms of impact on our society, this disease will certainly be the most important public-health problem of the next decade and going into the next century. On an international scale, it threatens to undermine countries, particularly in Africa.

—Dr. David Baltimore, microbiologist who was awarded a Nobel prize in 1975 for his work on viruses

The future is a race between "the likelihood of a successful medical solution [to AIDS], like a vaccine or a cure, and the political demands that will inevitably lead to the disruption of our free society."

—Neil R. Schram, M.D., Chairman of Los Angeles AIDS Task Force

It's a tremendous victory. . . . My only regret is that the employer got off too easy—they robbed him of two years of his life.

—Attorney for AIDS victim Todd Shuttleworth, commenting on settlement of lawsuit that cost the employer $196,000 and reinstated Mr. Shuttleworth to his former job

Contents

Acknowledgments

I wish to express my appreciation to Dr. Larry Cortez, associate head of the infectious disease department at Ochsner Clinic and epidemiologist for Ochsner Hospital, Elmer E. White, management attorney with Kullman, Inman, Bee & Downing in New Orleans, and Dabney Jacob, teacher, entrepreneur, and mother, for their efforts in reading the manuscript and providing me with valuable suggestions and contributions; to Ruth Neely, my efficient and skilled secretary, and Larisa Banta, my less skilled but lovely daughter, for typing the manuscript; and to Robert D. Bovenschulte, General Manager of Lexington Books, for his encouragement on this project.

Introduction

M y desk had almost been cleared of work late one afternoon when I received a telephone call from the corporate personnel manager of a restaurant that was a client of our law firm. A nineteen-year-old waiter with an absenteeism rate of 24 percent for the year had failed to report or call in for five consecutive days. However, he had appeared at the restaurant that morning armed with two letters. The manager, who had previously decided to terminate Charlie (not his real name) for absenteeism, read the letters. The first, signed by a doctor, stated that Charlie had the HIV virus and had been ill with various maladies during the previous three months, but that he did not have AIDS, he was physically fit to perform all the duties connected with his waiter's position, and he should be immediately reinstated. The second letter, from Charlie's attorney, warned that if Charlie were not immediately reinstated as a waiter, both the manager and his company would be sued.

The manager, bewildered and uncertain, sent Charlie home with the promise that he would be notified of a response within twenty-four hours. The manager then called the district manager, who expressed concern about fewer customers and declining revenues if the public learned an employee of the restaurant had AIDS, and suggested that they immediately fire Charlie.

The regional manager agreed that termination was in order, but emphasized that "the legal reason" was excessive absenteeism, not AIDS. Upon hearing the report, the executive vice president immediately called the corporate personnel manager who, in turn, called me, expressing compassion for a young man with a fatal condition. At 9:00 A.M. the next day all of the managers and I gathered around a conference table, read the letters from Charlie's doctor and lawyer, studied corporate personnel policies and the employee handbook, and listened to the manager describe a late-breaking development. Five employees had signed a petition the previous evening stating that they understood Charlie had AIDS and threatening not to work if Charlie were reinstated at the restaurant!

There were no easy answers, and the meeting was long. That afternoon, Charlie was told that his request for reinstatement was being granted, but that he was being assigned to cleanup and maintenance chores instead of his former waiter position, with a salary equivalent to his average compensation as a waiter and, of course, the same benefits. Charlie protested, threatened to call his lawyer, and complained to the district and regional managers, but, in the end, he accepted the assignment. Several employees voiced concern about his presence in the facility, but "educational talks" with them by the manager calmed the situation and prevented a walkout.

After five days of working as scheduled, Charlie missed the next ten days of work. A caller, who identified himself as Charlie's roommate, said he had pneumonia. Charlie returned with another letter from his doctor describing him as fit for reinstatement to his former position as waiter, and he loudly complained when he was told that the only position the company had for him was in cleanup and maintenance. He reluctantly accepted the assignment once again, but another absence occurred three days later. The roommate called the next morning with the sad explanation: Charlie was dead. No legal claim was ever filed against the restaurant by Charlie or his estate. The company's group health plan covered 90 percent of all medical bills, and its life insurance policy paid $10,000 to Charlie's parents.

This story of an actual situation presents, in a capsule, many of the legal issues, practical concerns, individual attitudes, and real-life tragedy of AIDS in the workplace. It raises a number of difficult questions on how an employer should proceed. Would it have been illegal to terminate Charlie? Does it make a difference that the manager had decided to discharge him for absenteeism before he knew that Charlie had the HIV virus? What if Charlie had cut his hand while working in the kitchen and his blood had dropped onto food later consumed by a customer? Could the customer contract AIDS? Is there any way that a customer or another employee could contract AIDS from Charlie on restaurant property, short of engaging in sexual activity or sharing a contaminated needle? What legal defenses would the restaurant have if a customer or an employee contracted AIDS or the virus and claimed that Charlie had infected them? May an employer take into account the possible spread of AIDS (real or perceived) or the anticipated loss of business if it were to continue an employee with the HIV virus on its payroll? Should an employee like Charlie be transferred to a job that does not include the handling of food? Could he be placed on leave of absence? Should the leave of absence be paid or unpaid? Does it matter that he has the HIV virus, according to his doctor, but not AIDS? Could the company insist upon an examination of Charlie by its own doctor? Should the company test Charlie and perhaps other employees for AIDS? Could the company terminate or transfer any employee who tested positive? Should the company discipline the employees who signed the petition registering their refusal to work with Charlie? What if the employees had carried out their threat not to work? Could they be fired or replaced?

Questions of what to do about employees with AIDS-related conditions are complicated by the many variables. For example, an employee may test positive for HIV antibodies but be quite healthy—as capable of performing job duties as ever—and never develop AIDS. Some people exposed to the virus have developed AIDS within two years while the hiatus for others has been six or seven. A recent study suggests persons infected with HIV have a higher probability of contracting AIDS in the *second* five years after exposure. An employee who tests positive for HIV antibodies or definitely has AIDS may be less infectious than an employee who has recently contracted the virus but has not yet developed antibodies. Regardless of whether or not, or when, the person has an active case of AIDS, the capacity of that person to infect others is indefinite or lifelong. Also, an employee may develop ARC (AIDS-related complex), which may or may not affect his or her ability to perform work, but never develop AIDS. Finally, it is impossible to categorize all employees who have AIDS. There are vastly different conditions, diseases, and stages which vary from patient to patient. In an early stage, which could consume two or three years, the AIDS victim might be physically capable of performing all the duties of his job, while in the late stages the employee could be entirely incapacitated for a long period of time. Between the early and late stages there are months and even years of widely fluctuating degrees of ability to perform work. Approximately 40 percent of AIDS patients suffer deterioration of mental faculties at some point, occasionally this deterioration is soon and severe. Others remain as mentally alert as ever through the final stage. Thus, there is no single answer or set of answers to the questions involving what to do with an applicant or an employee with an AIDS condition.

Managers desiring to approach AIDS-related questions in the workplace with sound judgment, sensitivity, and legal precedent are frequently confused by conflicting opinions and uncertain of what decisions to make. AIDS involves many different disciplines—medicine, law, business, psychology, and sociology—and it is a subject about which almost everyone talks much but knows little.

During the last two years, AIDS has become of paramount interest to the American public. This response is due to the serious concern about a fatal syndrome that is spreading at an alarming rate, the lack of a cure, and a continuous barrage of stories in the media. Headlines from various periodicals scream "No One Is Safe from AIDS" *(Life)*, "A Chicago Family Feud over AIDS" *(Newsweek)*, "AIDS: Is Anyone Safe?" *(Readers Digest)*, and "Tragic Tots Born to Die of AIDS" *(New York Post)*. Realizing that AIDS has all the ingredients of a long-running soap opera—sex, drugs, hysteria, and death—supermarket newspapers repeatedly exploit the topic. Medical journals frequently feature articles on AIDS, many of them contradictory and critical of each other. The June 1986 issue of the *American Bar Association* contains a lengthy article on the subject, with a photo of Rock Hudson on the cover. The August 11, 1986, issue of *New York Magazine* had a cover story on "The Death and Life of Perry Ellis," a famous fashion designer who died of complications related to AIDS. *Vanity Fair*'s March 1987 issue showed photographs of various artists, designers, actors, and entertainers who have died of AIDS in a story entitled "One by One." Personnel periodicals debate appropriate management responses.

While the vast majority of AIDS victims in the United States have been homosexuals, bisexuals, or intravenous drug users, approximately 2 percent of AIDS victims have contracted the disease from infected blood. High-risk groups are always excluded from the donor pool, but nevertheless bisexuals or homosexuals who prevaricate have passed contaminated blood into the banks. While this has been very rare since 1985 when the practice of testing all donated blood for HIV was adopted, in at least one recent case, a hospital patient was infected with the AIDS virus from blood that had been previously tested but showed no signs of the disease because the donor had given blood soon after a sexual encounter: he had not yet developed the antibodies that should have showed up in the test. Further, a 1986 study in Haiti revealed that 72 percent of AIDS cases were developed by heterosexuals who report that they had neither used contaminated needles nor engaged in homosexual activities. The U.S. Surgeon General has predicted that heterosexuals will account for an increasing percentage of future AIDS cases.

Thus, AIDS is affecting more and more people in the United States. By the beginning of 1987, the syndrome had struck approximately 30,000 people in the United States, with over 15,000 already dead and the remainder terminally ill. Table 1 breaks down

Table 1
Dramatic Increases in AIDS Cases in the United States

State	Total	1986	Percent
Alabama	66	30	45.4
Alaska	20	14	70.0
Arizona	160	83	51.9
Arkansas	40	32	80.0
California	6,226	2,825	45.3
Colorado	273	163	59.8
Connecticut	337	178	52.9
Delaware	38	22	57.9
D.C.	511	242	47.3
Florida	1,860	865	46.6
Georgia	552	302	54.8
Hawaii	97	60	61.9
Idaho[1]	N.A.	N.A.	N.A.
Illinois	682	372	54.6
Indiana	114	60	52.7

Iowa	34	21	61.8
Kansas	48	34	70.9
Kentucky	59	30	50.9
Louisiana	314	160	51.0
Maine	31	20	64.6
Maryland	396	187	47.2
Massachusetts	559	284	50.9
Michigan	223	124	55.7
Minnesota	142	90	63.3
Mississippi	33	22	66.7
Missouri	157	82	52.2
Montana[1]	N.A.	N.A.	N.A.
Nebraska	21	14	66.7
Nevada	60	38	63.3
New Hampshire	23	14	60.9
New Jersey	1,592	709	44.6
New Mexico	40	24	60.0
New York	8,823	3,666	41.6
North Carolina	158	76	48.1
North Dakota[1]	N.A.	N.A.	N.A.
Ohio	247	155	62.8
Oklahoma	75	46	61.3
Oregon	104	56	53.9
Pennsylvania	613	306	50.0
Rhode Island	46	29	63.0
South Carolina	100	55	55.0
South Dakota[1]	N.A.	N.A.	N.A.
Tennessee	94	70	74.4
Texas	1,700	929	54.7
Utah	47	24	51.0
Vermont[1]	N.A.	N.A.	N.A.
Virginia	312	153	49.0
Washington	341	164	48.0
West Virginia	19	7	36.9
Wisconsin	73	39	53.4
Wyoming[1]	N.A.	N.A.	N.A.
Puerto Rico	273	93	34.0

Source: National Centers For Disease Control

N.A. = not available

[1] = not included in report because less than ten cases reported

the distribution of the AIDS cases among the various states and demonstrates the frightening increase in reported cases during 1986. It has been estimated that 2 million Americans are carrying the virus and are potentially infectious. The U.S. Public Health Service projects that over 20 million Americans will have the virus and 2 million will have full-blown AIDS by 1991. In that year, it is predicted that 74,000 people will be identified as having either ARC or AIDS—approximately three times the annual incidence of polio at its peak thirty-five years ago. The most alarming prediction issued thus far was from the World Health Organization: the number of people in the world infected with the AIDS virus by 1990 will be 100 million. U.S. Health and Human Services Secretary Otis Bowen has predicted a worldwide death toll in the tens of millions, absent effective medical vaccines and treatment. Hospital administrators in the United States predict that by the year 2000, 40 percent of their patients will be AIDS victims. With the number of victims dramatically increasing, its spread in the heterosexual community, and no cure in sight, AIDS in the workplace is becoming a major concern to employers, employees, customers, and patients.

Who will pick up the tab? Hospital costs for AIDS victims are estimated at $100,000 per patient. As the number of victims skyrockets, so will the cost. One study projects that the cost for treating AIDS patients will total between $37 and $113 billion between 1986 and 1991. Employers attempting to contain rising insurance premiums may be tempted by insurance salespeople's pitches to exclude AIDS-related illnesses from coverage in return for lower premiums. Hospitals may refuse admission to AIDS victims without insurance. In these situations, increased regulation of insurance company practices by state and local governments will probably be used to achieve social objectives, including the protection of people with AIDS conditions from being discriminatorily deprived of insurance benefits and medical treatment.

Several states and local governments have enacted special statutes to restrict employer discretion in handling AIDS-related matters. The U.S. Department of Justice has issued an opinion on whether AIDS victims are handicapped within the meaning of existing federal laws, but the U.S. Supreme Court arrived at the opposite conclusion. Other courts are certain to issue their opinions on AIDS questions in case after case and appeal after appeal. Unions and arbitrators have already entered the arena. Finally, the National Labor Relations Board will soon be faced with the legality of companies' terminating employees who refuse to work with, treat, or serve people afflicted with AIDS.

This book reviews all the laws potentially applicable to AIDS in the workplace—federal, state, and local—and then analyzes specific AIDS issues in a practical fashion, identifying the pros and cons of alternative approaches and recommending courses of action that are both consistent with legal cases and protective of legitimate business interests. Special treatment is extended to the controversial subject of testing for AIDS. Included in the appendixes are sources for information, medical data, samples of legal pleadings, checklists for preventing and defending AIDS claims, and sample personnel policies and employee handbook provisions.

1
AIDS in
the Workplace:
General Considerations

S ince being identified in 1981, AIDS has presented challenges to doctors, lawyers, business managers, hospitals, ministers, and sociologists, among others. The questions, which cut across the lines of those disciplines, are complex, often interrelated, and largely unanswered. A basic understanding of the medical facts is essential background for solving AIDS-related problems in the workplace.

Medical Facts

The human T cell lymphotropic virus type III (usually written and spoken as HIV or HTLV-III) is the cause of acquired immunodeficiency syndrome (AIDS). Almost all persons infected with HIV manufacture antibodies, and thus far the majority of them have not developed complications. A minority eventually develop AIDS-related complex (ARC) and a smaller minority develop AIDS. It is presently unclear why and how the virus attacks the immune systems of the unfortunate people who develop AIDS, or how it breaks down immune systems and makes them vulnerable to recurring, fatal infections and other diseases. But there is no doubt that this is what happens. The AIDS victim typically has a maximum of five years between contracting the virus and death; the survival period from initial development of infection to death is an average of eleven to fifteen months. While the infections, diseases, and survival periods vary from victim to victim, the eventual result is invariable: death.

AIDS is a syndrome, not a disease. Technically, no one has died of AIDS or ARC, but thousands of people are dying every year from infections or diseases allowed to ravage their bodies unchecked, because their immune systems have been incapacitated by HIV.* This virus has been identified and medically isolated in human blood, semen, feces, bone marrow, lymph nodes, tears, saliva, and urine. There are documented cases of its transmission to other people by sexual contact (usually through anal intercourse, with infected semen breaking into the bloodstream), sharing of contaminated needles with infected blood or blood products being injected or escaping into the bloodstream, and perinatally from mother to infant. Medical experts emphasize that the virus cannot be transmitted through casual contact with an infected person, such as sharing toilets, food, and beverages or shaking hands. However, a few researchers have questioned the studies that led to those conclusions, arguing that the samples were too small and that an insufficient amount of time had expired between contact with the AIDS victim and the conclusion of the study.

It was originally believed that AIDS affected only the body's immune system. However, scientists have recently established that the AIDS virus directly attacks brain and lung cells, resulting in brain degeneration and pneumonia. While this finding is a development toward understanding and curing AIDS, it is also significant because the job performance of a victim with mental impairment could be affected and HIV could cause diseases and serious medical problems in a person who never develops AIDS. This new knowledge that AIDS can infect motor centers and other areas of the brain should have legal implications. Since a significant percentage of the victims have various neurological complications, including dementia (with resulting difficulty in concentrating and a tendency towards being apathetic and psychotic), employers faced with the decision-making process will be sensitive to the medical facts concerning a particular applicant or employee with an AIDS condition.

---

*The two most prevalent opportunistic diseases that develop from the AIDS condition are Kaposi's sarcoma (a form of cancer) and a protozoan infection of the lungs called *pneumocystis carinii* (pneumonia). Doctors refer to them as KS and PCP, and they are extremely rare in people with normal immune systems. Symptoms of AIDS include fatigue, fever and chills, loss of appetite and weight, swollen lymph glands, purple skin blotches or bumps, dry cough, persistent diarrhea, and a coating on the tongue or throat.

Tests are available to determine if a person has developed antibodies to the AIDS virus (referred to herein as either HTLV-III or HIV). If a positive test is confirmed, the individual has been exposed to the virus.* However, this does not mean that he or she has AIDS or ARC. In fact, the probability is high that the individual with a positive test will never develop AIDS or ARC. The Centers for Disease Control reported in an early study that only 10 percent of those with HIV had developed AIDS, and only 30 percent had ARC. More recent studies estimate higher percentages, but the majority of those with the virus are free of the symptoms or conditions of ARC and AIDS thus far.

There are serious problems, however, with the medical studies performed in recent years. As mentioned, medical science did not identify the syndrome until 1981—only a few years ago. Blood tests can identify the antibodies produced by the virus, but not the virus itself. Thus, it is significant that the body does not always produce the antibodies in a short period of time. Frequently there is a hiatus between contracting the virus and the manufacture of the antibodies; in some cases, the lag has been months. So a person who recently developed HIV through sexual contact may be accepted to donate contaminated blood because the test for antibodies was negative. Or a hospital employee, infected with the virus through being stuck by a needle, may continue treating patients with open wounds or preparing intravenous solutions because the test taken immediately after the accident was negative.† Some medical experts believe that the virus antibodies are undetectable for a few weeks, while others opine that people could carry the virus for up to eight months before finally testing positive. For this reason, most hospitals request that employees and patients exposed to HIV be tested at regular intervals for an entire year before concluding that negative test results mean they did not contract the virus.

---

*Most laboratories use the ELISA screening test to measure antibodies to the AIDS virus, but its accuracy has been questioned by the "false positives" established in a recent study (5 percent of the samples showing positive were actually negative when checked with the Western Blot assay test). Obviously, confirmation with the Western Blot test by a professional laboratory is mandatory before the result is communicated or relied upon in any way.

†Studies conducted thus far suggest it is difficult and rare both for a nurse to become infected with HIV through a needle stick and then to transmit the virus to patients and others. Comprehensive studies on these critical issues are continuing.

Once infected with HIV, the person will carry it forever. AIDS, then, is like syphilis—it will never be eradicated. Moreover, people with HIV who eventually develop AIDS are always moving forward to the next stage. They never step back.

Another medical fact is that viruses other than HIV or HTLV-III have been found to cause AIDS. LAV-11 and SBL 6669 V-11 are viruses linked to West African patients with AIDS. Individual diseases can and have been caused by more than one virus; three separate kinds of polio viruses, for example, can cause paralysis. The only virus that has caused AIDS thus far in the United States is HIV or HTLV-III.

The diagnosis and treatment of AIDS is especially difficult for doctors without experience. In response to the scarcity of literature and books and the lightning-like changes in the area, a service called "AIDS Physician Link" was established. It is a nationwide referral and assistance system for both doctors and AIDS patients which includes a computerized registry of physicians who treat persons with AIDS.

While medical science has identified the syndrome and the antibodies produced by the virus that is causing it in the United States, so far there is neither a reliable, utilitarian test that identifies HIV nor a cure for AIDS. The research and studies are continuing, and the death toll is mounting.

Social Considerations

AIDS-related issues have made a significant impact on the world community in a very short period of time. The tragic fact that affliction with AIDS is always fatal generates concern and fear. In the United States, AIDS is the twelfth leading cause of death among males. Obviously, though, these problems are not restricted to the United States. In France, 15 percent of gay men are infected, as well as 51 percent of all drug users. In Italy, the figures are 12 percent of gays and 28 percent of those who use drugs. Sweden has the highest percentage of homosexual males with the virus— 20 percent. The most staggering figure, however, is in the continent of Africa, where 4.2 percent of all people in urban areas of the central republics are infected.* Cases of AIDS have been reported in seventy-eight countries, including the Soviet Union and China.

In the United States, over one-half of the gay men in San Francisco and New York have HIV. The problem, however, is neither strictly male nor homosexual. Almost 7 percent of the total cases reported in the United States involve females, and each year more and more women are contracting AIDS, confirming the fear that the syndrome is being spread through heterosexual contact. Further, AIDS is having a disparate impact on minorities. One study concluded that 50 percent of the women and children with AIDS in the United States are black, most of whom contract the virus through intravenous drug use. In Chicago, a study revealed that 40 percent of AIDS cases involved blacks or Hispanics. A national study found that 73 percent of all female AIDS patients are minorities, and 75 percent of all heterosexual victims are minorities. Scientists expect AIDS cases among minorities to continue increasing, while those among Caucasians are predicted to decline. The Centers for Disease Control reports that over the past five years, 25 percent of all persons with AIDS have been black and 14 percent Hispanic, while the percentages of these groups in the overall population are only 12 and 6 percent, respectively. Only 1 percent of all AIDS victims have been children, but the tragedy of having babies and young children suffer from immune deficiencies and eventually die is especially poignant. Further, the number of child victims is growing; a doctor in Houston has noted the large increase in pediatric cases and termed it an epidemic. Public health officials predict that the next "high-risk" group for AIDS will be sexually active teenagers.

Scientists have described AIDS as the most serious epidemic of the past 50 years. In fact, AIDS is a pandemic, which is an epidemic involving multiple countries. The National Academy of Sciences predicts that by 1991, 270,000 Americans will have AIDS (54,000 of whom will die in that year), concludes that AIDS is a social

---

*Central Africa is believed by researchers to be the origin of the AIDS virus because a relatively high proportion of the population has it, and the Green Monkey carries a virus closely related to the HIV virus identified in humans. Recently, a virologist discovered HIV in the blood plasma of a man who donated it in Zaire more than twenty-five years ago.

catastrophe, and recommends a strenuous commitment to education and research. Dr. Mahler, head of the World Health Organization, was quoted by *Newsweek* as saying: "I thought, wait and see—maybe it is not as hot as some are making it appear. I definitely admit to a gross underestimate. We're running scared." Health and Human Services Secretary Otis Bowen says, "AIDS is the most serious health threat facing our nation." Surgeon General C.E. Koop has advocated that special sex and drug educational materials on AIDS be used in grade schools and high schools. The National School Boards Association responded with a declaration of war on AIDS and a recommendation that facts on AIDS be incorporated in high school curricula. The U.S. Health and Human Services Department has issued a plan for educating Americans on AIDS and preventing its transmission by a number of approaches, including abstinence, if single, monogamy, if married, and the use of condoms by sexually active people. Persons at high risk and women contemplating pregnancies are encouraged to have the test. President Reagan declared AIDS "public enemy number one" and promoted education as a means of preventing its spread.

In England, leaflets educating the public on AIDS and how it is spread were delivered to 23 million households. The literature warns against intravenous drug use and urges people to have only one sex partner or, at the least, to use condoms. AIDS cases in the twelve-state European Economic Community are doubling every nine months. In response to the speed of the spread, a central unit has been formed to gather and transmit facts and educational materials among the countries. Princess Diana was given extensive publicity when she visited a special ward for AIDS patients in Middlesex Hospital. A nurse who has become a carrier was moved when Diana, who was not wearing gloves, shook hands with her. In Switzerland, where the cases are doubling every two months, the government is using an extensive advertising campaign to educate its citizens. Sweden has implemented sending leaflets to all its citizens' homes, advertisements, and a hot line in a campaign to fight AIDS by stopping sexual promiscuity. In the United States, public interest groups and manufacturers of condoms were critical of the initial decision by television networks, *Time, Newsweek,* and *People* to refuse advertisements for contraceptives as a device to retard the spread of AIDS. Nevertheless, sales of condoms were up 10 percent in 1986, after a decline of 50 percent during the previous ten years. *Newsweek* has changed its policy and has accepted an advertisement from a condom manufacturer that pictures an attractive young woman saying, "I'll do a lot for love, but I'm not ready to die for it." The copy for the ad reads, in part:

> AIDS isn't just a gay disease, it's everybody's disease. . . . Especially since the Surgeon General recently stated: "The best protection against infection right now, barring abstinence, is use of a condom."

The stock of several condom companies has risen in value in proportion to the increased interest in AIDS.

The public's fear of contracting AIDS through blood transfusions has stimulated the use of commercial (as opposed to community) blood banks that charge a fee to freeze blood for a donor's own use and accept donations from relatives. A company has made and is marketing to the public a videotape entitled: "AIDS and the American Family." Advertisements invite people to use their Master Card or Visa in ordering the tape through an 800 number to "save your family."

The media has publicized and exploited the issue. Newspaper headlines read "AIDS Spreading to More Children." *People Magazine*'s cover says "First you find out your son is gay. Then you learn he's dying—EVERY PARENT'S NIGHTMARE." *Newsweek* runs a cover story entitled: "Future Shock—AIDS" with the opening: "By 1991 an estimated 5 million Americans may be carrying the AIDS virus." Another *Newsweek* issue has a story about two young girls with divorced parents whose mother will not permit them to stay overnight with their gay father for fear the girls will contract AIDS. After a court battle, the judge ordered the father to submit to a blood test, but the father refused. *Time, U.S. News & World Report, New York,* and *Business Week* all publish cover stories on AIDS issues. *The New York Times* writes "Heterosexuals Spreading AIDS In Haiti." The *Times* of London does a story on married women and children who have contracted AIDS. *USA Today* runs the following misleadingly broad headline: "Firing of AIDS

Carriers O.K.'d." AP and UPI have stories every week, such as "AIDS Attacks Brain Cells," "AIDS Rampant in Five Years, Agency Warns," and "AIDS: Two Get Virus while Handling Blood." *USA Today* runs an interview with a woman who contracted AIDS from her recently deceased male lover, and adds as a postscript that the woman died of AIDS complications just prior to press time. Columnist Bob Greene refers to AIDS as "an American apocalypse" and a "plague," before saying "AIDS must be addressed with the same magnitude as if we were at war with a super power nation." Tabloids claim that "cockroaches carry AIDS" and that Liberace's cat is infected with AIDS.

These stories, for the most part, are on page 2, but when a celebrity announces that he or she has AIDS or dies of AIDS-related problems, the story is on page 1. It is anticipated that Rock Hudson, Liberace, and designer Perry Ellis are only three of the many celebrities in the entertainment and fashion industries who have contracted or will contract AIDS. People in other industries and occupations are also vulnerable. Jerry Smith, a former professional football player with the Washington Redskins, publicly announced that he had contracted AIDS. Roy Cohn, a renowned attorney, recently died of complications connected to the virus. Terry Dolan, founder of the National Conservative Political Action Committee, proponent of Ronald Reagan and opponent of Frank Church, Birch Bayh, and George McGovern, died in January 1987 at the age of 36 of complications from AIDS. The technical causes of some of these deaths are instructive: Ellis—viral encephalitis (four months after his business partner and lover, who suffered from Kaposi's sarcoma, died of lung cancer); and Cohn—heart failure. Unfounded rumors about AIDS flourish—Burt Reynolds and Richard Pryor felt forced to deny vehemently and repeatedly that they had AIDS in press releases.

At least five plays have been written about AIDS, including "The Normal Heart," "As Is," "Beirut," and "Warren." For the most part, they describe, from a victim's perspective, the tragedy of contracting the syndrome and the inevitability of death. Harvey Fierstein, author of "Torch Song Trilogy" and "La Cage aux Folles," recently wrote "Safe Sex," a trilogy of plays dealing with the anger, fear, and frustration of being gay and worrying about AIDS. "Beirut" is about an internment camp for HIV positive people in a future with restrictions on contact with the "prisoners." Barbra Streisand will direct and produce a film based upon "The Normal Heart." A movie made for television, "An Early Frost," depicted a son with AIDS returning to his family. Television shows present characters with AIDS ("St. Elsewhere") and reduce sexual encounters to reflect the impact of AIDS on society ("Cagney and Lacey"). In a movie entitled "Dragnet" the hero, involved in a passionate embrace, reaches into a box of condoms, which is empty. He then decides to abstain from sex.

If, as predicted, AIDS kills 54,000 people in 1991, it will become a leading cause of death, behind only heart and lung disease, cancer, strokes, and accidents. A report by the Department of Health and Human Services, after noting that San Francisco and New York thus far account for 41 percent of all AIDS cases, predicts that those two cities will have less than 20 percent by 1991, because the syndrome will be spreading throughout the rest of the country. Suburban hospitals are quietly treating AIDS patients already.

Quite predictably, these devastating developments and the extensive publicity concerning them are having ramifications for the way people live. Gay groups counsel less sex with fewer partners. *Newsweek* reports that AIDS and the publicity generated by it are changing the way women approach sex: sexually active women are not as promiscuous, and other women have become celibate. A survey by *Glamour* magazine concludes that 47 percent of the women interviewed say they have changed their sex habits because of AIDS. *Time* runs a cover story on "The Big Chill—How Heterosexuals Are Coping with AIDS." A young lady dating a photographer with extensive exposure to gay men in his work wrote to Ann Landers that she feared contracting AIDS; her request that her fiance be tested for the AIDS virus was rejected as insulting. Was she reasonable in demanding a medical certificate?

Further, a woman in Minnesota has sued her former fiancé for $50,000, alleging that during their sexual experiences he exposed her to the AIDS virus. Specifically, she claims he knew or should have known that he had ARC and was negligent in failing to inform her. In part, his defense is that the plaintiff was contributorily negligent, and that she voluntarily and willingly assumed the risk of infection.

Another young married woman who wants a child writes "Dear

Abby" that she fears a former lover who was shy and inexperienced may have been bisexual. Could she have contracted AIDS from him? Abby's advice: get the test. A poll asked children between the ages of eight and seventeen to identify their worst fears. The top three: being kidnapped, nuclear war, and AIDS. Among adults, the top three health worries are cancer, AIDS, and heart disease—in that order.

A "folk legend" making the rounds at water coolers and watering holes across the country suggests that a man picks up an attractive woman at a bar, takes her to his place for the night, and wakes up the next morning to her absence and a message on his bathroom mirror written in lipstick: "Welcome to the world of AIDS!" This actual experience occurred in a "swing club" in Minnesota that provides members with "opportunities for social and sexual contacts"—during routine checks for venereal disease two female members who eschew drugs tested positive for HIV. The investigation disclosed that two male club members were bisexual. Dating services and social clubs are responding to the fear of AIDS among sexually active people. The "Peace of Mind" club issues cards when members test negative. Members of a dating service are informed of other members' test results. The American Institute for Safe Sex Practices (AISSP) will only accept into membership people who present a medical certificate stating an AIDS test was negative. Members, who are placed on a computer list available to the membership, must be retested every six months. A company called "Protection Connection" offers fast home delivery of condoms and spermicidal sponges. Customers frequently receive the goods within three minutes of the telephone order. AIDS figured prominently in a New York criminal courtroom when the defendant, accused of murdering his homosexual lover, argued that the murder was triggered by the lover telling him, immediately after two acts of sex, that the lover had AIDS.

Doctors and nursing personnel who treat AIDS patients are much more likely to suffer from anxiety and stress because of the lack of adequate treatment and the terminal nature of AIDS. (*Newsweek* had a cover story on a doctor who had treated 300 victims, over 200 of whom had died.) Two doctors filed a lawsuit in New York, claiming that they were denied the opportunity to purchase a cooperative apartment because one of them treats AIDS patients.

With the grim statistics, studies, and forecasts, and with AIDS penetrating outside the homosexual and drug-user categories, society as a whole is responding to the need for large sums of money to fund research. The U.S. government and other nations are expected to allocate millions of dollars. The Reagan administration budgeted $534 million for AIDS in fiscal year 1988 while the Centers For Disease Control allocated $3.7 million to six cities for work in preventing AIDS. The Design Interior Foundation for AIDS has thus far raised $400,000 in funds, with considerable assistance from such celebrities as Elizabeth Taylor, Brooke Shields, and Calvin Klein. The National Institute of Allergy and Infectious Diseases has awarded $100 million to fourteen universities and hospitals for conducting drug research to combat AIDS. The Robert Wood Johnson Foundation AIDS Health Services Program allocated $17.2 million among eleven cities and countries for more specialized or humane health services for AIDS patients. Nevertheless, the National Academy of Sciences laments that these and other programs are "woefully inadequate" and recommends that a national commission be established and that $2 billion be devoted for AIDS research and treatment. The stocks of laboratory companies striving to develop a vaccine or drug to battle AIDS have been volatile, as investors recognize the financial implications of a cure.

Politicians, as well as doctors, espouse various theories about AIDS. For example, Carlton Turner, former adviser on drugs to President Reagan, suggested that smoking marijuana leads to homosexuality, which in turn causes AIDS! While many experts have expressed considerable doubt about a causative link between marijuana and AIDS, Turner's views have received extensive publicity in the United States. In the Soviet Union, published stories accuse the United States of creating and spreading AIDS! Specifically, a Soviet magazine ran an article entitled "Panic in the West," which claimed that HIV was created by Pentagon scientists at a secret army laboratory in Maryland. Further, the Russian newspaper *Pravda* published a cartoon showing a U.S. Army figure paying money to a scientist for the AIDS virus!

The response of institutions and people to AIDS-related issues approach hysteria in some cases. Ryan White, a fourteen-year-old with hemophilia who contracted AIDS through a blood transfusion, was barred from attending school in Indiana because of the fear that he would infect fellow students. In California, Ryan Thomas, a kindergarten student who had contracted AIDS through a blood transfusion, was prevented from attending school after he bit another child. The parents of Ryan Thomas, in one of the first AIDS cases, sued and obtained an injunction requiring his readmission.

Membership at a weight-lifting and exercise club in Washington, D.C., plummeted because several members were gay. In New Jersey, a nine-year-old boy whose sister has ARC is perplexed because over half of the students at his school have been kept home by their parents due to his presence. In New York, a county jail inmate with a confirmed case of AIDS spat upon every guard and prisoner who came close to his cell; worried officials arranged a special plea bargain under which he was convicted of a misdemeanor, given a suspended sentence and released, even though he had been arrested for a felony involving stolen property. In New Orleans, business at several well-known restaurants in the French Quarter is considerably down because of rampant rumors that some of the gay waiters have AIDS. Moreover, Catholic priests all over the country have received inquiries and complaints from parishioners about the practice of common use of the cup connected with Communion; some worshipers have brought small, individual cups to the Communion rail for the purpose of preventing possible spread of the syndrome. The Rector of St. Patrick's Cathedral in New York City denied the request of a couple to be married there on the ground the groom had AIDS. The denial was overruled by the Archbishop and the ceremony was performed. The Vatican, which has been generally critical of the prohomosexual movement, sees AIDS as another reason to oppose homosexuality. A Vatican official has been quoted as saying: "In 1986, AIDS cannot be ignored in any consideration of the moral and ethical issues raised by homosexuality." Fundamentalist minister and presidential candidate Pat Robertson put AIDS in the lights of his "700 Club" television show by touching a victim and saying, "We rebuke this virus, and we command your immune system to function in the name of Jesus." Hospital administrators with declining numbers of patients debate the advisability of accepting and expanding treatment of AIDS patients: on the one hand, they help to fill empty beds, but on the other, their presence may send other patients to competing hospitals.

Doctors have been quietly testing and treating priests for AIDS since 1981. Recently, the fact that a minority of priests have an AIDS condition has been heavily publicized and has raised questions about celibacy and homosexuality among the clergy. Prisons are quite concerned about the 61 percent increase in the number of AIDS cases in 1986. A New York prison caused controversy when it granted early paroles to several prisoners with confirmed cases of AIDS. Taking a different approach, U.S. Secretary of Education William Bennett states that prisoners with AIDS who threaten to infect other people after their release should have their term extended.

Schools, churches, prisons, gymnasiums, restaurants, and hospitals are not the only institutions struggling with and responding in various ways to the AIDS dilemma. The military has decided to test every recruit and member for the virus in an attempt to keep AIDS out of the armed services. The American Civil Liberties Union (ACLU), previously the guardian of the civil rights of such diverse groups as blacks and neo-Nazis, is now rushing to the aid of gays allegedly suffering from discrimination due to AIDS. The National Restaurant Association (NRA) and other management groups have sponsored educational programs and disseminated factual material concerning AIDS for the purpose of allaying unfounded fears.

Even those perceived as possible candidates for the syndrome are being harassed and discriminated against. "Gay bashing" describes the practice in San Francisco and other major cities, where thugs from the suburbs drive into inner-city areas frequented by gays, locate a lone gay person, and physically beat him while shouting antigay slogans. One homosexual was brutally beaten by a teenage gang on a San Francisco bus; two of his teeth were knocked out and his eyes were closed with bruises. He did not have AIDS. In Los Angeles, paramedics paused before helping a heart attack victim because they thought—incorrectly—that he had AIDS. In New York City, an obviously gay manager was fired when he announced that he would be absent to see his doctor—because of a false rumor that he had AIDS. "The prejudice and violence AIDS has inspired is a scourge almost as terrible as the disease itself," said a rabbi in San Francisco who has many AIDS patients in his congregation. "I'm reminded of medieval times when Jews were made scapegoats for the plague."

Great Britain is considering a policy requiring all African visitors to submit to a test for the AIDS virus before being admitted. Under the proposal, those refusing or testing positive would not be allowed in the country. This is prompted by the facts that 90 percent of the AIDS cases reported in Britain and the United States have thus far involved men, while the proportion is equal among men and women in Africa, *and* that the African variety has not yet appeared in appreciable numbers in Western countries, although the threat is very substantial.

Aside from publicity, reaction and overreaction, hysteria, and discrimination, there is controversy. Should employers, public and private, have the right to terminate or suspend employees with ARC or AIDS? Should hospitals, doctors, and dentists be able to deny them access to treatment? Should hotels and restaurants be allowed to deny entrance to their establishments to those afflicted? Should those with confirmed cases of AIDS be quarantined? The Centers for Disease Control and almost all other public institutions continually preach care and concern, but warn of overreaction; AIDS and HIV cannot be spread through casual contact, they emphasize, and discrimination against victims is unwarranted. But psychologist Paul Cameron of Nebraska has publicly presented the view that gays (not just victims of AIDS) should be *quarantined* to prevent the spread of AIDS! And Mississippi health officials actually issued a quarantine for a male prostitute, also a transvestite, who continued soliciting men for sexual acts, while dressed as a woman, despite orders to refrain due to his AIDS condition. Specifically, the quarantine prevents the Jackson man from working as a prostitute or engaging in sex without first informing the partner of his AIDS condition. A judge in Florida also temporarily quarantined a sexually active fourteen-year-old boy who tested positive for HIV. And a female prostitute with HIV in Miami admitted during one of her fourteen court appearances that she lies to her customers about her AIDS condition.

Many argue that the Mississippi and Florida cases are examples of the principle that, until a cure is found, the health and safety of the general public should override concerns about individual victims. In another case, the Minnesota Department of Health has proposed confinement as a method of dealing with individuals carrying the virus who continue in activities, such as sex with multiple partners, that spread AIDS. The department acknowledges problems with two prostitutes infected with the virus who are continuing sexual relations, despite counseling and recommendations to the contrary.

Ethical Considerations

For understandable reasons most of the information on AIDS focuses on the perspective of the ill-fated victim. But what about the concern of the emergency room nurse who is asked to treat an AIDS patient with knife or bullet wounds? Or a patient undergoing a heart bypass operation with a surgeon or nurse who has ARC? Or the manager of a restaurant who believes it is wrong to have a chef with AIDS preparing food for unsuspecting customers? Or employees at any facility who sincerely fear that they may be infected by a fellow employee with a confirmed case of AIDS? Do employees, customers, patients, and members of the public have the right to be apprised of AIDS situations involving them? Do employers have an ethical obligation to inform employees, patients, and customers that an employee with AIDS is on the payroll? Morally speaking, should employees be able to refuse to work with, serve, or treat people with HIV, ARC, or AIDS for fear of contracting it themselves and spreading it to members of their family? Do doctors have an ethical duty to notify the spouses or sex partners of their patients who have the HIV virus?

There are many questions, but few answers. The area is unclear and subjective. Gradually, the law will settle many key issues, but the fundamental tension between the rights of a person with AIDS or HIV infection and the rights of those with whom he or she may come into contact will continue to raise troublesome ethical issues.

Ethical questions have arisen in research for a cure. As noted previously, the federal government has undertaken a $100 million program to test new drugs. One experimental drug called "azi-

dothymidine," or AZT, has proved effective in blocking the repro-
duction of the virus. More specifically, AZT failed to kill the virus
upon contact with cultures in the laboratory, but it stopped it from
spreading. In England, AZT was given to eleven AIDS and ARC
patients for six weeeks. Infections cleared up, fevers and night sweats
terminated, and most patients gained weight. Then AZT was utilized in treating AIDS victims at twelve medical centers in eight
U.S. cities. However, in order to test its effectiveness the responsible
doctors established two groups of AIDS victims: one group was
given AZT and the other a placebo. None of the victims knew
which group they were in. And the only way to have a chance to
be treated with AZT in 1986 was to be accepted into the study.
Critics complained that human beings were being used as guinea
pigs.

When AZT was approved by the Food and Drug Administration in 1987, the cost to the patient was $200 per week. This
expense was too high for many AIDS patients, and they were forced
to go without the one thing that could prolong their lives because
they could not afford it. The laboratory manufacturing AZT explained that they needed to recoup the millions of dollars devoted
to research and development of the drug. Further, AZT is unavail-
able to patients who, in the opinion of doctors, are too weak to
benefit from it. (The FDA did, however, release AZT for use by
some patients prior to official approval because not to do so, they
said, would be immoral.) It has been reported that "underground
clinics" dispense homemade, experimental drugs to AIDS patients
in several major cities. Emulating formulas for AIDS medications
not yet approved by the FDA, the clandestine clinics make their
treatments available on an inexpensive basis. In Texas, suit was
filed to stop a man from selling to AIDS patients the "service" of
injecting them with their own urine, which he claimed would fight
the infection.

Various blood banks are carrying out a "Look Back" program
designed to trace recipients of blood from donors later found to
have HIV. The idea is to locate recipients of contaminated blood
prior to 1985 (when blood banks began testing donations for the
antibodies), inform them that the donor of the blood they received
tested positive, and request them to submit to the test. Approxi-

mately 50 percent of the found recipients had become infected with the HIV virus. Several of those notified by the blood bank who tested positive then secured counsel and sued the bank. Should blood banks be expected to continue tracing and notifying those who received contaminated blood, when such action may well lead to a lawsuit against them? It is suggested that the banks have an ethical obligation to notify *all* recipients of infected blood, regardless of the possibility of litigation.

Throughout his illness, New York lawyer Roy Cohn said that he was battling liver cancer. After his death, friends and lawyers stated that cancer was the cause. However, investigative reporters Jack Anderson and Dale Van Atta ran a story a week prior to his death that quoted from documents surreptiously obtained from the National Institutes of Health (NIH). These documents revealed that Cohn was being treated with AZT and must, therefore, have had AIDS. Was this ethical? The privacy and dignity of a dying man were violated—for what valid purpose? On the other hand, *Women's Wear Daily* and *Variety,* which cover the fashion and entertainment industries, never report that prominent people in those fields have AIDS. Arguably, people who regularly have contact with AJDS victims in these industries would appreciate such reports, when they can be documented.

The death of Liberace also sharply illustrates the conflict between a patient's right of privacy and the public's right to know. While he was ill, Liberace's friends emphatically denied that he was suffering from AIDS. Upon his death, Liberace's personal physician certified that the cause was heart failure brought on by degenerative brain disease. When the Riverside County Coroner accused the doctor of "pulling a fast one on us" and announced that Liberace actually died of cytomegalovirus pneumonia due to AIDS, the nation chose sides. One group argues as follows: it's important to record and examine each case of and death due to AIDS; many states have laws against listing false reasons on death certificates, and people—especially those who knew him—should know the truth in situations like this in which the disease is infectious. Accurate reporting allows health department officials to track and inform sexual partners. False reports like this raise the question of how many AIDS-related deaths have been covered up in the past few years. The other group argues that a person who has suffered untold agony should be allowed a peaceful death, his reputation intact, without sensational stories pervading the media and tasteless jokes circulating around the country. The actual cause of death should be a private matter between the deceased and his or her family. In the case of celebrities, the public's motive for knowing is curiosity—a yen for gossip. What valid purpose is served by the coroner calling a press conference to inform the nation that Liberace had AIDS? The best approach may be to enact laws requiring physicians to report accurately both AIDS cases as soon as they are diagnosed *and* AIDS-related deaths to local health officials who, in turn, must report the figures to the Centers for Disease Control. While the law should provide stiff penalties for physicians who prevaricate, it should also insist that the reports be sealed, confidential, and without public access.

Legal Considerations

Hundreds of federal, state, and local employment laws give protective status to applicants and employees who are in the right groups. Thus, female applicants for construction jobs cannot be rejected because of their sex; blacks cannot be refused promotions to managerial positions because of their race; senior executives cannot be forced into retirement because of their age; employees upset with working conditions cannot be laid off because they signed union cards; and veterans cannot be denied reinstatement in their jobs because they have been in the military for the preceding six years. Special statutes protecting these groups from discrimination in the workplace have been enacted over the years, and agencies to enforce the laws have been created. However, at present, no federal laws and only a handful of state and local laws specifically restrict the discretion of management in the handling of AIDS in the workplace. Stated another way, there are few laws directly protecting people with AIDS conditions in the workplace, and no laws prohibiting applicants or employees with HIV, ARC, or AIDS from working.

Some employers have taken direct action against employees in AIDS situations. A sailor who refused to take an AIDS test required by the navy was court-martialed, found guilty, jailed for forty-five days, reduced in rank, and given a bad conduct discharge. When sanitation workers refused to work with a fellow employee with AIDS, the City of New York suspended them without pay for the day, *and* reassigned the AIDS victim to a watchman position on the night shift.

AIDS victims have been evicted from apartments and denied access to restaurants and hotels. They have been fired, isolated, and forced into leaves of absence from the workplace. Some dentists refuse to treat patients suspected of carrying HIV. The Cook County Board of Commissioners limited the staff privileges of a male physician with AIDS and excluded him from duties involving direct patient care. An AIDS patient with a serious heart condition was rejected for surgery by a Minnesota physician who was concerned that his operating team would be exposed to large quantities of infected blood. A Florida judge required a defendant with an AIDS condition to wear a mask in the courtroom. Discrimination stalks them even after death—a few funeral homes have refused to accept people who died of AIDS-related causes. Various political groups, including the National Gay and Lesbian Task Force, have launched publicity campaigns and lobbying efforts designed to enact legislation to protect gays in general and AIDS victims in particular against discrimination and harassment.

At the federal level, the U.S. Supreme Court has indicated that the law protecting the handicapped is applicable to people with AIDS and other infectious diseases, while the U.S. Department of Justice has ruled that discrimination against AIDS victims in the workplace is permissible *if* it is motivated by a sincere desire to avoid infecting others. States, which also have laws protecting the handicapped, have enacted limited legislation directly on the AIDS question, with testing and discharging for AIDS circumscribed. Most of the laws clearly protecting AIDS victims have been debated and passed at the local level. Thus, Los Angeles and San Francisco have ordinances specifically protecting AIDS victims from discrimination.

On the other hand, California is also the location of a referendum that would have added AIDS to a list of reportable contagious diseases, allowed victims to be quarantined, and permitted terminations from certain jobs. A total of 683,576 Californians signed petitions sponsored by the Prevent AIDS Now Initiative Committee (PANIC), a group with Lyndon LaRouche among its supporters, but the referendum failed at the polls.

Despite the small number of statutes and ordinances on the specific subject, the potential for lawsuits involving AIDS in the workplace is enormous. Here are a few possible causes of action against employers:

   invasion of privacy for insisting that an applicant or employee submit to an AIDS test or for asking whether he or she has the AIDS virus;

   violation of a state or local law protecting the handicapped from any adverse actions against them;

   breach of confidentiality of medical records, libel, slander, and defamation of character for communicating a test result or medical report or diagnosis involving AIDS to managers, supervisors, rank-and-file employees, or the public;

   wrongful discharge for terminating, transferring, or placing an AIDS victim on involuntary leave of absence;

   and violation of the duty to warn other employees, customers, patients, sex partners, or family members of fact that an employee has the AIDS virus.

A technical but significant procedural point to be resolved in AIDS cases is which side has the burden of proof. Should the victim who has been discharged, transferred, or had a test result communicated to the switchboard operator have to prove by a preponderance of evidence that a law has been violated? Or should the employer be obligated to present convincing proof that it was not? In a federal court case involving the admission of a child with AIDS to a public school, the judge placed the burden on the school board to prove there was a real danger of transmitting the virus from the child to other children in the school. The allocation of burden was highly significant because the school board was unable to submit persuasive proof of the danger that others would be infected, and the AIDS victim won an order requiring his admission. If the burden had been on the child to prove that his admission would not endanger or infect the other children, the result might have been different. In state court suits involving established laws, the burden of proof questions are well settled.

While legal challenges to employer decisions involving AIDS are expected to increase substantially in the near future, it is significant to note that thus far the number of claims is extremely low compared to the number of victims in the workforce. Apparently applicants and employees who perceive that they are victims of race, sex, or age discrimination are much less hesitant to file suit. Other than the reluctance of AIDS victims to publicly declare their condition in a claim, factors explaining the low number of cases include the absence of statutes on the subject and the efforts of employers to reach solutions that at least partially recognize the interests of the victims.

Business Concerns

What about the perspective of management, which has obligations to maximize profits and to protect the health of customers, clients, and other employees?

Suppose a restaurant manager sincerely believes that allowing an AIDS victim to continue working as a cook would discourage customers, reduce revenues, and jeopardize the health of customers. Or the owner of a large barber shop determines that a community rumor that one of his barbers has tested positive is true and worries that established customers will go elsewhere. What if an administrator reasonably concludes that admission of AIDS victims at his suburban hospital would drive down other admissions? Word of mouth communications that a neighborhood restaurant has an AIDS victim chopping carrots in the kitchen or that a shop has an infected barber shaving and cutting hair could have an almost immediate negative impact on revenue. And at least one hospital has suffered from unusually low admissions because it became branded as the "AIDS hospital" for both research and treatment. When businesses go into a tailspin or fail, people are adversely affected. Employees are laid off and investors lose money. How should the interests of institutions and people other than the AIDS victim be considered and treated?

The U.S. Department of Justice recognized concerns beyond

those of AIDS victims when it declared in June 1986 that employers covered by Section 504 of the 1973 Vocational Rehabilitation Act may discriminate against an applicant or employee with AIDS *if they believe he is capable of transmitting the syndrome.* That opinion has been compromised by the U.S. Supreme Court, as will be fully explained in the next chapter, but the health interests of other employees and the public have been officially sanctioned. What about the high economic cost of covering AIDS-related problems with the group insurance plan? Should management be able to exclude that coverage for the purpose of avoiding escalating premiums?* Is money—like the health of other employees and the public—a valid factor for consideration?

Does management have a legal duty or ethical obligation to disclose information about AIDS in the workplace? Suppose a manager learns that Fred (an employee) has AIDS and allows him to continue in his regular job. Is there an obligation to tell other employees about Fred's condition? If the answer is affirmative, does the obligation extend to all personnel at the facility or only those who work closely with him? Doesn't this answer overlook Fred's right of privacy? If the answer is negative, then what if the employees learn through others about Fred's and management's failure to disclose the situation to them? Wouldn't their anticipated anger and frustration be justified? What if another employee later contracted the virus (perhaps through sex or drugs) and sued the company, claiming that he or she contracted it in the workplace and alleging that management violated its duty to inform him or her and other employees of Fred's condition?

Business has legitimate reasons to be concerned about the impact of AIDS decisions on other employees as well as its customers. The refusal of some or all employees to work with an AIDS victim, causing disruption or discontinuance of operations, is only one of the many potential ramifications. Other unfavorable developments include employees:

---

*Insurers frequently attempt to exclude AIDS-related problems from health plans; both life and health insurance companies propose mandatory employee testing for AIDS and threaten higher premiums without the tests. They wish to charge much more for AIDS victims, just as they presently charge higher premiums for both high blood pressure and heart patients.

signing union cards and petitioning the NLRB for representation because they are upset with how management handled an AIDS matter, and they believe that an outside, third party can assist them (nonunion companies);

filing grievances on AIDS issues and processing them to arbitration (union companies);

submitting health and safety complaints to OSHA or state health agencies (both union and nonunion).

The Service Employees International Union (SEIU) and other labor organizations have disseminated written educational materials on AIDS to health care, food service, and other personnel, and are using the issue as a device to sign up new members. The SEIU suggests employer-employee cooperation in developing infectious disease programs as an approach to protecting the health of employees in the workplace. The pitch is that some companies are too lax in their infection control policies. The threat of AIDS, unions feel, is important to thousands of employees; potential members are promised that union representatives will promote infection control committees (with union representation) and require management to develop policies to protect employees fearful of contracting AIDS from patients, customers, or other employees. The SEIU also promises education of all workers and strong opposition to mandatory antibody testing. In fact, the AFL/CIO has adopted a resolution opposing the screening of workers for AIDS. The American Federation of State, County, and Municipal Employees (AFSCME) is lobbying OSHA to issue stringent standards that would protect health care workers from exposure to communicable infections such as AIDS and hepatitis B. This approach demonstrates action to current members and assists campaigns for new members. Business, therefore, finds unions as well as government and the courts looking over its shoulder as it resolves AIDS issues in the workplace.

In sum, a balancing act will frequently be required: The interest of protecting the applicant or employee with HIV, ARC, or AIDS from discharge, deprivation of insurance, or other discrimination should be weighed against the legitimate business concerns and health interests of other employees and the public. It is anticipated

that this tension between the desire to apply laws prohibiting discrimination against AIDS victims and the objective of protecting
the business and health interests of others will be examined repeatedly in administrative hearings and judicial opinions over the
next several years. Different facts and circumstances will produce
different results, but the approach for making the determination
will always be the same: a balancing of competing interests. And
one of those interests should and will be that of business.*

Health Care Considerations

While hospitals are certainly business-oriented and thus share most
of the concerns discussed above, some aspects of AIDS in the workplace are unique to health care facilities. With the proliferation of
hospital beds during the 1970s and early 1980s, and the federal
government's Diagnostic Related Groups (DRG) program, hospitals today are competing against each other for a declining number
of admissions to a surplus of beds. The fact that many hospitals
are experiencing a reduction of 20 to 40 percent in admissions has
sparked staff reductions, the closings of wings and floors, emphasis
on outpatients, and the utilization of sophisticated marketing tech-
niques, including advertising and "guest relations" programs designed to favorably impress patients. The image the hospital projects
is all-important in its battle to lure patients to their hospital and
away from a competitor's. In these circumstances, a public perception of a health care facility as an "AIDS Hospital" because it treats
a large number of AIDS victims and/or has a grant to conduct
research on AIDS could, with an uneducated public, be a prescrip-
tion for financial disaster.

Hospitals treating a significant number of AIDS victims are,
among other things, emphasizing previously existing infectious
control procedures, educating patients and the public on these procedures (sterilization, double-gloving, etc.), publishing articles about
hygiene and infection control, and keeping a low profile on their

---

*A few companies are profiting from the AIDS situation. Laboratories testing for HIV are
doing a booming business in some areas, while other companies make and market AIDS
antibody test kits.

role in treating AIDS victims or performing research on the subject. Administrators are not unhappy with increased patient census from the admission of AIDS patients, and they fully understand the predictions of large increases in the future. See Appendix A, documents 1 and 2 for special guidelines and recommendations concerning AIDS in the workplace—many of which relate to health care personnel—issued by the U.S. Public Health Service.

Another crucial point is that the high cost of treating AIDS patients (approximately $100,000 is spent for the hospital care of each) is not always covered by health insurance. Approximately 40 percent of AIDS victims receiving health care are on Medicaid, and only 1 to 3 percent qualify for Medicare. Incidentally, the federal government's share of Medicaid payments for AIDS victims in 1985 was $50 million. Less than one-half of AIDS patients are covered by private insurance plans. What about the hospital bills of AIDS victims covered neither by Medicaid nor by an insurance plan, who eventually die? A Public Health Service study predicts that by 1991 the annual cost of treating AIDS will be $60 billion! A hospital in an already precarious position would have an unacceptable amount of red ink. Total uncompensated care by hospitals in the United States doubled from 1980 to 1985—from $4.6 to $9.5 *billion.* AIDS may exacerbate an already precarious financial situation for some hospitals.

The American Hospital Association (AHA) speaks of "hospital death by AIDS" resulting from unpaid bills related to AIDS victims. A newspaper account of the AIDS crisis has the headline: "AIDS May Kill Hospitals." *Hospitals,* a trade magazine, recently had an article entitled: "AIDS—A Timebomb at Hospitals' Door." The problem is compounded by insurance companies that either exclude treatment for medical problems caused by AIDS or increase the premium to the point that the corporation agrees to exclude AIDS coverage for the purpose of cost control. Suppose a small community hospital had five nonpaying AIDS cases and declining admissions in the same year? A survey in California established that hospitals were losing $5,200 per AIDS admission—three times the amount of the uncollectibles on the average patient. Some fear that hospitals will engage in the "dumping" of AIDS patients— refusing admission and sending them to public hospitals. A former soldier was reportedly denied coronary bypass surgery at an army hospital near San Francisco because he had tested positive for the AIDS virus. He was later accepted by and successfully operated on at another hospital. Another AIDS patient with a serious heart problem was rejected for surgery at a Minnesota hospital well known for sophisticated heart operations.

Almost all hospitals, however, accept whatever AIDS patients seek admission. Further, many have competed for and gladly accepted grants from the federal government for conducting AIDS research. While most hospitals are very willing to accept and treat AIDS victims, those doing a significant amount of AIDS care are concerned about their reputation in the community. They well know the public's phobia of contracting the syndrome, the misinformation bandied about, and the exploitation of the issue by the media. Although hospital administrators and doctors understand that AIDS cannot be transmitted through normal contact in a hospital, the public does not.

Hospital doctors and administrators also know, however, that inadvertent needle sticks, blood splashes, and other errors and conditions associated with treating AIDS victims can lead to the transmission of the disease from patients to employees. And, further, it is at least theoretically possible for hospital workers who contract the virus to transmit it to patients. This is why hospitals, more than any other type of employer, are studying AIDS-related programs, developing policies, and educating employees.

Hospitals have a unique status among employers in many ways. Some believe they should be able to ask applicants if they have HIV and require employees to submit to testing because of concerns connected to job assignments. Employees treating and assisting AIDS patients have special vulnerability to infection, both HIV and the infections the patients pick up because of impaired immune systems. *Blood splash* (when blood from an open wound of an AIDS patient is splashed on an employee, causing concern that infected blood may enter the bloodstream of an employee through a cut or mucous membrane); *needle sticks* (the most common accident wherein infected needles accidentally scratch or otherwise penetrate the skin of an employee); *scalpel wounds,* and other means are a constant threat for some hospital employees. Should such potentially infected employees be required to submit to the HIV test? If not, it is very possible that they could contract the virus and be in a position to transmit it to other employees and patients in exercising their duties over a long period of time. Many hospitals recommend that employees so exposed submit to the test, and provide repeated applications of the test for a year without charge, but only a few actually require such submission. The Centers for Disease Control (CDC) has issued bulletins regarding AIDS, some of which relate to the workplace. Appendix A, document 3 contains the CDC Recommendations for Preventing Transmission of HIV in the Workplace. Thus far, however, these guidelines have not recommended *requiring* hospital employees exposed to HIV through needle stick or blood splash to submit to the screening test, which could easily be administered at the hospital during work time at hospital expense. Concern seems to be that such a requirement would violate the individual's right of privacy. However, what about the possibility of a recently infected nurse or lab technician unwittingly transmitting the virus to patients and employees as he or she continues regular duties for the next five or ten years?

How likely is it for hospital personnel to be infected with HIV by patients? How dangerous is it for a hospital employee exposed to the virus to treat patients and have regular contact with other employees, family members, and friends? The Centers for Disease Control in Atlanta conducts studies involving hospital employees who have had exposure to the virus through needle sticks, blood splashing, or other means. The tentative conclusion is that the risk is quite low. Hospitals should also carefully follow the continuing study by the National Institutes of Health to determine the risk of transmitting the AIDS virus from patients to health care workers. Hospital employees exposed to the blood or body fluids of infected patients have been studied in follow-up examinations to determine whether they have developed the virus. A tentative conclusion from the on-going study is that the incidence of developing HIV from a hospital exposure is less than two for every 1,000 exposures. An epidemiologist with NIH described the risk as present but low.

As indicated, the Centers for Disease Control also maintains statistics and conducts studies on AIDS issues. Of the first 20,000 AIDS cases reported in the United States, 5.5 percent involved people who were health care workers. While some of them contracted AIDS through drugs, sex, and other means unconnected with their work, a definite number were infected by incidents at work. Forty percent of these incidents, according to CDC, were preventable. Thus, 17 percent happened while incorrectly resheathing or recapping needles; 13 percent occurred when contaminated materials were being improperly disposed of; and 10 percent were due to contamination of open wounds or exposed tissue. Health officials emphasize the need for extra caution in caring for HIV patients and in handling their blood. Many recommend that gloves, masks, gowns, and goggles be worn. Health care workers, however, usually consider these recommendations to be unrealistic.

A 1987 report by the Centers for Disease Control described three cases of hospital workers contracting HIV through exposure to contaminated blood during their work. Each instance involved exposure unrelated to a needle stick: 1) an emergency room nurse applied pressure—with a chapped, ungloved hand—to a site with blood on a patient she did not know had AIDS; 2) a lab employee was sprayed with blood on her face and mouth when a vacuum-sealed test tube burst; and 3) a worker operating a blood-separating machine was splattered with blood when the machine broke. A separate CDC study of 1,500 health care workers exposed to HIV through needle sticks and other means revealed that only one tested positive.

While the medical associations, departments, and spokespeople almost all cite these studies to support their opinions that HIV is not going to be transmitted to others in the workplace except in rare, somewhat unique situations, many doctors, hospital administrators, and health care employees remain skeptical. They are waiting for more complete data before they endanger themselves or others. In New Orleans, a dietician sued her hospital-employer for $3.7 million after she tested positive for HIV following an accidental stick from a contaminated needle. Pregnant at the time of the accident, the plaintiff claims she was pricked by the unsheathed needle that had been improperly placed under papers on the food tray of an AIDS patient, and that she is suffering acute stress and severe depression due to the incident. A renowned heart surgeon in Minnesota refused to perform a complicated operation on an

AIDS victim because his surgical team of several physicians and nurses would have been exposed to substantial quantities of contaminated blood. A Chicago hospital suspended operating privileges of a surgeon who developed AIDS. Moreover, a major hospital chain reports that a significant number of hospital personnel are skittish about treating AIDS patients, and that some are actually hostile towards them. Researchers found that a significant number of admissions to the emergency room of Johns Hopkins Hospital had HIV, and recommended that emergency medical and rescue workers take greater precautions. All of those with HIV were actively bleeding and in need of multiple invasive procedures. A man in London contracted HIV through a skin transplant at a hospital. He had been badly burned, and the skin donated by another man was not tested for the virus prior to the operation. Donated organs, of course, should also be checked for HIV before transplant operations. Transplanted organs (a kidney and liver) infected two recipients with HIV recently, even though the test was performed, because the donor had received extensive blood transfusions prior to his death, causing a negative test result.

An indication of the importance of properly educating health care employees is the study at a New England hospital establishing that workers having the least contact with AIDS patients had the most fear and stress about treating and having them in the facility. Stated another way, the hospital employees who were in frequent contact with AIDS patients, treating them on a regular basis, had relatively little concern and worry about being infected. Hence, both education and increased exposure to AIDS patients should reduce the level of anxiety.

At the very least, hospitals must recognize the special AIDS-related questions confronting them and resolve the issues only after careful deliberations. The potential for employee unrest and litigation is enormous.

A real, uncontroverted risk for hospitals is the spread of secondary infections to AIDS patients from others. Since their immune systems are impaired, AIDS patients contract any of a number of infections, some of them highly contagious. Obviously, strict compliance with infection control procedures in the treatment of AIDS patients is critical. Related to this is the fact that hospital employees with AIDS are highly vulnerable to these secondary infections. Thus a health care employee with AIDS is in much greater danger of contracting a serious illness from patients and other employees than they are from him.

Another special problem for hospitals is the confidentiality of medical records. There are no regulations requiring special handling of records for AIDS victims, as there are for alcohol, drug, and psychiatric patients. Should hospitals treat records of AIDS victims as confidential? (Almost all do.) Should hospitals give results of the HIV antibody test to people other than the patient or employee being tested? Conflict can develop between the desire to keep a patient's condition confidential and the duty to inform others of a potential exposure. What if an employer or prospective employer seeks access to the medical records of a patient or ex-patient? Suppose an insurance company, trying to determine whether to cover a claim, asks for copies of medical records relating to AIDS? The National Gay and Lesbian Task Force is concerned that a positive test result could label the person for life and make him or her unemployable and uninsurable. Most hospitals already treat these records as confidential, although they are not required to, and continually refuse requests for data from potential employers and insurance companies. Obviously, they are subject to subpoena in the event of legal claims. Hospitals should be certain to segregate medical reports involving AIDS conditions from the personnel files, place them in a secure location, and limit access to them.

Some hospitals have converted substantial portions of the material disseminated by the CDC in Atlanta into special *policies* for handling AIDS issues. (See Appendix B, document 1.) One hospital has a written policy on "Caring for the AIDS Patient" and another for employees infected with HIV. (See Appendix B, documents 2 and 3.) Others, however, apply their regular policies and procedures on infection control or life threatening illnesses to AIDS, which many doctors and administrators believe is analogous in its communicability to hepatitis B. (See Appendix B, document 4.) A few hospitals have detailed policies that recognize the needs to prevent the transmission of HIV and to protect patients and employees as well as determine what is best for the victims. (See document 5 of Appendix B.) Some have developed policies, forms, and procedures for follow-up after exposure to the HIV virus. (See Appendix B, documents 6 through 9.) Most hospitals feel there is no need for a special AIDS policy on placement of an employee with an AIDS condition; such a policy could mandate a particular course of action in an unanticipated situation. They feel that it is preferable to stay with established, general policies on infection control and approach AIDS-related problems on a case-by-case basis. This point is especially significant under current circumstances, when there is virtually no legal precedent and many anticipated medical and legal developments in the future. An advisory committee of the American Hospital Association has issued a report on controlling infections in a hospital environment (See Appendix B, document 10.) A list of reportable diseases (most of them are communicable) hospitals have contended with over the years is in Appendix B, document 12.

Lurking in the background of treatment in this area by hospitals and doctors are potential lawsuits. The possible causes of action are numerous:

1. *Medical malpractice.* The area of diagnosis of AIDS is fraught with claims. A homosexual, worried about AIDS, visits his doctor for a physical examination. He is initially pleased with the report that he is in good health and free of disease, but most angry the next year when he becomes ill and is told he has ARC or AIDS and has been a carrier of the virus for years. Perhaps the doctor failed to test for the virus. Or did so but made mistakes in reading the results. Or the test yielded a false negative. Or the records revealed a positive test result that was never communicated to the patient. Suppose that the individual, under the false belief that he was free of AIDS-related conditions, infected his sex partners during the interim between the doctor visit and illness. Couldn't these third parties also have a claim against the doctor and the clinic or hospital with which he or she is associated? It may well be negligence not to report the positive condition to public health authorities and to fail to warn spouses or partners.

Another danger is that an individual admitted to a hospital with complaints and symptoms of AIDS is not properly diagnosed.

As a result, relevant treatment is not administered. The reverse situation is a false diagnosis of AIDS communicated to the patient. Plaintiff attorneys, of course, will be interested in any mental anguish that may result from these errors of omission and commission.

2. *Tort—informed consent.* Prior to drawing blood and testing it for antibodies to the virus, the hospital or doctor should secure informed, written consent. Torts like battery, negligent testing, and failure to inform of consequences could be alleged. Special checklists and forms should be utilized both to ensure that proper information on the purpose and meaning of the test is effectively communicated to the individual *and* to protect the hospital, clinic laboratory, and doctor.

3. *Tort—failure to explain or counsel.* There are serious ramifications of a positive test result, including alienation of family, loss of job, severe depression, and suicide. Any individual testing positive should be carefully counseled, and alternatives for medical and emotional assistance and treatment should be explained. Obviously, all counseling sessions should be well documented.

4. *Tort—failure to inform third parties.* Wives, children, friends, sex partners, or coworkers of the individual may claim that the hospital or doctor was negligent in failing to inform them of the individual's AIDS condition. The allegation would be that they became infected by continuing to associate with the individual after AIDS had been diagnosed because they were unaware of his or her infectious condition. Under current law in most jurisdictions, the plaintiffs would have considerable difficulty in proving a case. Consider, though, the law in California: a psychiatrist whose patient specifies the person the patient intends to kill has the obligation to breach the confidential relationship with the patient and inform the potential murder victim. Is this concept applicable to AIDS cases?

5. *Discrimination against employees who test positive.* Hospital employees with positive results may be discharged, transferred, or placed on medical leave because of the hospital's fear of infecting patients and other employees. Failure to promote and denial of salary increases are two additional claims that could be filed. Specific causes of actions and applicable laws are reviewed in later chapters.

6. *Breach of confidentiality of medical records.* Disclosure of

a positive test result for the AIDS virus or communication of the medical record of an applicant, employee, or patient with an AIDS-related condition could prompt claims for invasion of privacy, libel, slander, defamation, and breach of confidentiality. It is critical for hospitals and patients to cautiously adhere to all rules of confidentiality and avoid any breach in their communications and dealings with others.

7. *Failure to protect employees from being infected.* Suppose a hospital employee contracts AIDS and alleges that he was infected by a coworker who was allowed to continue working despite the hospital's knowledge that he was a carrier. Or a nurse assigned to treat AIDS victims is infected and files suit, claiming that the hospital failed to provide her with sufficient protective gear and that the hospital's procedures for treatment are inadequate. These possibilities suggest the importance for hospitals to implement infection control procedures, insist to the point of discipline that all appropriate personnel adhere to them, and to document their efforts in this area.

8. *Failure to protect patients from the virus.* A couple in Washington, D.C., has sued the hospital where their son was born for $15 million. The allegation is that three blood transfusions, contaminated with the AIDS virus, were administered to the baby soon after he was born. The boy died of AIDS at the age of 3 1/2. Suppose a patient claims to have contracted the virus from a needle stick, blood splash, or other means while in the hospital. Again, scrupulously adhering to established procedures for testing blood and controlling infection and carefully documenting the application of these procedures in AIDS situations should provide valid defenses to hospitals in most situations.

9. *Failure to disclose, resulting in emotional trauma.* Suppose that a patient learns after surgery or other treatment that the doctor who operated on him, or the nurse who dressed his wounds, had HIV, ARC, or AIDS. Suppose further that the patient then files suit, alleging emotional trauma, negligence, mental anguish, and worry about contracting AIDS.

One hospital exclusively for the treatment of AIDS patients has opened in Houston. While its losses averaged $800,000 per month during the first six months, it is continuing to operate. However, indigent patients are no longer being admitted. There also may be nursing homes only for AIDS victims because, in part, of the unique medical and legal aspects of the disease. The Catholic Health Association has an advertisement arguing that poor AIDS patients must receive the "physical, psychological, and spiritual help" they so desperately need, regardless of insurance. A partial answer is more hospices exclusively for AIDS patients, like one that is very effective in the Gulf South. People with AIDS-related conditions often develop serious dental problems but are unable to secure treatment. In response, a New York hospital opened a special dental clinic devoted exclusively to treating AIDS patients.

Hospitals are also much more vulnerable than other employers to employees who refuse to work because of AIDS patients. Refusals to treat AIDS victims, prepare their food, or clean their rooms would generate considerable labor problems, both legal and practical.

Conclusions

Despite the conflict, controversy, and competing interests, there is one thing on which doctors, lawyers, ministers, managers, and union agents all agree: *the need for education.* Anxiety about AIDS is epidemic. Fear of contracting AIDS is the cause of considerable disruption, panic, and hysteria among members of the public. The State of Washington postponed the adoption of antidiscrimination guidelines on AIDS following a public hearing that featured speakers stating that AIDS is spread by mosquitoes and fleas! The Human Rights Commission decided that the public has visceral reactions and misinformation on the topic. The proper antidotes for this ignorance and fear—largely unjustified—are facts. Employees should not refuse to work with an AIDS victim if they understand that the syndrome cannot be transmitted through casual contact. Customers will not boycott a restaurant if they understand that it is impossible for the head waiter, who may have ARC, to infect them during the performance of his or her duties.

Some employers have attempted to educate their managers and employees with in-house seminars. A few have brought in medical and legal experts to explain—in basic terms—facts and figures on the subject. A national teleconference on AIDS in the workplace, sponsored by the Public Broadcasting Service (PBS) and the Bureau of National Affairs (BNA) was presented to over 2,000 people at 100 locations throughout the country in 1985. Data on AIDS is available from numerous sources. (See Appendix E, document 1.) The Shanti Project, a group based in San Francisco, provides volunteer counseling for people facing life-threatening illnesses, including AIDS. Employers with Employee Assistance Programs (EAPs) are encouraging possible AIDS victims on the payroll to disclose their conditions and seek medical help (covered by insurance plans) as well as other assistance (counseling, and other support available under EAP). Employers are in a position to eradicate much of the misinformation about AIDS that exists through short, factual presentations at the workplace.

2
Federal Laws

No special federal laws protect AIDS victims from being demoted, transferred, placed on unpaid leave, fired, or even not hired because they have the HIV virus, ARC, or AIDS. Nor is it likely, given the political implications, that members of Congress will sponsor or enact new laws to specifically prohibit discrimination in the workplace against those with AIDS-related conditions. However, courts and administrative agencies could apply several existing federal laws for the purposes of protecting job applicants and employees with AIDS, respecting health and safety of other employees working with AIDS victims, and otherwise restricting employer flexibility in resolving these problems. (It should also be stated there are no laws *preventing* people with AIDS conditions from being hired or assigned to any job.)

Title VII of the Civil Rights Act of 1964

This federal statute proscribes discrimination against an applicant or employee on the basis of sex, as well as race, color, creed, national origin, and religion. The Equal Employment Opportunity Commission (EEOC), which was created to administer this law, has jurisdiction over *all* employers with fifteen or more employees. Claimants have the right to file a charge with the EEOC within 180 days after the alleged act of discrimination; an administrative investigation, determination, and possible conciliation are triggered by the charge. Regardless of the commission's conclusions, the individual claimant is given the right to file a lawsuit in a federal district court and to have his or her claims of sex discrimination fully presented to the federal judiciary. Class actions, where an individual applicant or employee claims to represent all others who are similarly situated, are not infrequent, and available remedies for successful claimants include back-pay, interest, payment of the plaintiff's attorney's fees, and injunctive relief.

At first blush it seems that a homosexual AIDS victim or even a gay male perceived to have AIDS who suffers discrimination on the job could file an actionable charge of sex discrimination with his local EEOC office. There is, however, a serious, if not fatal flaw, in any attempt to apply this law to an AIDS situation in the workplace. The prohibition against sex discrimination contained in Title VII definitely prohibits adverse action against a male or female employee because of sexual *gender,* but the law is clear thus far that discrimination by employers based upon sexual *preference* is not prohibited.

Enterprising plaintiff attorneys may argue that because approximately 90 percent of AIDS victims are male, any policy or practice that discriminates against AIDS victims would have a disparate impact against males.* Hence, discrimination on the basis of sex is established. Since, however, the large majority of male victims are homosexual, and homosexuality is a preference, any such claim would be highly vulnerable to dismissal by either the EEOC or the federal district court.

In a California case, three homosexual men and two lesbians filed suit against Pacific Telephone and Telegraph Company, alleging failure to hire, harassment, and discharge because of their sexual orientation. The male plaintiffs offered proof that alleged policies and practices on the job disproportionately and adversely affect men and argued this was sex discrimination in violation of Title VII. The federal courts rejected all claims and dismissed the lawsuit. The appellate court concluded that "Title VII's prohibition of 'sex' discrimination applies only to discrimination on the basis of gender and should not be judicially extended to include sexual preference such as homosexuality." *DeSantis v. Pacific Tel. & Tel. Co.,* 608

---

*According to the Centers for Disease Control, 66 percent of those with AIDS in the United States have been homosexual or bisexual males, while 17 percent have been intravenous drug users (mostly male), and 7 percent have been males who are both homosexual and IV drug users.

F.2d 327, 329 (9th Cir. 1979). The Federal Fifth Circuit Court of Appeals has flatly ruled that "discharge for homosexuality is not prohibited by Title VII or Section 1981." *Blum v. Gulf Oil Corp.,* 597 F.2d 936 (1979). See also EEOC Decision no. 76-115 (1976). There may be an opportunity under Title VII for an employee who believes he is being harassed on the job because of his status as a homosexual with an AIDS condition. *Joyner v. AAA Cooper Transportation,* 749 F.2d 732 (11th Cir. 1984). The cases on the issue of sex discrimination, however, establish that gays who are fired, not hired, or forced to take leaves of absence because of an AIDS condition can expect that Title VII claims of discrimination due to sex will be soundly defeated.

Applicants and employees of Haitian and African descent who believe they have been unfairly treated due to an AIDS condition may have a viable claim of national origin discrimination. The media have extensively reported that Haitians are a "high-risk" group concerning AIDS, and that large numbers of residents of certain portions of Africa have AIDS conditions. Suppose an employer refused to hire a Haitian or African immigrant because of the perceived connection between those areas and AIDS. Even though the Centers for Disease Control removed Haitians as a high-risk group, potential plaintiffs from Haiti and Africa could argue they were discriminated against because of their national origin.

The Vocational Rehabilitation Act of 1973

This federal law prohibits contractors with the federal government and other employers who receive federal financial assistance from discriminating in employment on the basis of an applicant's or employee's handicap. Section 503 of the act applies to companies having contracts or subcontracts with the federal government in excess of $2,500, while Section 504 is applicable to *all* employer-recipients of federal financial assistance (primarily hospitals and schools). The Office of Federal Contract Compliance Programs (OFCCP), part of the U.S. Department of Labor (DoL), has been given the responsibility under Section 503 to monitor compliance with this law by contractors and subcontractors. It is the responsibility of that agency to audit employers to determine if their Affirmative Action Plan (AAP) is sufficient under Executive Order 11246 and to investigate any complaints from applicants or employees concerning companies covered under the Executive Order or Section 503. If an AIDS applicant or employee filed a complaint of discrimination based upon handicap with the OFCCP, the first inquiry is whether the employer has sufficient connection with the federal government to satisfy the jurisdictional standards. The second, more difficult, issue is whether AIDS is a handicap within the meaning of the statute. A checklist for determining whether a private employer is a contractor within the meaning of the law and thus under the umbrella of the Vocational Rehabilitation Act of 1973 is contained in Appendix D, document 1. Further, copies of the texts of Sections 503 and 504 appear in Appendix D, documents 2 and 3.

The Department of Health and Human Services (DHHS) has overall responsibility for enforcing Section 504. Since there are no dollar limitations for jurisdiction, the first procedural question is whether AIDS is a handicap, assuming an AIDS-related complaint. Individual claimants have the right to secure counsel and pursue complaints in federal district court under both Sections.

A person with a "handicap" has been legally defined as one who: 1) has a physical or mental impairment that substantially limits one or more of his or her major life activities; 2) has a record of such impairment; or 3) is regarded as having such an impairment. The statute states that an employee whose current use of alcohol or drugs prevents him from performing the duties of the job in question is not within the definition, but it is silent with respect to applicants and employees with AIDS-related conditions. There is no specific exclusion or inclusion of contagious diseases in the definition of handicap.

In order to establish eligibility for assistance, the individual must also demonstrate that he or she is a "qualified handicapped person." More specifically, the burden is on the individual to prove his or her capability, with reasonable accommodation, to perform the essential functions of the job in question without endangering the health and safety of the individual or other employees in the workplace.

Civil rights organizations and attorneys for people with AIDS conditions make a strong argument that AIDS is a "protected handicap" under this law. An applicant or employee with ARC or AIDS obviously has a medical impairment with a supporting medical record. Those with a positive test result for HIV antibodies, but not exhibiting any physical manifestations of ARC or AIDS, are not actually impaired, but they may well be included in the definition of a handicapped employee as people who are "regarded as having such an impairment." Handicapped persons covered by the law who successfully prove discrimination are eligible for both protection and remedies under the 1973 statute. Specifically, it is illegal for an employer to discriminate against applicants or employees or treat them differently from nonhandicapped individuals solely because of their handicaps. If an applicant or employee is debilitated by the impairment to the point that he or she cannot perform all the duties of the job, the law requires the employer to reasonably *accommodate* the employee as long as this accommodation does not constitute undue hardship. The burden is on the employer to show that special adjustments or accommodations would cause unreasonable problems in its operation. Remedies for successful claimants include back pay, interest, and attorney fees. Penalties for guilty employers include loss of federal funds and contracts; employers that have substantial contracts either with the federal government or with companies that do risk being barred from consideration for future work.

The two pertinent questions are: 1) is a person with an AIDS condition "handicapped" within the meaning of Section 504, and 2) if so, is he or she "otherwise qualified" for the job in question? The debate with respect to (1) has subsided since an important decision was reached by the U.S. Supreme Court, but (2) remains almost wholly unanswered. In 1986, the U.S. Department of Justice, in response to a request from the Department of Health and Human Services, issued a formal opinion which recognized an employer's right to discriminate against AIDS victims where there is a concern that the syndrome will be transmitted to others and exonerated employers in those situations from the reach of Section 504. Specifically, Justice concluded that while it is certainly true that "discrimination based on the disabling effects of AIDS" violates Section 504, if the employer can prove that the adverse action against the AIDS victim was motivated by a belief that he is capable of transmitting the disease to others, the discrimination would *not* violate the law, even if the employee is a qualified, handicapped person. Thus, according to the Department of Justice, dismissal of AIDS victims based upon a fear of contagion is permissible, as far as Section 504 is concerned.

The Opinion immediately stirred up a hornet's nest. First, the Department of Health & Human Services (DHHS), the very group that requested the Opinion, repudiated it, with an assistant secretary of health saying it "does not reflect new scientific or medical information on AIDS." The CDC also criticized the conclusion, reiterating its position that an employee with AIDS poses no risk to individuals in a workplace setting. The American Medical Association (AMA) took a formal position against it, and the American Public Health Association passed a resolution urging the Justice Department to rescind it. Various lawyers representing the American Bar Association (ABA), including management attorneys, criticized the Opinion as illogical and contrary to the intent of Congress in enacting Section 504. Since the number of employers affected by Section 503 is far greater than those under the jurisdiction of 504, there is considerable interest in the opinion of the OFCCP. Thus far, however, the OFCCP has not taken a position as to whether concern that employing persons with ARC or AIDS may transmit the syndrome to other employees, patients, or customers justifies discrimination under Section 503.

Both administrative agencies and courts have ignored and repudiated the Opinion. DHHS has formally accused Charlotte Memorial Hospital and Medical Center (North Carolina) with violating Section 504 by dismissing a male from his position as registered nurse, and then refusing to consider him for any other position, because he had AIDS. A nine-page letter from DHHS detailing the accusations and findings was received by the hospital in early August 1986, almost exactly two years after the complaint was filed and six months *after* the nurse had died of complications connected with AIDS. DHHS is seeking back pay and possibly benefits for the family of the deceased charging party *and* a "collective action plan" from the hospital, which would be designed to protect the rights of applicants and employees with AIDS in the future.*

With respect to whether the Vocational Rehabilitation Act regulates AIDS in the workplace for employers who either have contracts with the federal government or are recipients of federal funds, the only opinion that really counts is that of the U.S. Supreme Court. In the seminal case entitled *Arline v. School Board of Nassau County,* 480 U.S.—, 94 L Ed. 2d 307, a 1987 Supreme Court decision, a third-grade teacher was fired because of repeated problems with tuberculosis. Her lawsuit under Section 504 was quickly dismissed by the lower federal court on the ground that a contagious disease was not a handicap. The Supreme Court disagreed, ruling that people with contagious diseases such as tuberculosis may be considered handicapped within the meaning of the act. The school board and the U.S. Department of Justice argued that Arline's relapses of a communicable disease posed a threat to the health of school children and others, but the Supreme Court brushed this aside, saying:

> The fact that *some* persons who have contagious diseases may pose a serious health threat to others under certain circumstances does not justify excluding from the coverage of the Act *all* persons with actual or perceived contagious diseases. Such exclusion would mean that those accused of being contagious would never have the opportunity to have their condition evaluated in light of medical evidence and a determination made as to whether they were "otherwise qualified."

The Court then remanded the entire case to the lower court to determine whether Arline is "otherwise qualified." Stated differently, the question of whether Arline's medical condition or contagious disease represents a health hazard remains open and relevant. If the school board can present persuasive medical evi-

---

*The RN filed a complaint with DHHS on July 9, 1984, claiming that he was forced to take a medical leave of absence because he was *perceived* to have AIDS, although he did not in fact have it. During the long period of time that the complaint was being administratively processed or ignored by DHHS, the RN did contract AIDS, and as noted, died in early 1986.

dence that Arline's recurring tuberculosis would be a threat to the health of children and others at the school, her suit should be dismissed and the school board's position upheld. If, on the other hand, the preponderance of medical evidence at the trial suggests the absence of such a threat, Arline should win reinstatement to her third-grade position, back wages, and attorney fees. The Court explained that resolution of the "otherwise qualified" issue is a two-step journey. First, listen and defer to "reasonable medical judgments of public health officials." Second, considering the medical testimony, ask if the employer can reasonably accommodate the employee.

The Justice Department has directly injected the issue of AIDS in the *Arline* case by arguing that persons with HIV were contagious but neither physically impaired nor suffering from other symptoms of AIDS. However, the Court declined the opportunity for a sweeping decision involving AIDS by observing:

> The argument is misplaced in this case, because the handicap here, tuberculosis, gave rise both to a physical impairment *and* to contagiousness. This case does not present, and we therefore do not reach, the questions whether a carrier of a contagious disease such as AIDS could be considered to have a physical impairment, or whether such a person could be considered, solely on the basis of contagiousness, a handicapped person as defined by the Act.

There are several significant points about the Supreme Court's decision in *Arline* to bear in mind in attempting to apply it to AIDS situations: 1) Arline herself suffered from a definite physical impairment—her tuberculosis was diagnosed as "acute," she had been hospitalized, and "her major life activities were substantially limited by her impairment"; 2) the Court expressed concern about the continuing need of states to enforce public health laws and to regulate communicable diseases, and voiced the hope that its decision will "complement rather than complicate" those efforts; 3) persuasive medical evidence that employment of the plaintiff would be a real and substantial threat to the health of other employees should result in a dismissal of the suit, as the Court said:

> A person who poses a significant risk of communicating an in-
> fectious disease to others in the workplace will not be otherwise
> qualified for his or her job and a reasonable accommodation will
> not eliminate that risk. The Act would not require a school board
> to place a teacher with active, contagious tuberculosis in the class-
> room with elementary school children.

and 4) the Court emphasized that regardless of the threat-to-the-
health-of-others issue, the employee with the contagious disease
must be able to perform the essential functions of the job in question; if not, the question becomes whether a "reasonable accommodation" by the employer would be appropriate; the legal
explanation is that accommodation is not reasonable if it requires
fundamental changes in the job or imposes unreasonable financial
or administrative burdens.

The Supreme Court's decision in *Arline* raised more questions
than it answered. Lower federal district and appellate courts will
soon be faced with many issues involving the application of Section
504 and the Supreme Court's decision in *Arline* to specific factual
situations involving AIDS in the workplace. For example, is an
applicant with a positive test for HIV antibodies who is not hired
covered under the law? Unlike Arline, he or she has no physical
impairment. What about a male employee who is obviously homosexual and who is rumored to have AIDS, but in fact he does
not? Suppose an employee with AIDS in an early stage is physically
capable of performing all the duties connected with his or her job
and is not physically or mentally impaired, but due to periodic
display of the symptoms, has an extraordinarily high absenteeism
rate. Does the employer have to "accommodate" the employee by
retaining him or her on the payroll? What if the employee is physically capable of performing most of his or her duties, but not
lifting, one of the job's main duties? Or what if he or she can
perform all the essential functions for only eight hours, but the job
has a ten- or twelve-hour shift. Suppose a computer operator who
regularly works with sensitive, critical data is physically healthy in
his or her early stage of AIDS but suffering from dementia. Does
Section 504 protect this person? What if a male RN in the operating room of a hospital contracts AIDS and insists on continuing

his duties. Must the hospital leave him in that position or can it legally, as an accommodation to the victim, patients in the operating room, and other employees, involuntarily transfer him to a position where he is less likely to transmit the syndrome? Can an employer move an assembly line employee with AIDS to an isolated area of the warehouse, where the employee continues his or her regular job at the same pay and benefits? Is it permissible to have the employee perform all of his or her work at home, without loss of pay or benefits?

A critical procedural question remains to be resolved—who has the burden of proof? Typically, the plaintiff in Sections 503 and 504 cases has the burden of proving 1) that the employer is a supplier or contractor within the meaning of the Act; 2) that the plaintiff's specific medical condition (HIV, ARC, or AIDS) is a handicap; 3) that the plaintiff is otherwise qualified, meaning that he or she is capable of performing the essential functions of the job with or without a reasonable accommodation, and that his or her condition is not a threat to the health and safety of others; *and* 4) that he or she was discharged, transferred, or not hired because of this handicap. Will the burden be reallocated in any way for AIDS cases?

With respect to remedies, should the parents or "live-in" of an AIDS victim who died before his or her legal victory became final receive back pay that would have been awarded to the victim had he or she been alive? Should a hospital be enjoined from treating future employee-AIDS victims in particular ways, regardless of the situation? Is it permissible to ask AIDS patients if they can lift materials connected with the job, or whether they can work ten-hour days? Can the personnel manager describe the duties of a particular job to an applicant with an AIDS condition and ask whether he or she can perform them? If the applicant answers in the affirmative and is hired, but the employer quickly determines that he or she is physically incapable—contrary to the applicant's assertions—can the newly hired employee be discharged?

There are several cases pending in the federal courts which squarely face issues including AIDS and Section 504. In Florida, Todd Shuttleworth, a budget analyst for Broward County, was fired shortly after he developed AIDS. The county candidly acknowledged that the motivation for the discharge was his AIDS condition and explained the rationale: possible infection of fellow employees or others who would be in the office. Shuttleworth, thirty-four, had been promoted just prior to his discharge on the basis of outstanding performance reviews. Although he later developed pneumonia and became physically unable to work, it is undisputed that he was fit to perform the duties of his job at the time of discharge. Shuttleworth retained counsel and filed a charge with the Florida Commission on Human Relations (which has upheld his claim, as explained later) and a $15 million lawsuit in federal court for lost wages, medical and legal expenses, and damaged reputation. He has also successfully solicited media coverage of his cases. The cases were settled shortly before trial on the following terms: Shuttleworth was offered reinstatement in his former job and paid back wages and benefits estimated at $190,000, including medical costs not to exceed $100,000; his life and health insurance were reactivated; and his attorneys were paid $56,000 in fees and expenses. The court, however, denied the plaintiff's requests for damages connected to alleged emotional distress and mental anguish on the basis that they are not available in Section 504 actions.

In another federal court case, a licensed practical nurse (LPN) at a state affiliated hospital had a "roommate" who was admitted to the same hospital for an AIDS-related condition. The roommate later died. During his friend's illness, the LPN informed a supervisor that he might have contracted AIDS and agreed to submit to tests to determine whether he had been exposed to HIV. The LPN took the tests but refused repeated requests from the hospital to divulge the results. While continuing to refuse, he missed three days of work and was terminated. He then filed suit in federal court, alleging violations of multiple statutes, including the Vocational Rehabilitation Act, and requesting unspecified monetary damages. Not incidentally, his LPN duties required occasional invasive procedures. A copy of the lawsuit, filed by the ACLU, is presented in Appendix D, document 4.

A former employee of the Parkland Blood Bank in Dallas has filed a complaint under Section 504 with DHHS, claiming that he was refused reinstatement after he quit because of a positive test for the AIDS virus. The blood bank's defense is based partly on the assertion that employing someone who has tested positive would undermine public confidence in the bank and deter donations.

The National Gay Rights Advocates filed a charge under Section 504 with DHHS on behalf of a surgical technician who was placed on indefinite leave of absence by a hospital in Orlando. The technician, who claimed he was able to perform all the duties of his job, said that after the hospital learned he had a positive test result, he was given a choice of the following options: resignation, termination, or medical leave. Since continued insurance coverage was important to him, he chose the leave, but his preference was to continue his regular duties.

In California, a male guard was discharged from his position at a female prison shortly after he refused a transfer to another job. The transfer order was implemented when the prison learned that the guard had AIDS. After suit was filed under Section 504, the attorneys for each side successfully negotiated a settlement providing for continued medical insurance coverage as long as he suffered from AIDS-related maladies. There was neither reinstatement nor back wages paid, although the plaintiff received accrued vacation pay.

A special education teacher with AIDS was placed on a leave of absence with full pay and all benefits. Dissatisfied, he secured and presented a letter from a state health official saying he could be reinstated. The school board refused, suit was filed, and the court ruled in favor of the teacher.

In a suit raising the issue of whether a person who tests positive for HIV, but does not have ARC or AIDS, is handicapped within meaning of the law, the plaintiff entered a hospital's substance abuse treatment program to save his job. However, he was forced out by a hospital official after testing positive for HIV. ACLU attorneys filed a claim under Section 504 in his behalf, and the case is pending.

Employee Retirement Income Security Act

In passing the Employee Retirement Income Security Act (ERISA), Congress decided to prohibit discharging or otherwise discriminating against employees for the purpose of interfering with their right to claim benefits under an employee benefit plan. As previously noted, the medical cost of treating AIDS victims is significantly high. Suppose an employee with an AIDS condition is terminated, allegedly for the purpose of avoiding health care or medical claims to which the employee would be entitled under an ERISA-qualified plan. The definition of "benefit plan" is broad, including any health, disability, or life insurance policy or program. Employers who discharge employees testing positive for HIV antibodies or present medical documentation of ARC or AIDS for the purpose of preventing costly insurance claims and the increase in premiums likely to follow could be in violation of this federal law.

In a case involving the discharge of an employee allegedly because she contracted multiple sclerosis which would increase the company's insurance premium, the court ruled that discrimination in those circumstances violates ERISA. Enterprising plaintiff attorneys are certain to utilize this approach in AIDS cases in the near future.

Occupational Safety and Health Act

This federal statute, enacted in 1970, requires employers to provide a safe working environment for their employees. The Office of Safety and Health Administration (OSHA) of the U.S. Department of Labor has the responsibility to administer this act.

In general, employers have the duties under the act to comply with all promulgated standards and regulations and to furnish a workplace "free from recognized hazards that are causing or are likely to cause death or serious harm. . . ." Moreover, a provision in the statute prohibits employers from retaliating against employees who refuse to perform assigned work which they reasonably believe poses a danger.

While there have not yet been reported cases on this particular issue, suppose a group of employees files a complaint with OSHA to the effect that their employer has violated this law by allowing employees with AIDS to work with them and expose them to the virus. More particularly, suppose a hospital employee is exposed to HIV through a needle stick, but declines the hospital's offer to be tested for the virus with the statement, "Why should I go through the test every month for the next twelve months? Even if I'm positive, there's nothing I can do about it." The employee, then, is allowed to continue in his or her duties, and fellow employees file a charge with OSHA, alleging an unsafe working environment in that they are possibly being exposed to the virus as they continue handling the same needles, working with the same laboratory specimens, and otherwise having contact with a potential AIDS carrier. Is allowing employees in these situations to continue in their regular jobs "hazardous" within the meaning of OSHA?

Under current law, the probable answers to all these hypotheticals are negative. Hospitals, however, should be certain to apply all appropriate infection control procedures and satisfy all such standards; failures in this area would make one vulnerable to OSHA charges by employees or others.

National Labor Relations Act

The National Labor Relations Board (NLRB) and U.S. Supreme Court have recognized the right of employees to protest working conditions by refusing to work, circulating petitions, or other concerted activities. A decision by their employer to discharge them for engaging in such a protest is an unfair labor practice (Section 8(a)(1) violation) and would result in reinstatement of all employees with full back pay plus interest. The NLRB is without jurisdiction over public employers, so this section is applicable only to nonpublic situations.

Known as "protected concerted activity," this doctrine applies to action by two or more employees without union initiative, activity, or involvement. The only two requirements are that the employee action be concerted (usually two or more employees) and for the mutual aid or protection of employees. Examples of protected concerted activity include circulating a petition to protest a decision to work on a holiday; refusing to work scheduled overtime; walking off the job to display dissatisfaction with machinery not being properly maintained; and leaving job stations and gathering in the break room because it is too hot, too cold, raining, snowing, or the vending machines are broken again. A recent case involved an individual truck driver refusing to drive because of his belief that the fleet of trucks was not properly maintained, and it was therefore unsafe for *all* truck drivers (the doctrine can be applied even though the protest was only by one person because it involves a condition affecting a group of employees).

Over the years, hundreds of managers and supervisors have run afoul of this doctrine because of their sincere belief that employees had engaged in insubordination and were deserving of discharge. Supervisors feel embarrassed, chagrined, and undermined when employees they previously fired for disobeying instructions to work overtime in the dark or perform electrical work when it was raining file charges with the NLRB and eventually achieve reinstatement with full back pay and interest. Further, Section 502 of the National Labor Relations Act extends protection to union workers in situations where their safety is threatened by "abnormally dangerous" work conditions.

At the present time, groups of employees throughout the country are refusing to work with fellow employees who have AIDS. In New York City, thirty-nine sanitation workers refused to work with an AIDS victim, with the result that all thirty-nine were suspended without pay for one day. One hundred and fifty tons of garbage were not collected that day, but when the AIDS victim was reassigned to another position (watchman on the 12:00-8:00 A.M. shift), the other employees returned to work.

Paul Cronan, a repairman for New England Telephone Company, was released shortly after contracting AIDS. A $1.5 million lawsuit resulted in a settlement providing for his reinstatement approximately one year later. However, on his first day back at work a sign was painted on the wall—"Gays and bisexuals should be taken to an island and destroyed"—and twenty-nine of forty-four fellow repairmen refused to work because of his presence! Cronan complained that he was "treated like a leper." A few nurses have refused to treat AIDS patients for fear of contracting the syndrome and transmitting it to their families. Laboratory technicians and other medical personnel have refused to handle needles used to inject AIDS patients. Food service and housekeeping employees have announced that they will neither deliver food to nor clean the hospital rooms of AIDS patients. Almost always, the manager or supervisor who gave the instruction or possesses the overall responsibility becomes enraged with what he perceives as insubordination. This reaction is particularly true of doctors who expect nurses and other hospital personnel to place the medical treatment of patients above and beyond any concern for personal safety. Doctors and health care administrators take the position that hospitals are inherently hazardous in that the potential for contracting disease always exists. But they feel, as long as long-established precautions are taken, the risk is minimal and necessary; hence, any hospital employee who refuses to follow orders or carry out normal duties vis-à-vis AIDS patients should immediately be fired.

It is inevitable that the NLRB will be asked to decide numerous cases on the question of whether concerted activities by employees refusing to work with or treat AIDS victims is "protected." Employers will undoubtedly argue that while such a refusal by a group of employees may be concerted, it should be deemed "unprotected," because the interests of the AIDS victim, complying with the Vocational Rehabilitation Act and applying the company's normal rules and policies in the assignment of work should override unfounded concerns of health or safety on the part of the protesting employees.

Part of the difficulty with this doctrine is that the employer's representative often feels he must make a quick decision on the spot: either fire the employees or allow them to continue their protest. Managers believe that if the activity is truly protected and concerted, they must allow the protest to continue or face sanctions from the NLRB; on the other hand, if they conclude the employee protest is unprotected, then they believe they should immediately discharge the employees or their authority will be undermined. However, the best approach to defusing the situation and resolving possible protected concerted activity problems is usually neither to fire nor to allow the protest to continue. Instead, employees withholding their services should be told very clearly and definitely, in front of witnesses, that they must either return to work and carry out the duties in question *or* leave the employer's premises. No law or regulation requires employers to allow employees refusing to work and protesting conditions to continue on the employer's property. A nurse refusing to treat an AIDS victim, a maintenance crew refusing to repair a machine manned by a homosexual rumored to have AIDS, the clerical staff refusing to work with a bookkeeper whose brother has a confirmed case of AIDS could all be ordered to perform the duties they were assigned or leave the employer's premises. If they refuse to leave, they should be told that they are subjecting themselves to disciplinary action, up to and including discharge, for violating the order to vacate the premises; either security or the police could then be called. If discharge becomes necessary, it is motivated by their refusal to obey an order to leave the employer's property and not for any protest connected to AIDS.

In 95 percent of the cases, if the matter is handled well, the employees will obey orders to leave the employer's property. Once the employees have left, the employer has the legal right to hire permanent replacements for the protesting personnel. If permanent replacements are hired and in place before the protesting employees return to work, the employees can be legally told that their positions have been filled in their absence with permanent replacements, and if they wish to seek reinstatement to their former positions, they must complete an application for reinstatement by leaving their names, addresses, and telephone numbers. The employer is not required to discharge the permanent replacements to make room for the protesting employees. Instead, the employer's only obligation is to offer the protesting personnel who have declared their desire for reinstatement an opportunity to fill openings for which they are qualified that accrue in the future, prior to hiring from the outside. This obligation to employees on the recall list is indefinite.*

It is important, then, for supervisors, department heads, and managers who may be faced with employees' refusal to work in an AIDS situation to be trained *not* to make snap decisions, *not* to fire employees, and *not* to allow demonstrations or refusals to continue with employees on the property. Instead, the appropriate human resource or other manager should be called, regardless of the

---

*To prevent a replacement from later claiming that he had an employment contract with the company on the basis of his being told his services would be "permanent" in duration, inform the newly hired employees that they are "regular" and not temporary.

day or hour, and approaches to the AIDS problem that incorporate these principles should be taken.

Set forth below are a series of AIDS-related situations in the work force involving the doctrine of protected concerted activity. Included in each is a situation presenting the problem (ask yourself how you would handle it), an assessment of whether the protest is protected or unprotected under an NLRB law, and a suggested response for management. In dealing with real AIDS situations in the workplace, remember that there is no substitute for advice from a labor lawyer fully apprised of applicable laws and pertinent facts.

Example 1

Situation. A group of twenty production employees sign a petition demanding that a janitor, a male homosexual, be fired. When presenting the petition to the superintendent, the group leader (Don) says that the janitor is rumored to have AIDS and that none of the production employees want to use bathrooms cleaned by him. Don adds that if the janitor is still in that job the next morning, all twenty and probably more employees will walk out.

Protected Concerted Activity? No. A demand by employees that another employee be removed from a job should not be and is not protected under U.S. labor laws. There is no evidence in this case that the health or safety of the employees has been threatened in any way. A rumor that the janitor has AIDS is insufficient to demonstrate a legitimate employee concern.

Management Response. The superintendent and personnel manager (two managers) should ask Don into an office and inform him in a firm manner: "If you or other employees have detailed information on any illness the janitor may have and how it may threaten the health or safety of others, please pass it on to us. At the present time there is no evidence or report that either the janitor has AIDS or that the health of you or others is threatened in any way by him. In these circumstances, you and the others must follow the regular work schedule—if you don't you'll be subjecting yourselves to being permanently replaced." Then go to the production floor and individually give the same message to others who signed the petition. Begin reviewing applications so you can quickly contact, interview, and perhaps hire twenty or more employees if a walkout occurs.

Example 2

Situation. Edna, a housekeeping employee at a hospital, informs the department head that she will not clean room 5B01 because its current patient is being treated for AIDS. When the department head points out that the hospital has been treating AIDS patients for several years and neither she nor any other housekeeping employee has ever refused, Edna replies that her husband has just learned that she cleans the rooms of AIDS patients from time to time and last night he ordered her never to do it again, because of a fear that she might contract it and transmit it to him and their five children.

Protected Concerted Activity? No. Once again the NLRB should dismiss an unfair labor practice charge, if filed. Here, the activity is not concerted: only Edna is refusing to perform a duty assigned to numerous housekeeping employees. There is no indication that others have authorized Edna to speak for them; Edna (or her husband) may argue that she is expressing concern that affects or threatens other employees, but in those circumstances the NLRB should conclude that the activity (refusing to perform assigned duties) is definitely not concerted and may not even be protected (there is no indication that simply cleaning the room of an AIDS patient is infectious).

Management response. The department head and personnel director should meet with Edna and inform her: "Your assigned duties will continue to include the rooms of AIDS patients, and you'll be expected to clean those rooms in the same manner as the others. We hope you'll agree to this; if you refuse to carry out your duties, you'll be guilty of insubordination and subject to being permanently replaced."

Example 3

Situation. The office manager discovers most of his clerical staff discussing a newspaper article about a male politician in town who has just resigned from his office with the announcement that he is suffering from AIDS, which he contracted through injecting illegal drugs. The wife of the politician, Shirley, works as the office manager's secretary. One of the clerical workers tells the office manager: "It has been proven that AIDS is transmitted through sexual contact. This means Shirley may well have AIDS. And she's here every day, getting water from our drinking fountain, using our restrooms, and serving *you* coffee and lunch. What are *you* going to do about it?"

Just then Shirley walks up and says: "Last week the children and I were tested for the AIDS virus, and I just learned that while the results were all negative for the kids, mine was positive. The doctor assures me that I don't have AIDS now and may never have it. I feel fine and want very much to continue working. My husband is expected to die before the end of the year, and with the loss of his paycheck, medical bills, and four children, I really need my job."

One of the clericals shouts: "Well, that's not good enough for me. Any of us could catch it from Shirley and then give it to our husbands, just the way her dopehead husband gave it to her. I'm going to the break room and won't return to work until Shirley leaves and never comes back." The other clerical staff follow her to the break room, leaving the office manager and Shirley.

Protected Concerted Activity? Probably not. There is no indication that AIDS can be transmitted through casual contact in the workplace. Even if Shirley eventually develops AIDS, the CDC and almost all doctors say that she will not infect other staff members or her boss through carrying out her office duties and having normal contact with them. And to date, she does *not* have AIDS. On the other hand, the employees, who are definitely engaged in concerted activity, have a sincere concern about the health and safety of themselves and the members of their families. Medically, their fears appear to be unfounded, but they neither understand nor believe that. The NLRB would probably conclude the concerns of the clerical staff were unreasonable and their refusal to work unprotected.

Management Response. Education is in order here. Send Shirley home with pay, after expressing sympathy and concern. Then meet with all the clerical staff, bringing in a nurse or doctor if appropriate (as well as materials) for the purpose of informing them of basic facts about AIDS and answering their questions. At the end of the session, explain in no uncertain terms that Shirley will be at work the next day and that all of them will be expected to report and work as scheduled; those who don't will be subject to being permanently replaced. (Consider moving Shirley to a work location that is at least partially isolated from the other clericals.)

Example 4

Situation. When a nurse inquires about the past or present medical problems of a patient in the emergency room who was injured in an automobile accident, the patient reports that he has AIDS. Word spreads to the other five nursing personnel on duty in that department, all of whom refuse to treat the accident victim, who is bleeding profusely. All five nurses refuse orders from both doctors and the department head to assist in treating the patient.

Protected Concerted Activity? Probably yes. The refusal is obviously concerted, so the only question is whether it is protected. The hospital can argue that it should not be, because nurses have an obligation to carry out orders in emergency treatment situations, but the NLRB could note the risk of blood splashes and other exposure to the virus and rule the refusals to be protected.

Management Response. Be certain that the orders to assist in treating the AIDS patient are clear and understood, and that the refusals are definite, heard by witnesses, and documented. Then send the nurses home. Do *not* allow them to treat other patients or to be transferred to another area. Hire permanent replacements as soon as possible (this may be difficult to accomplish in a short amount of time). Follow NLRB rules concerning permanent replacements and applications for reinstatement. Obviously, educational efforts are very much in order.

Example 5

Situation. A plant manager places a notice on the bulletin board of a manufacturing facility stating that effective the next day all employees are subject to random testing for AIDS. The following morning 50 percent of the employees on the first shift walk around the plant with petitions protesting the AIDS test instead of reporting to their machines. The manager announces over the loud speaker system that all employees are ordered to their machines and any who don't comply will be fired. The announcement is repeated three times. Ten minutes later the manager appears on the plant floor with security guards, informs the twenty-five protesting employees that they are fired, and orders them off the property.

Protected Concerted Activity? Yes. The AIDS test is certainly a condition of employment, and employees have the right to register their objection by withholding their services and informing others of their protest. The activity is obviously concerted. While the employer could argue it should be unprotected because it occurred during working time, interfered with work by employees who began their assembly assignments as scheduled, and generally disrupted operations, the NLRB would probably dismiss those arguments.

Management Response. The manager made a series of mistakes. The decision to test production and maintenance employees randomly in a manufacturing facility is founded neither on logic nor on the law. If the employer is a federal government contractor or in a state or city that has either a general handicap law or a special AIDS ordinance, it probably is engaging in illegal conduct. Aside from the law, it is poor employee relations to implement any new policy with a one-day notice. In this case of a controversial rule, there should be a minimum hiatus of thirty days between the announcement and the implementation. Moreover, meetings with employees to explain the rationale and inviting their questions and comments would be in order. Finally, the manager should have reminded employees of the rule prohibiting solicitation while they are supposed to be working and instructed them to report to their machines. Assuming that is ignored, the employees roaming the plant with petitions should be ordered either to report to their job stations and begin work or to leave the company's property. Those who continue the protest should be escorted off company property.

None of them should be threatened or told that they are fired. The message is quite simple: if you aren't going to work, you must leave. After escorting them out of the plant, apply the rules and procedures for protected concerted activity.

The Constitution—Equal Protection and Due Process Clauses

Persons with AIDS conditions on the payrolls of the federal, state, or local governments could consider suits under the Fifth or Fourteenth Amendments to the U.S. Constitution. The Fifth Amendment protects applicants and employees from being deprived of "property" without due process of law by the U.S. Government, while the Fourteenth Amendment extends protection to state and local government employees. Specifically, Amendment Fourteen prohibits states from depriving its citizens of "property" without due process of law, or from denying them equal protection of the laws. Since the equal protection clause essentially means similarly situated people must be similarly treated, a policy or practice by a state hospital to discriminate against AIDS applicants or employees may violate the Constitution. Further, the Fourth Amendment protects governmental employees from unreasonable searches and seizures. This has already been applied to void discharges for positive drug test results, and it is at least equally applicable to tests for HIV antibodies.

State and local government employers should be especially sensitive to lawsuits grounded to Constitutional theories.

3
State and Local Laws

Buford Jones was adept at climbing the corporate ladder. Hired immediately out of college as an assistant manager by a restaurant chain, Buford was promoted to manager within one year, and then to district and regional managerial positions in rapid succession. At the tender age of twenty-eight, Buford—known as the executive vice president's fair-haired boy—was promoted to vice president over all Florida operations. One of the secrets of Buford's success, he often boasted, was that he always checked corporate policy before effectuating a decision. There were several voluminous policy manuals on every conceivable business subject, and Buford often advised associates that if you went by the book, you could never make a mistake.

When Buford inspected one of his newly acquired restaurants in Florida during his first week as an officer of the corporation, he was amazed to find an elderly lady working as the cashier. The manager informed him that "Granny," who was eighty-four years old, had worked at that restaurant for thirty-two years. Buford reacted quickly. Turning to chapter 9, paragraph 2 of the corporate personnel policy manual, he pointed out to the manager that the mandatory retirement age was seventy, admonished him for allowing Granny to work fourteen years beyond the limit, and ordered the manager to effectuate her "retirement" by the end of the week.

Ten days later, the company was served with an age discrimination lawsuit filed in state court, a development that was played up by the local newspaper. At 5:00 P.M. on the day following the newspaper story, a group of fifteen previously regular customers began picketing the entrance to the restaurant, protesting unfair treatment of Granny, and demanding her return. The executive vice president, director of human resources, and general counsel called Buford from corporate headquarters, heatedly informing him that while corporate personnel policy correctly reflected the status of federal law as of that time (1985),—that is, mandatory retirement after seventy as permissible—the state of Florida had a special statute that protects employees from involuntary retirement regardless of age!

Since reinstating Granny with full back pay, extending a public apology, and paying her attorney's fees, Buford has decided to check local laws as well as corporate policy before effectuating personnel decisions.

Until recently, managers concerned about possible labor laws needed only to bear in mind any applicable federal statutes and how they are interpreted by federal commissions. During the last five years, however, states, counties, and cities have exercised legislative discretion by enacting statutes and ordinances to protect applicants and employees from employment discrimination and by creating human rights commissions to administer their laws. Greater protection at lower governmental levels than federal has been extended to cover such areas as maternity, age, sexual preference, and AIDS. In fact, AIDS is a subject that has generated considerable debate in local legislative bodies. Hence, prudent managers with multistate and city facilities must become aware of any state and local laws that may pertain to AIDS before effectuating decisions or drafting policies on this topic.

There is a higher probability of a state or local law disposing of an AIDS-in-the-workplace issue than a federal one. Normally, state statutes cover all employers with more than a handful of employees, while, as noted, the Vocational Rehabilitation Act of 1973 applies only to some public employers and private companies with sufficient federal government contracts or subcontracts. Stated another way, thousands of private companies, exempt from federal laws on the subject, are covered by state or local laws applicable to AIDS situations.

States

A few states have enacted legislation specifically pertaining to AIDS. Florida, Wisconsin, California, and the District of Columbia all prohibit or restrict the use of results from the HIV virus test in employment decisions affecting applicants as well as employees. California and Wisconsin also mandate that the test results are confidential and prohibit their disclosure in order to protect the privacy of the afflicted employee. States can be expected to debate hundreds of laws involving AIDS during the next several years. After discovering that AIDS has infected 0.83 percent of its population, the State of Texas recently enacted a law requiring that couples wishing to obtain a marriage license be tested for the HIV virus.

Most states, like federal agencies and courts, are using existing laws to protect victims from discrimination. Thus, a Massachusetts superior court has ruled that AIDS is a handicap under that state's law. The plaintiff, a repair technician with New England Telephone, alleged that he was forced to disclose a diagnosis of ARC to his supervisor after a series of medical absences led to interrogation. Eventually he quit, after unsympathetic coworkers threatened to lynch him. The technician filed suit, claiming that he was handicapped within the meaning of state law and thus deserving of reinstatement and full back pay. Justice Rouse specifically rejected the U.S. Department of Justice's position that employer actions taken against AIDS victims that are based upon fear of contagion are permitted, and she ruled that the definition of handicap includes individuals with AIDS "who are not a threat to co-workers, but whose co-workers erroneously consider them unemployable." In response to the employer's argument that the plaintiff was not technically suffering from AIDS as such, Judge Rouse ruled that an employee with ARC "would be handicapped regardless of whether he was presently suffering any adverse physical effects of AIDS. It is the potential to contract other illnesses that constitutes the handicap." This case, like most other AIDS suits, was settled short of trial, and the plaintiff was reinstated to his former position. *Cronan v. New England Telephone.* (As explained in the previous chapter, plaintiff Cronan's reinstatement sparked harassment and a walkout by fellow employees.)

The Washington State Human Rights Commission has specifically recognized AIDS as a disability under that state's discrimination law and has proposed policy guidelines for preventing discrimination against victims of AIDS in employment. One guideline stresses that the agency "does not currently recognize any job classification where a diagnosis of AIDS would prevent the hiring of any person who has the syndrome" and indicated that employers are obligated to "reasonably accommodate disabled persons, including AIDS victims, unless the disability prevents proper performance on the job."

Michigan, Ohio, California, and Florida are among the twenty-one states that have formally classified AIDS as a handicap, whereas Kentucky's legislature specifically concluded that AIDS is not a handicap within the meaning of its discrimination law. The California Fair Employment and Housing Commission ruled in 1987 that its law protecting the handicapped is applicable to persons with AIDS and ordered that back pay and interest be given to the estate of an employee with AIDS who was denied reinstatement by Raytheon before he died. However, in 1986 a bill classifying AIDS, cancer, and other specific diseases as physical handicaps and extending special protection to people with these conditions was vetoed by the governor of California. As indicated in chapter 2 Todd Shuttleworth filed a charge with the Florida Commission on Human Relations after being discharged by Broward County. The Commission concluded that AIDS is a handicap within the meaning of that state's law.

Since forty-two states and the District of Columbia have statutes protecting the handicapped from discrimination, considerable litigation involving AIDS matters is anticipated. A graphic artist filed suit against his company, claiming violation of Virginia's handicap law, when he was first placed on mandatory leave of absence and eventually terminated, allegedly to protect other employees. There have been at least two suits in Louisiana, one by a waiter fired after he allegedly disrupted the hotel by announcing to fellow employees and guests that his roommate had AIDS, and another by the credit manager of a television station who claimed that he was physically and mentally able to perform his job but was fired after his ARC condition progressed to AIDS. (Copies of the hotel and television station lawsuits can be found in Appendix D, documents 5 and 6.)

Suppose the applicant is not presently impaired in any way, but the employer has medical knowledge that he has ARC or is in an early stage of AIDS, with the inevitability of impairment and eventual replacement after his death. Anticipating extensive absenteeism, a short return on training time and cost, heavy use of health insurance, and then a life insurance payment, all within the relatively near future, may the employer refuse to hire or promote the person? In *State Division of Human Rights (New York) v. Xerox Corp.*, the court rejected the employer's argument that an obese applicant was unacceptable because his physical condition would deteriorate. Similarly, in *Chrysler Outboard Corp. v. Wisconsin Department of Industry,* the court addressed the claim of an applicant who was denied employment because he had acute lymphocytic leukemia. Relying upon a report from the medical consultant that the applicant's condition posed a high risk of infection from minor injury, a risk of prolonged recuperation, and a risk of complications from the disease, all of which would result in lost time, the employer rejected the applicant. The court, however, concluded that the disease was a handicap and observed, "The employer's contention that the complainant may at some future date be unable to perform the duties of the job is immaterial."

A Wisconsin court relied upon the state's law banning discrimination on the basis of sexual orientation in ruling that an employer's policy excluding persons with AIDS was illegal. The rationale— since most victims are gay males, the policy has a disparate impact on a group because of their sexual orientation—was rejected by *federal* courts in applying federal law, but this is a separate, *state* law.

Plaintiff attorneys, always resourceful, are not limited to statutes specifically covering AIDS handicaps or sexual orientation. In Michigan, a man who had been employed for fifteen years was terminated two days after discussing his AIDS condition with an executive of his company. He was allowed to retain health insurance coverage but deprived of life insurance, he alleges. His attorney has sued for $10 million, claiming breach of employment contract and intentional infliction of emotional distress, as well as discrimination against the handicapped.

State court tort actions should be anticipated in an environment where jokes and rumors about AIDS are endemic. A hotel was sued by an employee who claimed he suffered severe emotional distress due to false gossip and talk at work about his having AIDS. Wishing to avoid publicity, the employer quietly settled the suit for a substantial sum. Defamation, slander, and libel are possible causes of action against an employer whose agents maliciously and falsely state, orally or in writing, that a gay or other employee has AIDS. In Pennsylvania a hospital, church, and minister were sued by a patient with these allegations: hospital employees falsely told a minister that the patient was suffering from AIDS, and the minister repeated the erroneous information to others, including several in the congregation. The suit seeks damages for emotional distress, embarrassment, lost wages, and medical expenses.

In Chicago a woman at O'Hare Airport attempted to board a plane without a boarding pass. When the American Airlines agent refused her passage, causing her to miss the flight, she allegedly grabbed his arm. The agent then supposedly kicked her in the shins and bit her. When the agent later tested positive for HIV, the woman's lawyer filed suit against American Airlines for negligently hiring an AIDS victim and failing to safeguard its passengers from exposure to employees with contagious diseases. The woman is seeking $12 million in damages!

The obligation, if any, of an employer to inform an applicant, an employee, or others of an AIDS condition is an issue certain to receive considerable attention. In *Dornak v. Lafayette General Hospital*, the plaintiff was referred to the hospital's physician for a pre-employment physical examination after completing her application for employment as a nurse's aide. The hospital hired her but failed to disclose that a chest X-ray revealed tuberculosis. Later she experienced persistent coughing and other symptoms which caused consultation with her personal physician, who diagnosed her tubercular condition and determined that the X-ray in her personnel file showed it. Plaintiff filed a tort action, claiming the hospital was negligent in not telling her of the tuberculosis and asserting she would have secured medical treatment for that condition during the almost three years between the pre-employment X-ray and her doctor's diagnosis. The Supreme Court of Louisiana ruled that the hospital breached its duty to disclose the result of the X-ray. Specifically the court said:

> While we do not consider that the hospital had any obligation to give plaintiff a pre-employment physical examination, once it undertook to do so and subsequently employed her, she was entitled to and did rely upon the expectation that she would be told of any dangerous condition actually disclosed by that examination, especially considering the fact that she was employed by the hospital to perform duties placing her in contact with co-employees and hospital patients.

A question to ponder—what if the victim, ignorant of her condition, infects others after the test but before the diagnosis? Would the infected third parties have a cause for action against the employer? It seems definite that if an employer tests an applicant or employee for antibodies to HIV, any positive result should be communicated to the person. This should be accomplished even if the applicant is not hired. Note, though, the court's emphasis upon placing an employee with a "dangerous condition . . . in contact with co-employees and hospital patients." While there is a legal duty to disclose the condition to the employee, is there a corresponding obligation to inform co-employees and patients?*

Marc Christian, a homosexual lover of Rock Hudson, has sued the Hudson estate for $14 million, alleging that Hudson continued to have sex with him after Hudson's AIDS condition was diagnosed, thus subjecting Christian to fears that he will eventually contract it. The gravamen of the suit is that Hudson had a legal duty to disclose that he had AIDS. Apply the concept to the employment arena: suppose that an employee, patient, or customer learns that an employee who treated or served her, or worked closely with her for a long period of time, has or had AIDS, and that the

---

*Legislatures, as well as courts, can be expected to display concern for people infected without knowing it. Florida, for example, has a statute requiring notification to those who are infected with the HIV virus.

employer had knowledge of the employee's condition and allowed him to continue his duties without notifying others. The person then sues the employer, claiming anguish over the possibility of being infected or actual infection as demonstrated by a positive test result, and arguing that the employer committed a tort by failing to inform the plaintiff (and possibly members of her class) that its employee had AIDS. A Washington State Court of Appeals has ruled that a nonsmoker may maintain a suit against her employer for negligence in allowing her to be exposed to tobacco smoke in the workplace with the result that she developed a pulmonary disease. In allowing the common law action for negligence to stand, the court stated the employer violated its duty to provide "a safe and healthful place of employment. . . ." An enterprising plaintiff attorney with a client who may have contracted HIV from someone in the workplace is bound to argue this doctrine is applicable.

The employer's defenses would be that AIDS cannot be communicated through casual contact, that the doctrine is inapplicable in AIDS situations, and that there was a superseding obligation to maintain confidentiality concerning the AIDS victim. Such disclosures, if made, could stimulate discrimination against and harassment of the victim. Suppose, though, that the person with AIDS was a nurse involved with invasive procedures, or a laboratory technician regularly handling blood, and a patient or employee actually contracted HIV. These circumstances would strengthen plaintiff's case. In fact, a plaintiff may argue that the legal duty of the employer goes beyond disclosure to the actual removal of the infected employee from those and similar jobs. However, there is no precedent for such a strong ruling, and plaintiffs in these cases would have a heavy burden of proof. Any employer considering disclosure of an employee's AIDS condition to fellow employees, patients, or others should consider the possible claims against it for breach of confidentiality, improper communication of medical records, libel, slander, and defamation by the AIDS victim. An employer weighing the risks of disclosure should conclude in most situations that the probability of losing a suit is significantly higher if disclosure is made. Where feasible, an employer that decides that disclosure is appropriate in a particular case should obtain an authorization for it from the employee with AIDS.

There is no substitute for a precise and careful analysis of the facts in every situation where the rights of an employee with an AIDS condition may conflict with those of fellow employees or others. The most probable place for this tension between two rights is a health care facility. Suppose Tom is a patient with an advanced case of AIDS at Riverview Hospital. Not only is he positive for the HIV virus, he is contagious with respect to a variety of secondary infections, including rubella, brought on by his impaired immune system. A severe shortage of nurses caused by the hospital's inability to recruit replacements and unusual absenteeism causes Riverview to assign Cathy, on an overtime basis, to the ward in which Tom and other AIDS victims are located. Suppose further that Cathy is pregnant. Certainly Cathy would not be asked to directly care for Tom, and the hospital would disclose Tom's conditions to her if she were working in the general area of his room. Now suppose a reversal—Tom, still a victim of AIDS and slowed down, but not stopped, by contagious secondary infections, is the *nurse* and Cathy, pregnant, is the *patient*. It is again obvious that Tom would be removed from Cathy's ward. In fact, Tom would probably be removed from all patient care duties. If, however, Tom worked in a small office without exposure to patients, and doctors treating his secondary infections certify that the few employees with whom he has contact are not endangered, there would be neither disclosure nor removal. The probability of persons with AIDS in later stages developing secondary infections injects an important factor in the equation. Serious, contagious infections may dictate removal of the employee from a particular job while disclosure to fellow employees may suffice for others. Thus, there are situations where removal of an employee with an AIDS condition is necessary, other situations where disclosure of an AIDS condition is appropriate, and many more situations where neither should be effectuated and, instead, the employee with HIV, ARC, or AIDS is simply allowed to continue working without any action or publication of his or her condition. It is impossible to draft and rigidly apply previously adopted procedures or rules in these situations. Instead, management should analyze the rights and facts in the specific situation, rely heavily upon medical evaluations, and document the decision-making process.

In summary, there are a number of torts contained in established state laws that could easily be applied to AIDS in the workplace situations. These include *negligent hiring;* infliction of *mental anguish* and *emotional distress; slander, defamation,* and *libel* (oral or written communications stating an applicant, employee or ex-employee has AIDS, ARC, or the virus); *invasion of privacy; breach of confidentiality of medical records* (a personnel manager or clerk shows employees, a customer, patient, or other member of the public medical records describing the AIDS diagnosis of an applicant or employee); and *duty to disclose* (employees working side by side with an AIDS victim claim their employer should have notified them of the medical condition of the employee with AIDS).

While some lawyers may not be interested in representing AIDS victims, a few firms and several organizations are actually seeking such cases. The American Civil Liberties Union (ACLU) has been very active in this area, filing numerous suits in federal and state courts, and it is anticipated that the National Association for the Advancement of Colored People (NAACP)—largely because a disparate number of AIDS victims are black—will become involved. These organizations, primarily interested in making or changing the law, are expected to continue prosecuting cases through the various levels of courts, even after a plaintiff's death, to achieve their goal.

Perhaps the most entertaining legal development among the states in this area is the PANIC initiative in California. PANIC is an acronym for Prevent AIDS Now Initiative Committee. Supporters of Lyndon LaRouche and other members of the group collected 683,000 signatures to place a proposal on the ballot in that state that would categorize AIDS as an infectious disease like measles or TB, and allow health officers to use the full range of protective powers to safeguard the interests of the public—including a quarantine. Proposition 64 would have barred anyone with a positive test from schools and jobs that involve food handling. While the initiative was unanimously denounced by almost every politician and political party and soundly rejected by the voters on November 4, 1986 (71 percent voted against), it is an indication of the volatile emotions on the part of the public.

Finally, with different states taking varied and sometimes contradictory approaches to AIDS situations, employers must be careful of a special area of the law called "conflict." Suppose Ted, a resident of Indiana, works at a restaurant in Chicago that is owned by a large corporation based in California. Ted, fired after the manager hears a rumor that he has AIDS, wants to sue. The law of which state or city would apply?

Cities

Cities have also been active in this area. Los Angeles, Sacramento, and West Hollywood, California, and Austin, Texas, all have enacted ordinances that expressly prohibit discrimination against applicants or employees with AIDS. The City Attorney for West Hollywood has said, "The West Hollywood law is broad enough to allow us to find discrimination under certain circumstances involving people telling jokes about AIDS!" The Los Angeles and San Francisco ordinances move considerably beyond all employment discrimination laws, which provide for compensatory damages only, by allowing claims for punitive damages. Jessica's Nail Salon has been formally charged with violating criminal provisions of the West Hollywood law for canceling a pedicure appointment with a victim of AIDS. Conviction could lead to a jail sentence of six months, a fine of $1,000, or both. The small business' defense is that blood accidently drawn from an AIDS victim during a pedicure could infect others. The Austin ordinance proscribes AIDS-based discrimination in housing, as well as in employment and public accommodations. The Mayor of Boston avoided controversy with the city council by issuing an executive order that protected all city employees with AIDS conditions from discriminating in hiring, promotions, and employee benefits.

The Legal Aid Society of San Francisco has filed a complaint with that city's Human Rights Commission, alleging that Neiman-Marcus violated the ordinance protecting AIDS victims by terminating a salesman one month after he was diagnosed as suffering from AIDS. The specific claims are that the department store refused his request for unpaid medical leave (which would have allowed insurance coverage to continue), harrassed and humiliated him, and communicated his condition to other employees, thereby violating his right of privacy. The company's position is that the salesman had used all of his sick days, the medical plan he selected could not be converted into a private policy, the regular approach for resolving medical problems was used, and that there was no violation.

New York City's Human Rights Commission has rejected the U.S. Department of Justice's opinion that fear of contamination justifies discrimination in some cases, and instead has pledged to prosecute any employer that discriminates against AIDS victims. In fact, the New York City Human Rights Commission has a special AIDS Discrimination Unit for investigating and processing complaints. Other counties, parishes, and cities have considered statutes or ordinances to prohibit discrimination against AIDS in the workplace or to regulate employer responses to the issue.

Chattanooga is using AIDS as a justification for increasing its regulation of adult movie and entertainment facilities. Citing the threat of AIDS and the need to protect public health, a new ordinance requires licenses and permits for the facilities and regulates how they are operated. Courts, which in the past have frequently nullified attempts to regulate these establishments as violative of the First Amendment, have thus far approved laws like this as valid exercises of the city's power to protect and promote public health.

Persons with AIDS conditions who feel they are victims of improper discrimination have not hesitated to utilize city laws. In 1986 the numbers of charging parties with AIDS complaints filed with these human rights commissions are as follows: New York City, 317; Los Angeles, 140; and San Francisco, 65.

Employment-at-Will

The employment-at-will doctrine is that employees without an employment contract are on the payroll at the discretion of their employer, and can be fired "at will" for good reason, bad reason, or any reason, as long as the reason is not proscribed by law. This means that any plaintiff protesting a termination by filing a lawsuit in state court should have that claim dismissed unless a specific statute or employment contract can be identified that protects him or her. For example, a minority man might claim that he was fired because of his race; a woman would argue that she was terminated because of her sex; a sixty-eight-year-old, long-service employee could claim that he was forced into retirement because of his age; a young female could say that she was constructively discharged (forced to quit) because of sexual harassment in the office; or a newly hired vice president, fired after a disagreement with the president, could claim a letter describing his annual salary and benefits is an employment contract.

Over the years, numerous lawsuits have been dismissed by judges because terminated employees were unable to connect their termination to a particular type of discrimination that was protected by law. However, during the last five years, there has been a serious erosion of the employment-at-will doctrine. The Texas Supreme Court carved out the only exception to the employment-at-will doctrine in that state by ruling that a plaintiff would have the right to go to trial on a claim that he or she was terminated for refusing to perform an illegal act. Other cases have given protection—absent special statutes—in circumstances when whistle-blowing employees were fired after they reported illegal conduct at their companies to the authorities. Employment contracts, convenants of fair dealing, and requirements of good faith have been implied in several states to give an unfairly discharged employee his day in court. The employment-at-will doctrine has almost been completely eroded in California while—thus far—it remains strong in most southern and midwestern states.

It is suggested that employees with HIV, ARC, or AIDS who are not hired or are terminated by an employer that makes no attempt to accommodate them may have an opportunity to create additional exceptions to the employment-at-will doctrine. In their efforts to represent applicants and employees with AIDS conditions, creative plaintiff attorneys and organizations like the ACLU can be expected to exploit the softening of the employment-at-will doctrine that has occurred in recent years. Judges, impressed with the inequity of an employee summarily fired simply because he has developed AIDS or is positive for the HIV antibodies, may imply a covenant or stretch a doctrine to protect the plaintiff.

Multiple Claims

The ACLU and plaintiff attorneys will not limit themselves to a single, federal, state, or local law when filing a legal challenge on behalf of an AIDS victim. To the contrary, they should be expected to use the shotgun approach of listing every conceivable law to support their claims, hoping that the court will agree that at least one pellet has hit the jurisdictional mark. Appendix D, document 7, presents a letter mailed to the administrator of a hospital by an attorney representing a terminated AIDS victim. The letter threatens suit under three separate laws, one state and two federal. Note the involvement of both the ACLU and Lambda, an organization formed to promote the legal rights and interests of homosexuals.

Of considerable interest is the AIDS Civil Rights Project, administered in San Francisco by the National Gay Rights Advocates, which provides a full-time lawyer to assist those claiming AIDS discrimination. Advice, information, and technical expertise on filing and processing AIDS-related claims is available. Further, legal pleadings, law review and other articles, and general data on AIDS from across the nation are being placed in a computer database that will be available to claimants.

Jurisdiction or Coverage

Regardless of whether the law is city, county, state, or even federal, questions always arise of whether it covers the particular applicant or employee filing the claim (jurisdiction over person) *and* the particular conduct of the employer in failing to hire, terminating, demoting, or placing the charging party on leave of absence (jurisdiction over subject matter).

While it appears that most, if not all, of the laws discussed thus far would, directly or indirectly, be applicable to victims of AIDS or ARC, suppose the person filing the charges has neither but is positive for the antibodies to the HIV virus? As previously noted, probability suggests he or she will never develop full-blown AIDS, and he is not impaired in any way—should he or she be covered because his employer ascertained that he or she is HIV positive and took action adverse to him? The hotel case (Appendix D, document 5) raised the question of whether a roommate of an AIDS victim should enjoy the protection of a law designed to help victims of AIDS. Finally, should homosexuals and drug addicts who are perceived by their potential or actual employers to be candidates for AIDS be able to take advantage of these laws, assuming they are not hired or fired because of their homosexuality or drug addiction?

With respect to subject matter jurisdiction, an employer's action in refusing to hire or in discharging a victim of AIDS would probably be covered by the statutes. Suppose, however, that the employer merely transfers the AIDS victim to another job, which has less exposure to customers, patients, or employees, without a reduction in wages. Should a suit with those facts be dismissed for lack of jurisdiction or be allowed to go to trial on the merits? Assume an employee with AIDS at a hospital or restaurant is placed on involuntary leave of absence with full wages for four weeks, half wages for the next four weeks, and one-quarter wages for the next two weeks, pursuant to that employer's disability policy. Should the employee have the right to legally address his or her irritation with being taken off the job because of the affliction? Assume further that a victim of AIDS is placed on leave and assigned to a company's employee assistance program (EAP), just as victims of alcohol and drug abuse have been in the past, with the right to be reinstated in the future. Once again, is he or she entitled to a day in court?

Finally, should the prohibition against discrimination be interpreted to prohibit asking an applicant or employee if he or she has AIDS? Or should the statute be triggered only if the employer takes action that involuntarily deprives the person of employment at his or her regular wage rate? Employers may argue that questions about and tests for HIV are to assist in legitimate decisions about job placement, and not to discriminate impermissibly.

These and related questions will be debated in courts and administrative hearings for years to come. It is anticipated that those with the HIV virus and others perceived by employees to be candidates for AIDS will be given protection under the various laws. AIDS victims transferred or demoted, as opposed to discharged, will also be protected as long as they can show they were adversely affected by their employer's action.

Potential Remedies

The typical approach by a court or administrative agency in an employment discrimination case is to make the victim whole. That is, the discriminatee should be given restitution and placed in the situation he or she had prior to the illegal discrimination. Managers who made decisions that turned out to be illegal do not go to jail, and the companies do not pay a fine. Thus, the remedies are compensatory, not penal. Specifically, victims of employment discrimination would be reinstated to regular jobs or placed in the positions for which they applied—with full back pay plus interest. The victims are restored, whether terminated, demoted, or transferred— to their former positions, without monetary loss. Their attorneys' fees are often reimbursed by the losing employers.

There is a practical problem with this approach in AIDS cases. Due to the seemingly inevitable delay in litigation, cases often consume at least one or more years between filing the claim and final resolution. It is highly probable that during the time the case is being processed through the legal channels, the AIDS victim will die or at least become permanently incapable of performing the duties of his or her former job. In these circumstances, is the only remedy back pay from the time the victim was deprived of employment until death or the date at which he or she became physically unable to work? And, assuming that the victim has died, to whom should the back pay award be presented? While these questions will be debated for some time before being resolved, courts are expected to require awards of back pay to family members of the victim and restitution of life insurance benefits that the victim would have had it not been for the termination or for the failure to hire. In extreme cases a judge may issue a temporary injunction, compelling the employer to reinstate or return the plaintiff pending the trial and decision. Permanent injunctions prohibiting persons with AIDS conditions other than the plaintiff from being discriminated against may also be issued, with the court retaining jurisdiction for a year or two to be certain the discrimination is not repeated.

Criminal Cases

Another development is that many long-established state and local criminal laws, seemingly unrelated to the AIDS phenomenon, have been utilized in AIDS situations. The application of some of these laws has been especially strained and bizarre. For example, the city of San Antonio officially warned seven males under treatment for AIDS that they would be criminally prosecuted if they had sex with healthy persons. The basis of the letter, issued by the Bexar County Health Director, is the state's Communicable Disease and Prevention Control Act of 1982, which gives local health officials the power to control unspecified contagious diseases. Specifically, the letter warns the men against engaging in sexual intercourse with anyone not having a confirmed diagnosis of AIDS, sharing needles with other people, or donating blood, body organs, or tissues; it threatens two to ten years in jail for any violation.

In Michigan, police had trouble subduing a man who spat on them during the arrest. When it was confirmed that the arrestee was suffering from AIDS, a new charge was added to the blotter—attempted murder! In Fort Lauderdale, a defendant bit his guard's finger while being escorted to court. When the defendant tested positive for HIV, he was charged with attempted murder. Another attempted murder allegation was lodged against two prison inmates who surreptiously obtained blood serum contaminated with AIDS and poured it in a deputy's coffee, which he later drank.

A private in the U.S. Army was accused of aggravated assault for allegedly having sex with other soldiers after being told he was positive for the HIV virus. Query: is the virus a weapon? Members of the legislature in Louisiana answered in the affirmative when they proposed a bill that would require murder charges be filed against a person who knowingly transmitted HIV to another person. It died, however, after arguments that it would adversely affect AIDS education and voluntary testing programs. Several cities have struggled with the question of what to do with prostitutes, positive for HIV, who continue plying their trade after warnings and counseling that they are a threat to public health.

Public Health Laws

Almost all statutes and ordinances dealing directly or indirectly with AIDS in the workplace are designed to protect the victims. But what about the public? Every state's workers' compensation law emphasizes the state's general duty to protect and promote the health of its citizens. Many states also have special health and safety laws and, of course, Congress enacted the Occupational Safety and Health Act (OSHA) at the federal level many years ago. Is there a legal obligation on the part of employers to be certain that persons with AIDS conditions do not work in sensitive jobs, such as chef, operating room doctor, nurse, or laboratory technician in a blood bank? Should states, in exercising their power to protect public health, require employers to disclose, at least to employees in the same department, the fact that a particular employee has contracted AIDS or to remove employees with HIV, ARC, or AIDS from certain jobs?

Two states and at least three cities have considered bills that would require all food service workers to present medical documentation that they are free of infectious diseases. Further, the PANIC referendum in California emanates from the view, held by many, that the state should demonstrate at least some concern about the health of its citizens who are not yet infected with HIV. New York City health officials closed the Mine Shaft, a notorious gay bar where promiscuous sex was reportedly common, for the purpose of protecting public health. Laws proposed—but not enacted—in some legislatures: it would be a felony for gays to donate blood; people with AIDS could not work in health care or food service jobs; and all AIDS patients would be quarantined. All states do require both hospitals and doctors to report AIDS victims to health authorities. Further, Colorado law requires doctors and hospitals to report the names and addresses of all individuals testing positive for antibodies to HIV to the state board of health. Colorado also has delegated to state and local health officials the authority to take "restrictive measures" against people with HIV or AIDS who are "an imminent danger to public health."

There is a strong precedent for states exercising their broad police powers to control communicable diseases and protect the public's health. Here is what some states have done to limit the spread of AIDS: Georgia—convicted prostitutes may be required to submit to tests for the HIV antibody; Florida—a prostitute with AIDS was ordered by a court to wear an electronic monitor that signaled the police if she went more than 200 feet from her telephone; and Texas—the threat of AIDS is a rationale for retaining the law prohibiting sodomy. It is interesting to note that South Korea has announced that it will enact strong anti-AIDS laws to protect the health and safety of the thousands of people expected to attend the 1988 Olympics.

When the state's interest in promoting safety conflicts with an individual's rights to privacy and protection from discrimination, where should the proverbial line be drawn? The courts will have ample opportunity to draw that line as they attempt to balance the various interests in AIDS cases.

Nursing employees who regularly treat AIDS victims at San Francisco General Hospital demanded special equipment for carrying out their duties. When the hospital denied their requests for gowns, masks, and gloves, they were transferred to other positions. They then filed complaints with the California Health and Safety Commission, alleging multiple violations of the regulations promoting the health and safety of employees. After consideration of the complaints, the commission approved the hospital's action in effectuating the transfers and rejected the nurses' claims. In another indication that the laws on this issue will not be exclusively for the victims, a bill was introduced in the U.S. Congress that would legally authorize health care workers to wear the type of protective clothing demanded by the nurses at San Francisco General while treating AIDS patients at federally funded hospitals. A second bill provides that hospitals knowingly permitting health care personnel with AIDS to continue working are ineligible for federal funds; since the vast majority of hospitals are heavily dependent upon Medicare and Medicaid reimbursement, this bill, if enacted, would be a strong stimulus to regularly test personnel for HIV and carefully observe those who are positive for signs of AIDS. It should be anticipated that numerous attempts will be made in the near future at all levels of government to pass laws designed to prevent the transmission of AIDS and protect employees, patients, customers, and the public from being infected. Few, though, will be enacted.

Insurance

A complex, sensitive issue with AIDS in the workplace is insurance. Suppose an employer has a group life insurance term policy of $50,000, disability insurance that pays full salary for ten weeks and half salary for twenty weeks, and a generous health insurance policy. Typically, an AIDS victim would have medical costs and claims between $50,000 and $100,000; the disability benefit would be used because of the victim's inability to work during the later stages of the syndrome; and eventually he or she would die, thus using all three policies. The "experience" and ratings of this particular employer would be adversely affected, especially if other AIDS victims were on the payroll with the result that the premium would escalate or—more probable—the policies would not be renewed.

The Health Insurance Association of America (HIAA) reports that a few employers have experienced medical insurance claims of $300,000–$500,000 for individual AIDS patients, and points out that since the insurance industry did not even know about AIDS until recently, revenues have not been allocated for these claims. Many insurance companies are attempting to specifically exclude from coverage medical problems related to or caused by AIDS. If employers accept these terms, probably for the purpose of retaining the remaining coverage at the same premium, AIDS victims will be without insurance, and hospitals will either refuse to admit and treat them or be forced to extend uncompensated care. Another approach being utilized is to deny claims for illnesses during the early years of the policy on the ground that they are caused by a "pre-existing condition."

Life insurance companies believe that AIDS victims have purchased and will continue to purchase policies in large amounts after learning that they have the syndrome. A recent study disclosed that a disparate percentage of AIDS death claims were filed within two years of the policy's being issued. Specifically, 33 percent of the AIDS claims involved policies purchased within the previous two years, while only 1 percent of total claims occur within that period. One hundred and twenty-five of the AIDS-related policies had a death benefit of $100,000 or more, and three were in the amount of $1 million each.

Some companies require the HIV antibody test before issuing such policies. A few ask AIDS-related questions on their application forms, and depending on the answers, then require the antibody test before issuing the policy. Suppose an insurance company asks questions related to AIDS and requires the test only of male applicants who are unmarried and living in urban areas with significant numbers of homosexuals, such as New York, San Francisco, Los Angeles, Houston, and New Orleans? Should the company be able to use data on sexual preference, use of drugs, living arrangements, and type of occupation in determining insurability? The National Association of Insurance Commissioners has recommended that these and related questions on the applicant's "sexual orientation" not be asked, but has approved inquiries on past diagnosis and treatment of sexually transmitted diseases. Transamerica Occidental Life Insurance Company requires AIDS testing for large policy applicants in selected states. Some argue that just as men and women pay different rates for the same life and health insurance because premiums are based on risk, people in "high-risk" AIDS groups, such as gays, should pay higher premiums than heterosexual males.

These approaches of insurance companies often fly in the face of recent laws, including one in California that prohibits testing for AIDS unless the individual consents to the use of blood tests to determine insurability. Wisconsin has a law specifically prohibiting insurance companies from using AIDS test results in making decisions on policy coverage. The California Insurance Department has rejected a request by Blue Cross of California to offer group health insurance policies that would exclude coverage for AIDS and other sexually transmitted diseases. The District of Columbia

Council approved a bill prohibiting insurance companies from denying coverage to people testing positive for exposure to AIDS. Groups are campaigning against efforts by insurance companies to exclude coverage for AIDS-related medical problems. For example, the National Gay Rights Advocates filed a sex discrimination lawsuit against Great Republic Life Insurance Company, alleging that it denies coverage to unmarried males in certain occupations—including florist, hairdresser, and antiques dealer—and requesting damages in the amount of $10 million. The same group has sued an HMO (health maintenance organization) for allegedly refusing to accept applications from residents of San Francisco because of the higher probability of their contracting AIDS.

More litigation involving insurance and AIDS is anticipated. William Horner was distressed to learn that the claim he filed for medical costs connected with his AIDS condition was rejected by his insurance company on the ground that AIDS was a "pre-existing condition." Horner filed suit, alleging unlawful denial of benefits, and obtained a settlement that reinstated his medical coverage. However, he died two weeks after the settlement became final.

Another area for litigation may arise as insurance companies challenge laws that limit or prohibit them from testing applicants for HIV. The insurance industry feels that it should be able to approach AIDS in exactly the same manner as other illnesses and diseases, including requiring a medical test for its existence at the time application is made for coverage, with premiums keyed to the risk. Wisconsin, which has expressed a strong desire to protect AIDS victims from discrimination, considered a regulation that would permit insurers to use a series of HIV antibody tests in writing individual life, health, and accident policies. The restriction would be that the testing of applicants must include two ELISA and a Western Blot assay for confirmation. It is expected that, after considerable debate, most states will enact regulations allowing insurance companies to test under regulated conditions.

4
Unions, Arbitration, and Compensation

In addition to federal and state laws, courts, and commissions, employers with unions representing employees with AIDS, ARC, or HIV must be worried about union representatives and labor arbitrators looking over their shoulders. Futher, issues involving AIDS and both workers' and unemployment compensation are likely to surface.

Unions

Under the National Labor Relations Act, unions have a legal duty to fairly represent their members. After all, one of the primary reasons why members pay dues is for union agents to represent them against management when they need help. A member with HIV, ARC, or AIDS who is discharged, transferred, or involuntarily placed on leave expects a union steward to speak and act for him or her. A union that fails or refuses to process a grievance by an AIDS victim risks an unfair representation claim. Technically, the aggrieved employee member would be filing two claims in one suit—against the employer for lack of just cause in taking adverse action because of AIDS, and against the union for failing to vigorously argue the case. The union, as well as the employer, would be vulnerable to an award of damages including back pay, interest, and the employee's attorney's fees. An example of a complaint that could be filed in Federal District Court under Section 301 of the National Labor Relations Act against both the employer and union is found in Appendix D, document 8. A sample unfair labor practice charge that would be filed by a member against his or her union with the NLRB is in Appendix D, document 9.

From a legal standpoint, unions have the rights to refuse to process grievances and to dismiss employee claims short of arbitration as long as they are not acting arbitrarily. But practically speaking, it is easier and considerably less expensive for a union simply to speak for the protesting employee, present the case to management and the arbitrator, and let the neutral third party decide the issue. Hence, employers with unions should expect arbitration on almost any issue involving involuntary action against an employee with AIDS.

Unions also, however, have a strong duty to protect the health and safety of their membership. Suppose that 90 percent of the membership signs a petition seeking union assistance in removing an employee with AIDS from the workplace. Union representatives could take a page from management's book and attempt to educate their members on how AIDS is transmitted and assess the risk of infection at near zero, but many members are likely to dismiss the facts and press for removal. One or more members could retain an attorney or approach the NLRB with an argument that the union is breaching its duty of fair representation to them. If the union represents the interests of most members of the bargaining unit and presses management to remove the afflicted employee, it and its officers are open to a legal claim by the AIDS victim. If the union relies on factual information indicating that the employees' fears are groundless to reject or ignore the petition, and instead supports the right of the victim to continue in his or her regular job, the union and its officers are vulnerable to irritated members, who may replace current officers at the next election, resign (in right-to-work states), withhold their dues or attempt to decertify their union under NLRB procedures. In other words, unions have strong practical incentives to satisfy the majority of their members. The conflict between legal obligations and practical incentives will present many dilemmas on this issue.

What if employees walk off the job to protest an AIDS victim being allowed to continue working? Management can be expected to immediately contact the union officers, point to the ban on strikes in the current collective bargaining agreement, and ask the union to order its members to return to work. If the union accedes to the employer's demand, members may follow some or all of the paths described above: resignation and attempts to replace officers or even the union. In fact, employees may file a claim against the union charging that it is failing to defend and support their efforts to protect their health and safety. If, on the other hand, the union supports the illegal strike—either actively or passively—it almost surely will be sued by the employer for both an injunction requiring a return to work and for damages for lost revenue due to the unauthorized shutdown. It is significant that Section 502 of the National Labor Relations Act allows individuals or employee groups to ignore no-strike clauses and walk off the job when they have a good faith belief that there are abnormally dangerous conditions in the workplace. The U.S. Supreme Court has ruled that such strikes must be supported by ascertainable, objective evidence that the conditions are abnormally dangerous. It is highly unlikely that employees concerned about patients or employees with AIDS could satisfy this standard.

The admission of AIDS patients to a nursing home in Philadelphia was substantially delayed due to protests and problems raised by the union representing the health care employees. A union official threatened to strike the home if the problems could not be resolved. Specifically, union officials sought assurance that their members would not be exposed to AIDS, and that if any of them contracted the HIV virus while caring for patients, the employer would assume full financial responsibility. The president of the local union explained that while some employes at the home didn't object to caring for the AIDS patients, the majority did. The pragmatic union officials decided to represent the majority of its constituency.

Unions, as well as employers, will have confusing issues and conflicting demands to resolve concerning AIDS. Union officials can expect claims and lawsuits from members dissatisfied with their responses or lack or responses to AIDS-related conditions and decisions.

An example of union efforts to improve infection control procedures at health care facilities is the petition filed with the Occupational Safety and Health Administration (OSHA) by the

Federation of Nurses and Health Professionals requesting emergency, temporary standards to protect health care workers from AIDS and other infectious diseases. Similar petitions were filed with OSHA by the Service Employees International Union (SEIU), the National Union of Hospital and Health Care Employees (NUHHCE), and the Hospital and Health Care Employees Union. The petitions emphasize that health care personnel possess a higher risk of being exposed to and developing AIDS, and special standards and procedures designed to protect them should be issued and required by OSHA. Specifically, the unions argue that exposure of health care personnel to HIV could be prevented if OSHA would issue standards requiring health care facilities to follow infection control procedures on the topic as recommended by the Centers for Disease Control (CDC).

Another approach for unions wishing to promote the health, safety, and protection of its members from AIDS is to propose special policies and procedures for infectious diseases in general or AIDS in particular. During negotiations for a new contract, the union could demand data from the employer about rules, policies, medical records, and other information relating to the transmission of communicable diseases. Since health and safety are conditions of employment within the meaning of Section 8(d) of the National Labor Relations Act, the employer would normally be obligated to produce records that are pertinent to bargaining subjects and negotiate in good faith on union proposals for special policies, rules or standards. For example, the union may demand medical records of employees who have an AIDS condition. The employer would probably object on the grounds of private property and employee rights to privacy and confidentiality. In at least one NLRB and court case involving a medical issue other than AIDS, the employer was ordered to turn over the medical data with the names of specific employees removed.

Unions can also be expected to try to protect their members from employer efforts to infringe upon the civil liberties of employees in the name of preventing AIDS. Thus a union may propose a contractual provision prohibiting the employer from testing for the HIV antibodies. Or unions could object to and attempt to block employer efforts either to interrogate members about exposure to

AIDS or to require submission to the test. The American Federation of Government Employees has filed suit against the U.S. State Department and the U.S. Information Agency, challenging the new policy requiring HIV antibody testing of applicants, employees, and dependents of employees.

The AFL-CIO recognized the double and sometimes conflicting obligations of unions in Resolution No. 84, distributed to potential and actual union members in 1985:

> The AFL-CIO recognizes that unions have the dual concern of seeking to protect the health and safety of workers occupationally exposed to AIDS and the rights of workers who are AIDS victims and individuals who may be at high risk.

Labor Arbitration

Assume that an employee at a union facility is terminated, placed on involuntary leave of absence, or transferred to either another job or to an isolated area of the facility. Understandably upset, the employee can trigger a legal process against his or her employer without calling a lawyer or spending a penny. All he or she has to do is file a grievance. The employee's union, rather than risk his or her wrath and a possible claim for failing to prosecute, will almost certainly process the grievance to arbitration.

Thus far, very few arbitration awards have involved AIDS in the workplace. United Airlines decided to place a flight attendant afflicted with AIDS on an unpaid leave of absence. The male attendant, who wanted to continue working, filed a grievance protesting the action with his union, which took the issue to arbitration. The company argued that the health and safety of passengers and other employees justified its decision, but the arbitrator disagreed, ruling that United had violated its collective bargaining agreement and that the attendant must be given back pay for all the work days he missed. However, the arbitrator extended partial credence to United's position in concluding that the attendent was not eligible for reinstatement until he successfully completed a physical examination by a qualified doctor.

In another case, the arbitrator expressed concern about a nursing home employee grievant with AIDS transmitting the virus to others and criticized CDC guidelines as inadequate. He ruled that the proper course of action was to place the infected employee on medical leave of absence until it expired, and then on suspension until he or she no longer had a communicable disease. The arbitrator acknowledged that he was, in effect, prohibiting the grievant from returning to work, but the previous decision to discharge the employee was nullified and his insurance was reinstated.

Numerous cases involving involuntary, adverse treatment of employees with an AIDS condition will be presented to arbitrators in the future and it is anticipated they will follow this approach:

1. The overall question is whether the employer had *just cause* to treat the employee as it did. Almost all collective bargaining agreements expressly provide that the employer must have just cause to support disciplinary action against a member of the bargaining agreement. Arbitrators are certain to imply a just cause standard if a contract lacks one. If there are special contractual clauses or policies on the topics (transfers, demotions, or leaves of absence, for example), then the issue could be whether the contract was violated. The distinction between a just cause discipline case and a dispute over the interpretation of contractual language is important because the burden of proof is on the employer in the former case and on the union in the latter. It is anticipated that most arbitrators will place the burden of persuasion on the employer to justify its action in AIDS cases.

2. What is the specific evidence on the employee's medical condition? Is he or she simply positive for antibodies to HIV but mentally alert and physically fit? Or is he or she suffering from dementia? Perhaps a serious physical ailment has disabled the employee. If there is an impairment, is it temporary or permanent? Is the employee presently physically and mentally capable of performing the specific duties of his or her job? Did the employee present a doctor's letter confirming that? Was there medical testimony or evidence about the employe's condition? What objective evidence does the

company have that the employee could not satisfactorily perform his or her duties? (The *opinions* of managers are virtually worthless.)

3. Would there have been a medically documented danger to employees, customers, or patients if the employee had been allowed to continue working in his or her regular position? What objective evidence of the health and safety danger does the employer possess? (Again, documentation and the evaluations of experts are far superior to the subjective opinions of managers.)

4. What was the grievant's length of service? The longer the length of service, the more sympathetic to the grievant the arbitrator will be.

5. What is the past work record of the grievant? The better the work record, the more likely that the arbitrator will be supportive of the grievant. On the other hand, if the employer can show numerous write-ups, perhaps a disciplinary suspension, and extensive absenteeism or tardiness prior to the grievant's contracting AIDS, the employer's position is slightly bolstered.

In almost all cases involving involuntary action against an employee with HIV, ARC, or AIDS, the employer will carry a heavy burden of proving that its decision to terminate, transfer, or place on leave was justified by legitimate business considerations. The arbitrator's sympathy will be with the grievant, and absent compelling, objective evidence of physical incapacity of the victim or risk of infection to others, the grievance will likely be sustained.

It should be noted that unions do not represent either applicants or newly hired employees still in their probationary period. In fact, most collective bargaining agreements specifically state that probationary employees may be discharged without regard to the grievance and arbitration provisions of the collective bargaining agreement. Thus, a union employer's decision not to hire an applicant with HIV or to fire an employee who has not completed the probationary period and who has developed AIDS could not be grieved or reviewed by an arbitrator. However, as previously noted, that person probably has other available forums.

The grievance and arbitration processes are not limited to employee-victims of AIDS. Instead, other employees—upset with having to work with, serve, treat, or otherwise have contact with people who may be contagious—will be voicing their displeasure by pressuring employers to protect them from contracting HIV or AIDS. Union employers will frequently find themselves in a "damned if you do and damned if you don't" position when confronted by an employee with AIDS: if the employee is terminated, transferred, or placed on leave of absence to protect others from possible exposure, he or she could claim discrimination; on the other hand, if the employee is accomodated and left in his or her regular position, one or more employees with regular exposure to the victim may claim unfair, dangerous, or illegal conduct.

An example of the latter type of claim is *AFSCM v. The State of Minnesota,* an arbitration case involving the discharge of a prison guard who refused to carry out his regular duty of "pat searching" an inmate with a confirmed case of AIDS. The grievant guard persisted in his refusal after consultations with several superiors and attendance at an educational session, during which a prison nurse told the guards that AIDS cannot be contracted through casual contact. Eventually, he was terminated, whereupon he filed a grievance, and the case was presented to an arbitrator. The guard explained his refusal by testifying that he was "scared to death" of becoming infected, despite the nurse's explanation. The arbitrator, whose award is presented in Appendix D, document 10, ordered that the guard be reinstated without backpay. Thus, an employer that provided education for its employees, rejected hysterical and factually unfounded claims of an insubordinate employee, and gave the employee numerous opportunities to change his mind, had its decision reversed by an impartial third party!

In an unusual case, an insurance salesman had an employment contract with his employer that provided arbitration as a means of resolving certain disputes. While it is uncontested that he was dicharged after he contracted AIDS, the company said that it was for nonperformance, while the salesman claimed that the reason assigned was a pretext and that the decision was truly motivated by his AIDS condition. While the matter was pending, the salesman died. After hearing evidence from both sides, the arbitrator awarded over $16,000 to the estate, representing back pay from the date of discharge until his death.

Workers' Compensation

Every state has a law granting special compensation to employees who miss work due to injuries or illnesses contracted on the job. These laws also impose upon employers a general obligation to protect employees from hazards or unsafe conditions in the workplace. What if an employee files a workers' compensation claim, alleging that he contracted AIDS from an employee, patient, or customer in the workplace? Suppose a group of employees required to work in the same department as an AIDS victim file a claim requesting the state's Department of Labor to order the employer to take special precautions to prevent the spread of the virus?

With respect to the former case, the employee should be eligible *if* he or she can prove that he or she was exposed to and infected by HIV at the workplace. The obligation should be on the afflicted employee to establish a causative link between the job and the virus. A worker in California filed a claim against his construction company alleging that he contracted ARC while in a hospital because of a work-related injury. The connection between the employee's work on a construction site and the AIDS condition may seem strained to some, but the most tenuous relationship between work and AIDS is probably the Morrison Knudsen case. An employee of that company was not allowed to take his family with him while on duty in Zaire. After contracting HIV, apparently from prostitutes in Africa, he filed a workers' compensation claim. A hearing officer in California ruled that the company condoned sexual encounters with prostitutes by barring spouses from accompanying work crews, concluded that AIDS was a job-related "injury" in this situation, and awarded the employee disability in the amount of $197.12 per week.

There are numerous other possible claims by employees who contract AIDS. While workers' compensation is generally inapplicable to pre-exisiting conditions, a claimant may argue that the

condition was aggravated during employment. For example, suppose that Harry develops AIDS while working at ABC Company.
After extensive absences, he is fired. Then he applies at and is hired
by Baptist Hospital. With an impaired system of immunity, Harry
is highly vulnerable to diseases. Soon Harry comes down with
pneumonia and files a compensation claim against Baptist. The
hospital's defense would be that AIDS was a pre-exisiting condition
requiring a dismissal of his claim. However, as the above cases
indicated, the judge may find a way to award compenation to Harry,
perhaps by ruling that the condition was "aggravated" at Baptist.
Actually, the hospital may be fortunate that Harry filed a workers'
compensation claim instead of a lawsuit in tort alleging 1) failure
to test for or inquire about AIDS; 2) violation of the hospital's
duty to inform him that infections abound in the hospital; and 3)
negligent hiring. The potential for monetary recovery is much higher
in tort than in workers' compensation. Since workers' compensation is the *exclusive* remedy for work-related injuries, the hospital
may not contest the coverage in these circumstances.

A nurse in San Fransisco filed a claim alleging that her ulcer
was caused by stress from worry that she would contract AIDS
from the patients for whom she was caring. The hospital acknowledge that she was temporarily disabled from stress due to working
with AIDS patients, and the claim was settled for $5,000.

These and related issues under these statutes are bound to be
litigated.

Unemployment Compensation

To extend monetary protection to people who are deprived of their
jobs, every state has procedures for unemployment compensation.
Those who lose their jobs because a plant is shut down, or a department is eliminated, or a layoff is effected, are obviously eligible
to file for and receive unemployment money. Almost all states,
however, take the position that employees who are terminated for
misconduct, who voluntarily leave their employer, or who are
physically or mentally incapable of performing the duties of the job
are ineligible for this compensation.

Victims of AIDS who are forced by illness to quit work may

be eligible for medical compensation under their employer's disability or medical policies, but they ordinarily would be ineligible for unemployment compensation because of their inability to perform the duties of their position. If the AIDS victim is physically and mentally able to perform the duties of his or her job at the time of discharge, he or she may be ruled ineligible because he or she voluntarily resigned. Of course, sympathy for the AIDS victim may motivate the referee or commission to award the compensation. Consider the case of a healthy, capable partner of a homosexual AIDS victim who voluntarily quit his job for the purpose of caring for his dying partner. Should that employee be eligible for unemployment compensation? In 1985 the California Unemployment Insurance Appeals Board ruled in the affirmative from its Office of Appeals in San Francisco, concluding that the claimant left his job "with good cause" and therefore compensation must be paid.

5
Testing for AIDS

There is currently no labor relations issue more controversial than employment testing, including the polygraph, psychological stress evaluator, and paper/pencil tests probing honesty. Of the available tests, none stimulate more intense debate than the screens for drugs and AIDS.

All agree that testing for AIDS is valuable in identifying contaminated *blood,* preventing it from getting into community blood supplies, and enhancing the safety of transfusions. Recognizing that the same test can be utilized to identify *people* who are carrying the virus, the U.S. Public Health Service has recommended that all persons in the "high risk" groups undergo periodic testing for the purpose of counseling those with positive results to reduce the spread of AIDS to others, particularly sexual partners. The federal government's definition of "high risk" includes homosexual and bisexual men and intravenous drug users.

The controversy concerns testing by employers to screen applicants and employees with the virus. The U.S. Department of Health and Human Services (HHS) has opined that there is no need for routine AIDS testing. The Centers for Disease Control (CDC) says employment testing is unwarranted because AIDS is not transmissible in the workplace, including hospitals and restaurants, and that such testing would discourage people from seeking counseling and testing and thus thwart efforts to fight the disease. U.S. Surgeon General C. Everett Koop has said mandatory testing is unwise, because the people who need the treatment would avoid the test. A congress of scientists, epidemiologists, and civil libertarians met in Atlanta in 1987 and labeled required testing impractical and an invasion of privacy. Civil and gay rights organizations are highly critical of testing applicants or employees for AIDS.

A few local jurisdictions have proscribed AIDS testing in employment on the grounds that it invades the privacy of applicants and employees and leads to discrimination. However, other legislators in many areas of the country have called for mandatory testing, arguing that states already mandate blood testing and screening for other sexually transmitted diseases before issuing a marriage license and to include AIDS would be easy and informative. U.S. Secretary of Education William J. Bennett is a shrill proponent of AIDS testing. The Reagan administration strongly supports mandatory testing of federal prisoners, immigrants, refugees, and people either entering a hospital or getting married. The American Medical Association backs required tests for prisoners and immigrants, but balks at testing those entering a hospital or securing a marriage license.The U.S. Senate killed a bill that would have forced testing of immigrants and applicants for a marriage license.

Numerous employers—both public and private—have adopted mandatory testing for HIV in some capacity. In 1985, the Pentagon announced that recruits for all the armed services must be tested, and any with confirmed positive readings would be rejected. Further, the army, navy, air force, and marines have a program for mandatorily testing all 2.1 million current military personnel, with those having positive results being referred for medical treatment or limited service and medical observation programs, depending on the circumstances. Over 2,500,000 people have been screened by the military thus far, with thousands more to be tested in the future. In 1987, the U.S. State Department began testing foreign service applicants, employees, and their families for the virus.* Positive applicants are rejected, while employees and their dependents who are carrying HIV will be restricted from working abroad. Applicants for the Federal Job Corps program are also being tested. In the private sector, many employers are utilizing mandatory testing

---

*Local 1812, American Federation of Government Employees, filed suit on behalf of their affected members, challenging this new testing policy, alleging that it violates the Constitution, the Administrative Procedure Act, the Privacy Act of 1974, the Vocational Rehabilitation Act of 1973, and the Foreign Relations Act of 1980.

in selected situations. According to a recent poll, the public enthusiastically endorses testing for AIDS: 87 percent believe high-risk groups should be tested, 71 percent think it's a good practice for sensitive jobs, such as health care workers and food handlers, and an astounding 52 percent agree that everyone should be tested. Another poll concluded that people believe all patients entering a hospital (74 percent), job applicants (37 percent), and all present employees (34 percent) should be tested. A third poll found 42 percent of the public in favor of testing applicants for the HIV virus. Thus, while there are some exceptions, the battle line has been drawn, with public health officials and gay and civil rights organizations on one side, and employers and the public on the other.

Types of Tests

There are various types of AIDS-detecting tests. Testing for AIDS is never easy and can be unreliable. Unlike the urinalysis screen for drugs, AIDS testing is an invasive procedure, relying upon a sample of blood drawn from the person. The most popular test thus far is ELISA—enzyme-linked immunosorbent assay—which detects antibodies indicating the person has HIV. However, ELISA, which was developed to screen blood donors, is quite sensitive and has been heavily criticized for inaccurate readings. ELISA should be regarded as simply a preliminary test with unacceptable false positives (result is positive but person does not actually have the antibody). A positive result from ELISA or similar tests must be subjected to confirmation by a more sophisticated test—usually the Western Blot. Only when a reliable test like the Western Blot produces a positive result should a decision be made that affects the employment of the person being tested. Determinations of whether an applicant should be rejected or an employee transferred cannot and should not be made on the sole basis of preliminary test results. The Food and Drug Administration licensed a commercial kit utilizing the Western Blot test in 1987.

As previously indicated, some companies perceive a profit potential in the AIDS crisis. Murex is only one of several laboratories attempting to develop a simple to administer "home tests" for AIDS.

Murex has announced it has a portable test that produces a result in ten minutes and sells for only $10. However, additional study and review by the Food and Drug Administration (FDA) are necessary before the test can be marketed. It utilizes the Single Use Diagnostic System. Advertisements placed by laboratories suggest stopping in for a test "for your peace of mind" and claim that only a few minutes of your time in submitting to the test "could save your life."

All AIDS tests rely upon blood samples. The theory is that a substance placed in a sample of blood attracts antibodies to HIV and binds with them. Confirmation of this occurrence during a laboratory examination of the blood sample yields the conclusion that the person being tested has developed antibodies to and is carrying the HIV virus.

It should be strongly emphasized that no test identifies AIDS or even ARC. The only fact established by the test is whether the person has antibodies to the HIV virus. A person who recently contracted the virus but had not yet manufactured antibodies would produce a negative result. Typically, there is a six- to twelve-week hiatus between developing the virus and manufacturing the antibodies that can be detected. Thus false negatives (person tests negative but is carring HIV) are a possibility. No AIDS test, including the Western Blot, can predict whether a person testing positive will ever develop ARC or AIDS. It is quite probable that an applicant or employee with a confirmed positive result does not have AIDS, will not develop ARC within the next five years, and may never develop AIDS. However, a person with HIV is infectious, and will remain infectious with the virus until he or she dies.

While a few localities prohibit testing in the workplace, a more persuasive deterrent for public and private employers is the cost. ELISA, the preliminary search for the HIV virus, has an average cost of $60.00 per person. Since the error rate or number of false positives with ELISA is unacceptable, a second ELISA test should be administered if the first is positive. Those who also fail the second should be administered a third, confirming test—usually the Western Blot, which costs around $80.00. Finally, those with repeatedly positive results should be subjected to a clinical examination, usually consisting of skin tests and cell analysis in a hospital. Obviously, this is much more expensive, and the total cost for those with positive results can be prohibitive. However, the overwhelming majority of tested applicants and employees are negative on ELISA. The extra costs are only incurred with the extremely few who are positive with that screening device. The small but growing number of employers who utilize ELISA and like tests believe they are a small price to pay considering the potential problems of unwittingly hiring a carrier of HIV and assigning him to a job where he could infect other employees, patients, customers, or others.

Arguments Pro and Con

The arguments in favor of and contrary to AIDS testing are frequently emotional, subjective, and polemic. At one end of the spectrum, a law professor at the University of Nebraska favors mandatory AIDS testing for the entire population of the United States as the first step towards stopping the spread of AIDS. In direct opposition to that position is the opinion of the representatives of the American Medical Association, who are entirely against mandatorily testing anyone: "The best evidence available indicates that mandatory testing would be counterproductive because of the possibilities of false positives and breaches of confidentiality." An organization staking out part of the vast territory between those extremes is the American Nurses' Association (ANA) which "opposes the routine serologic screening of health care workers for the HIV antibody" but supports employer testing "to document on-the-job exposure to HIV after an occupational accident." The National Education Association (NEA) first approved and then voted to oppose mandatory testing of teachers for HIV. The president of the Association of Life Insurance Medical Directors says life insurance companies should be able to test all applicants because of the drop in life expectancy for those who test positive and to prevent discrimination against all homosexuals.

Gay rights and like groups urge a ban on testing in the workplace. They fear that identified carriers will not be hired, or will be fired, blacklisted, branded unemployable or uninsurable, and possibly quarantined. They argue that thousands of carriers who will never develop ARC or AIDS will be discriminated against, without valid reason. A representative of Lambda Legal Defense Fund has said:

> AIDS is not airborne. It's not waterborne. It's not foodborne. People who wish to protect themselves can do so if they have the correct information.

On the other side of the fence, William F. Buckley has advocated:

> Everyone with AIDS should be tattooed in the upper forearm to protect common-needle users, and on the buttocks, to prevent the victimization of other homosexuals.

As previously noted, the tests identify carriers. Without a test, a person could work as a chef, laboratory technician, or surgeon for years without knowing he had the potential for infecting people. Men and women could have multiple sex partners, transmitting the virus to many others who, in turn, infect still others, all the while ignorant of their condition. Women could become pregnant and not realize they had HIV until their babies develop AIDS. As Dr. Donald Hopkins of the Centers for Disease Control in Atlanta explained:

> Most people that test positive are infectious. We think it is important for them or their partners to know whether they are positive or not.

There is little agreement and some indecisiveness on what testing, if any, should be done. William Masters, well-known researcher on human sexuality, President Reagan, and Vice President George Bush are among those arguing that the test should be a requirement before a marriage license can be issued. U.S. Surgeon General C. Everett Koop advocates that women contemplating pregnancy be tested; scientists estimate that there is an 80 percent probability that an infected mother will transmit the infection to her child. Pediatricians who have unsuccessfully treated babies and children born with HIV, and helplessly watched them die, have strongly encouraged—but stopped short of requiring—that women be tested for exposure to the virus before becoming pregnant. The Centers for Disease Control first proposed mandatory testing for all persons applying for a marriage license, seeking admission to a hospital, or being treated at a venereal disease or drug-withdrawal clinic. However, after a conference and debate among various health officials, the proposal was withdrawn. All speakers denounced mandatory testing for various reasons. During the conference, a doctor from Harvard Medical School suggested that the Reagan administration was the catalyst for the proposal and that their real goal was to identify and quarantine all Americans exposed to HIV. Various hospital associations support the medical consensus against mandatory testing, but encourage voluntary testing. Georgia's proposal for mandatory testing of all convicted prostitutes was challenged as unconstitutional by the ACLU.

Prior to examining the specific pros and cons concerning testing, consider what is virtually undisputed:

1. All persons donating blood *must* be screened for HIV antibodies. Those with positive results should be rejected as donors. (Currently only 1 in 10,000 donors is testing positive; donors were not tested for the virus prior to April 1985.)

2. All women contemplating pregnancy should be encouraged (but not required) to be tested.

3. Persons worried that they may have contracted HIV from a sexual or drug experience or a blood transfusion prior to 1985 should be encouraged to submit to the blood test and they should encourage their partners to do the same.

4. Health care workers or others exposed to contaminated blood or semen through an accident such as a needle stick or blood splash should be encouraged to report the incident and voluntarily submit to the test.

5. The present ELISA test occasionally has false positives, and no decision or action should be made or taken with a positive result until a confirmation is secured from the Western Blot.

6. Since there is a hiatus between the exposure to the HIV virus and the production of antibodies, those who test negative should be retested at monthly intervals for at least six months following the initial test.

7. The test results should be treated with the utmost confidentiality—access must be severely restricted.

8. It is desirable to have numerous, reputable places for people who wish *voluntary* testing, which should be accessible and inexpensive; the government should subsidize the cost and consider making it free of charge for the purpose of encouraging testing on a voluntary basis; finally, *anonymous* tests should be widely available for those concerned about breaches of confidentiality.

Here are arguments in favor of mandatory testing:

a. Testing can be of enormous help in preventing the transmission of AIDS and reducing the predicted numbers that will be afflicted. If a carrier is not tested he may infect hundreds of others through sex and drugs without realizing it. Those identified as positive can be given immediate counseling and advice on the critical need for responsible behavior. Their cooperation can be solicited in tracing other possible victims.* Spouses and lovers of those who test positive have a right to know that fact. Hospital workers who treat people in the emergency room, frequently coming into contact with their patients' blood, would greatly appreciate knowing whether the patients are infectious. Studies suggest that significant numbers of homosexual males almost immediately curtailed sexually promiscuous behavior upon learning detailed data on AIDS. Accordingly, the spread of

---

*The Heterosexual Contact Tracing Program in San Francisco has identified over 100 people who had sexual relations with those infected by HIV. Those notified are given the opportunity to be tested. The organization uses the same approaches for tracing and identifying that are utilized with other sexually transmitted diseases. The names of all contacts are kept confidential. Tracing is not considered feasible for male homosexuals because so many have had numerous partners.

HIV in homosexual communities has been dramatically re-duced in several large cities. Learning that one is infectious would hopefully retard promiscuity or increase the use of condoms, which in turn would stem the spread of the deadly virus.* Widespread testing in various situations would help researchers determine the extent to which HIV is spreading into groups other than homosexuals and intravenous drug users, and would allow the focus to be on the virus and its cause, instead of on AIDS, the syndrome which frequently doesn't develop for five or more years.

b. Testing opens the door to treatment. Recently discovered drugs seem to be effective in arresting the destruction of the immune system, and certain drugs can be administered that reduce the chances of opportunistic infections ravaging the body. None of this can be done unless the person and his physician have knowledge of the HIV virus.

c. The individual with HIV, ARC, or AIDS can now plan the remainder of his or her life. If the individual is simply pos-itive for HIV, he or she may want to continue with his or her job and life style but secure frequent medical evalua-tions. If the individual has ARC, he or she may decide to check into a clinic that does substantial work on AIDS-related problems and benefit from the best, most up-to-date treatment. If the individual has full-blown AIDS in an ad-vanced stage, he or she may elect to go home for a reunion with his or her family. Or he or she may not do any of these things—the individual would be free to decide. But without the test, the individual lacks the opportunity to make these critical decisions until his or her secondary illness is so ad-vanced that he or she sees a doctor and AIDS is finally diagnosed.

d. There is precedent for mandatory testing. History estab-lishes that when epidemics such as syphilis and tuberculosis strike, testing has been heavily utilized, especially before a

---

*Lyndon LaRouche has said, "Members of the counterculture . . . have no right to carry a species-killer variety of contagious infection, any more than they have the right to fire a machine gun indiscriminately in a public place."

cure is found. Today donated blood and organs, of course, are carefully screened for various infections, including the HIV virus. Also, since AIDS is a sexually transmitted syndrome, why not utilize the same medical and legal measures that have been effective for gonorrhea and syphilis?

e. The cost is dropping as testing becomes more extensive, and it would be inexpensive for the governments to test prisoners and applicants for a marriage license routinely and to allow employers, including hospitals, to test applicants and patients.

Opponents of mandatory testing vigorously argue:

a. It violates an individual's right to privacy.

b. It is violative of the Fourth Amendment's right to be free of unreasonable search and seizure. (This principle is especially effective for governmental employers.)

c. It doesn't determine whether the person has or ever will have AIDS; all it does is identify HIV positive people who will probably never develop it.

d. The tests are sometimes inaccurate—there are both false positives *and* false negatives. Further, they show negative for a recently infected victim who has not yet produced antibodies.

e. Since as of yet there is no cure or vaccine, the test is useless—regardless of whether the result is positive or negative, there is nothing useful or significant that has been accomplished or can be done. (Until effective treatment of syphilis became available, for example, mandatory testing was not helpful.)

f. It is impractical. Mandatory testing of large groups of people would be too expensive, difficult, and time-consuming.

g. Persons identified as positive may have extremely unhealthy psychological reactions to that news, including depression and contemplation of suicide. Thus, the test has social and psychological ramifications, as well as medical and legal.

h. Mandatory testing would require identification of those who are positive and keeping a record of their location. It may motivate tracing of past sex and drug partners. In these circumstances, the concept of confidentiality could easily be compromised with the result that HIV positive people would be branded, discriminated against, and possibly quarantined. The discrimination could involve housing, insurance, and employment. Thus, people with the HIV virus who are very healthy and may never develop AIDS could be the victims of unfair and discriminatory treatment.*

i. Requiring testing would stimulate the above concerns about confidentiality and discrimination among homosexuals and drug abusers, with the result that the very people who could benefit the most from testing, counseling, and treatment would find ways to avoid the tests.

j. Testing will divide our society into two groups—those positive and those negative—with conflict and antipathy between the two developing to a greater degree every year.

One Company's Testing Policy

ENSERCH Corp., a company based in Dallas that is heavily involved in oil and gas, began testing its food service applicants and employees in 1985. The employee unit in question, consisting of approximately twenty people, serves food to an oil and gas workforce of over 1,000. All applicants are required to take screening tests, and any who turn up positive will not be hired as food service workers. A representative of the company was quoted as saying, "We're not going to hire someone as a food service worker who

---

*As previously indicated, both Roy Cohn and Liberace wished to die without their AIDS condition being known. The breaches of confidentiality in their situations seriously concern opponents of mandatory testing. In 1987, a confidential list containing the names of five hundred people who were tested for AIDS was reported missing from a health clinic in Washington, D.C., leading to speculation of theft, blackmail, breach of confidentiality, and discrimination.

has any infectious disease, not just AIDS." Employees with positive test results are referred for medical assistance, but not fired. A series of three tests are administered to detect communicable diseases, including AIDS. The same procedures are followed regardless of whether the identified condition is AIDS, hepatitis, tuberculosis, kidney ailments, or parasites. The overall goal is to protect the people being served. In response to company policies like this one, a representative of the Centers for Disease Control reiterated that office's position that there is "no evidence that AIDS is spread through food."

Gay rights advocates have heavily criticized ENSERCH, but more and more employers are using AIDS testing in areas where it is not regulated. Any employer making the decision to test should treat the results as extremely confidential, discuss both medical and employment considerations with those who test positive in a sensitive and caring manner, provide counseling, and make a definite, sincere effort to accommodate those with the virus, taking into consideration the marked distinctions among those who have the virus, ARC, and AIDS.

How to Implement Testing Policies

Most employers will not use AIDS testing because, for their particular operations, it is unnecessary, expensive, and likely to stimulate problems. For those, though, that decide to adopt testing, consider this advice.

With respect to applicants, explain to them most clearly that an AIDS test will be done as part of their pre-employment physical examination. Require them to execute a simple form giving the employer or its agent the right to conduct the test. Any positive results should be communicated to the applicant. A form signed either as an applicant or as a newly hired employee recognizes the right of the employer to require AIDS testing during his or her employment, and pledges to cooperate upon penalty of discharge.

There should be a hiatus of several weeks between the communication about a new AIDS testing program to employees and its implementation. A significant number of employees may resent the idea of an AIDS testing policy and resist it, especially if it involves random tests. Ample opportunity for questions, comments, and discussion should be afforded employees before they are required to give blood to be tested for antibodies to the HIV virus. Serious employee relations problems can emanate from implementation of mandatory testing. It is significantly less troublesome to adopt testing for applicants than employees. Also, testing employees only after an accidental exposure to infected blood or upon reasonable cause to believe the employee is positive would be less likely to offend personnel. Random testing of employees is especially sensitive from an employee relations perspective.

It must be remembered that blood testing is an invasive procedure. To protect against lawsuits alleging a battery or other tort, it's important to secure a release executed by the person, waiving all rights to sue, *before* the test is administered. If an applicant refuses to sign, he is not considered for employment. If an employee refuses to execute, he should be reminded of the message previously given to him that submitting to the test is a *condition* of his employment. Any who continue to refuse should be discharged for violation of the employer's policies.

Conclusions

Almost all states have laws requiring hospitals and doctors to report to the state board of health the names and addresses of all individuals who test positive for the HIV virus. This is a reflection of the threat of AIDS to the health of the general public. A few states prohibit employers from testing, reflecting concerns about confidentiality and privacy.

Numerous people and groups have a legitimate interest in knowing whether any person is positive: the individual himself, anyone with whom he or she has a sexual experience or shares a needle, the individual's family, and, not incidentally, employer, potential or actual. Identification will not necessarily lead to discrimination, but it can and should stimulate education, counseling, and prevention. Legislatures and courts should recognize the important distinction between securing data and using it. Determining whether a potential or actual employee has the virus can be a valid exercise; it is what the employer does with that determination that should be scrutinized and regulated. For example, hospitals or restaurants having knowledge of an HIV test result could decide more effectively on the placement of an applicant or employee. Often the person with an AIDS condition may agree that a nursing job at the ward desk instead of in the emergency room, or a hotel room inspector position instead of assistant chef, would be more appropriate. Or, if he or she lacked knowledge of an AIDS problem prior to the test being administered and financed by the employer (which is usually the situation), the individual may withdraw his or her application to seek medical treatment at a hospital in another area or to return to his or her family in another city. This knowledge may also stimulate the individual to seek counseling or other assistance. If he or she wishes to be hired or retained in his or her current job, and the employer decides that the individual cannot be accommodated, then—and only then—is there a conflict. The problem, if one develops, is not caused by the test, which yielded valuable information, but by a disagreement between the victim and the employer as to his or her employment status. Any legal inquiry should be triggered by an employer's decision after the test that is opposed by the victim, and not by the test itself. Testing can be a valuable tool for identifying carriers, leading to treatment and counseling, and making more intelligent and effective decisions regarding their employment status. There are numerous nonwork situations in which testing should be required: prostitutes and drug users convicted of crimes (the test result would be provided to the judge prior to sentencing); individuals seeking treatment at clinics for sexually transmitted diseases; and prisoners convicted of sex crimes, both before entry into prison and prior to their release. Employers, as well as the state, should be allowed some discretion here.

Since the legal validity of mandatory testing will be uncertain for years to come, there should be immediate and extensive encouragement of voluntary testing. Centers for testing which are administered or subsidized by the government should be established and publicized in all major cities. Because of the genuine concern for confidentiality, procedures for anonymous testing should be set up. Counselors should be trained and dispatched to the testing centers to advise those who test positive. With a syndrome that has killed thousands, threatened millions, and frightened everyone, testing should be viewed as a small, positive step toward identifying those who have the potential for developing it, giving them an opportunity to receive appropriate medical evaluations and treatment, and counseling them to abstain from conduct that would spread the deadly virus.

6
Practical Problems and Solutions for Employers

Framework for Analyzing Problems

Recent chapters have emphasized the legal perspective, but practical problems abound with employees on the payroll who have AIDS, ARC, or the HIV virus. This chapter shall raise and attempt to resolve some of the troublesome questions.

The problem of maintaining health, disability, and life insurance for AIDS victims under the employer's regular policies is enormous. On the one hand, employers would like to cover employees with AIDS, just as they cover employees with any other medical malady. As indicated, however, insurance companies—overwhelmed with the astronomical costs of paying off medical, disability, and life insurance claims filed by AIDS victims—are moving toward either denying coverage to AIDS victims or sustantially increasing premiums for policies that cover them. In response, a few state and local governments have restricted exclusionary practices. The impact of these laws is a general across-the-board increase in employer premiums.

As previously indicated, other practical problems include employees—angry at having to work side-by-side with an AIDS victim—quitting, collectively refusing to work until the person with an AIDS condition is removed, slowing down, or otherwise adversely affecting productivity. Employers' fear of lawsuits by other employees, and their potential cost, is another factor motivating decisions. The practice of using prison inmates on road gangs was terminated in Alabama because a citizen might be infected by a prisoner with AIDS and then sue the state. While, from a medical standpoint, the chances of a member of the public having sexual contact or sharing a contaminated needle with a convict on a road crew and thereby becoming infected with AIDS are, at best, highly remote, the point is that the practice was stopped because of AIDS. A hospital could conclude that continuing to utilize a registered nurse who tested positive in the operating room would subject it to lawsuits from any patient of the hospital who might later contract AIDS, and that the nurse should therefore be removed. Potential loss of customers and patients because of their fear of contracting the syndrome from currently infected employees, regardless of whether the fear is founded, should also be analyzed.

An employer with an AIDS problem wants to obey whatever laws may apply and treat the infected employee with kindness and sensitivity, but there are practical, often countervailing, considerations of productivity and profit. What should an employer do? Upon what factors should the decision be based? What decision-making approach would be appropriate? The suggested solution is *risk and impact analysis*. The probability that the action contemplated by the employer against the person with an AIDS condition violates the law, and the severity of any penalty, should be balanced against the potential legal and practical ramifications of ignoring the AIDS condition and either hiring the applicant or leaving the employee in his or her regular job.

Advocates for plaintiff victims of AIDS can and will argue that any type of discrimination against their clients should be illegal. Yet, as indicated, there are almost endless possible scenarios that face employers in this area. Variables include: 1) whether the victim is merely a carrier of the virus and without any type of impairment, is beginning to display signs of ARC and suffering mild mental or physical incapability, or has an advanced case of AIDS with dementia and periods of complete physical impairment; 2) what industry is represented by the employer (manufacturing, banking, food service, or health care); 3) what are the exact duties of the job in question (crane operator, surgeon, file clerk, janitor); and 4) are doctors in agreement about the victim's physical and mental ability to perform work, or are opinions in conflict? In these circumstances of widely fluctuating, individual situations and competing interests, it would be improper and unfair to employers for government to adopt a rule that discrimination in employment against an applicant or employee with an AIDS condition is wrong per se. Taking an extreme case to illustrate the point, it should not be illegal for a hospital to cancel staff privileges of a surgeon carrying the HIV virus.

Discrimination has become an ugly word in the employment arena. Somehow it is fashionable to be "discriminating" in the selection of clothes, cars, spouses, and friends, but improper to discriminate against applicants and employees. Yet every day employers discriminate against hundreds of employees—legally and with legitimate reasons. Thus, a personnel manager discriminates against twenty qualified applicants for a secretarial position in selecting the twenty-first who typed slightly faster than the others. A supervisor discriminates against two warehouse employees for fighting on company property by firing them. A department head, ordered to reduce her staff by five, discriminates in favor of a less senior but better-qualified computer operator, with the result that older, more-experienced operators are laid off. It must also be recognized that people with AIDS cannot be categorized with the groups that have been extended protection by our laws. While it can be flatly stated in our society that an employer cannot discriminate against a minority because of race, a female because of her sex, or a senior citizen because of age, people with the various AIDS conditions should not be given the same protection because of the critical differences between AIDS on the one hand and race, sex, religion, age, and so forth on the other. The medical facts that people with HIV virus are capable of infecting others, that those with ARC and AIDS will become physically and perhaps mentally impaired in the near future, and that applicants and employees with AIDS will die within the relatively near future require that AIDS employment problems be considered separately and independently.

It would be far simpler to have hard and fast rules, for example, stating that any type of employment discrimination against an AIDS victim is illegal, or, in view of the current epidemic that our society is facing, that employers may refuse to hire, may fire, or likewise discriminate against them with impunity. Simple, rigidly applied rules, however, often produce complex, unacceptable results. As H. L. Mencken said, "For every problem there is one solution which is simple, neat—and wrong." It is preferable to articulate an approach for resolving problems with AIDS in the workplace that takes the competing interests into consideration and yields solutions that are responsible and defendable.

The following eight points comprise a suggested framework for employers to analyze the risk and impact of options involving an applicant or employee with HIV, ARC, or AIDS.

1. *Is there a statute or ordinance (federal, state, or local) that directly applies to the situation? Does it clearly prohibit taking any action against the applicant or employee?* (The "action" would usually be rejecting the applicant or terminating the employee, placing the employee on leave of absence, or transferring him or her to another job.)

If the answers to these two questions are in the affirmative, no further analysis is required; the law must be obeyed. If, however, there is sincere and serious doubt about whether the law in question applies to the particular situation facing the employer, then the following two inquiries should be answered:

How valid are the defenses?

What are the penalties if a violation is found?

The stronger the defenses, and the milder the penalty, the more likely an employer will be to take action against the victim.

2. *Are there court or administrative cases suggesting that laws on related subjects may directly apply to the situation?* (An example is the probability that federal and state laws protecting the handicapped are applicable to AIDS.) If so:

How valid are the defenses?

What are the penalties if a violation is found?

Suppose a state or city ordinance regulating treatment of the handicapped has language that is ambiguous, is arguably inapplicable to the specific facts, has never been relied upon in an AIDS situation, and there are no cases or opinions interpreting it. Once again, this is a point in favor of action adverse to the person with an AIDS condition.

3. *If the HIV-positive applicant is hired or the employee with AIDS is left in his or her regular job, can it be reasonably anticipated that any of the following groups would take legal or other steps against the employer's interest: employees, customers, or patients?* Specifically, would they sue for being exposed to the virus? Refuse to work with the victim and perhaps encourage other employees to also withhold their services? (If so, was education of these employees attempted?) Cease doing business with the employer? How effective or successful would be their efforts against the employer?

If the answers to any or all of these inquiries are affirmative, the employer will be more inclined to move against the person with the AIDS condition.

4. *If the victim is allowed to work in the job that he or she wants, what is the probability that others may be infected?* Grounded to this is an analysis of the specific job applied for or occupied by the victim. Is it an office or clerical job, or that of a nurse regularly treating patients with open wounds? Is the position in sales, finance, or education, or in food handling? Only exceptional jobs present reasonable opportunities for infecting others, and the employer should bear the burden of proving the danger, relying upon a sincere, as opposed to an unrealistic, concern. Interviews with and documentation from medical doctors would be important here.

5. *If the contemplated action against the person with AIDS is not taken, what is the reasonably foreseeable impact on the "bottom line?"* Specifically, will potential customers or patients really go to another restaurant or hospital, causing substantial loss of business and profit, or are these fears speculative or unwarranted? How costly would it be to hire or retain the AIDS victim in his or her current position?

A slight impact on cost augurs no discrimination against the AIDS victim. Any employer claiming substantial adverse impact should be prepared to prove it with objective evidence.

6. *What is the impact of the contemplated action on the applicant or employee?* Will he or she be deprived of needed insur-

ance coverage? Will this be a devastating emotional blow at a time when the victim requires support and sensitivity? Or will he or she be grateful to take a leave of absence or transfer to another position? As indicated, there may not be a conflict between what the employer thinks is best for business and what is acceptable to the victim; there is no substitute for clear communication, during which the employer's representative noncoercively explains the options, solicits the victim's views, and documents the interview.

Suppose that the employee with an AIDS condition strongly desires to continue working as long as he or she is physically and mentally able, and that the victim's only financial resources are wages and insurance connected with the job. These facts, of course, support continuing the victim's employment in some capacity.

7. *What is the specific ability of the person with HIV, ARC, or AIDS to perform the duties of the job in question, both presently and in the near future?* Does he or she have ARC, fully developed AIDS, or is the victim simply a carrier of the virus? Is he or she physically or mentally impaired in a way that would interfere with job performance or reduce productivity or work quality? If the employer concludes that there is or soon will be an impairment, what objective, medically supported proof is available? Can the employee be reasonably accommodated? Are there available jobs in other areas, perhaps somewhat isolated from the public or other employees, that he or she can perform?

The burden will be on the employer to substantiate claims of impairment and lack of reasonable accommodation with clear, direct, and objective testimony and exhibits.

8. *Finally, carefully balance the risk and impact of being held in violation of the law and assessed the penalty if the action is taken, against the damage and disruption that are likely to occur if no action is taken and the person with an AIDS condition is hired or allowed to remain in his or her regular job.*

Caution: As noted above, clearly applicable laws must be complied with, regardless of the possible damage and disruption. It is respectfully submitted, however, that genuine ambiguity and doubt will cloud most legal issues for years to come, and in these situations, this framework for analysis should be helpful.

Effect of COBRA

A new federal law is quite relevant to the analysis of whether it is proper to terminate AIDS victims. The Consolidated Omnibus Budget Reconciliation Act (COBRA) requires employers with twenty or more employees to offer to continue medical insurance coverage at group rates for up to eighteen months to any employee who quits or is discharged for reasons other than gross misconduct. Those accepting the offer must pay the entire cost of insuring themselves. Further, the same obligation of continuing insurance coverage applies to a spouse or dependents if the employee dies. The penalty for failure to comply is stiff: loss of the tax deduction for contributions to all health plans.

Application of COBRA to AIDS situations can produce results like this: A restaurant with twenty-four employees ascertains that the chef has AIDS. Attempts to accommodate him by transfer are unrealistic considering the size of the facility and the lack of job openings; moreover, assume there is no leave of absence policy. The chef could be discharged with the security of having his health insurance continued for at least eighteen months, which will—in most cases—be sufficient time to cover all medical costs. Moreover, the spouse and dependents of an expired exemployee would appreciate the substantial hospital costs being covered by the company policy. If the employer thought it appropriate, the cost of the continued coverage could be absorbed by the company instead of by the AIDS victim or the victim's family.

Testing Applicants or Employees for the Antibodies to the AIDS Virus

Bearing in mind the substantial background on this controversial issue that was presented in the previous chapter, the risk and impact assessment discussed above should be implemented. Is there a law—federal, state, or local—that would expressly permit or prohibit mandatory testing? If not, there are several factors to take into account: 1) since mandatory testing is emotional, controversial, and currently receiving considerable publicity, decisions not to hire or to fire based exclusively on a test result have a high probability of being legally challenged by the irate person deprived of a job simply because of a positive report; the adversely affected individual is more likely to seek counsel, and the plaintiff attorney is more apt to view this as an opportunity to enhance his or her reputation, as well as collect a fee; 2) the judge to whom the case is assigned will not have ample precedent to guide his or her decision; instead, the judge will enjoy considerable discretion in deciding a case on the first impression—usually a dangerous situation for the employer; 3) the plaintiff will be in a position to stimulate considerable sympathy for his or her plight—either the employee is only positive for antibodies to HIV, without impairment, and perfectly able to perform the job or he or she is suffering from serious impairments and facing imminent death; and 4) an employee, as opposed to an applicant, would have support from fellow employees and possibly both supervisors and a union, especially if he or she had long length of service and an excellent past record.

These factors suggest that unless and until mandatory testing becomes accepted and prevalent—which is most doubtful in the near future—employers should use it sparingly and selectively, if at all. For almost all jobs, mandatory, routine testing of all applicants or random testing of employees would be an unwise expenditure of effort and expense. Further, such testing would stimulate legal claims and stir up employee unrest.

There are specific circumstances involving health care and food service personnel where mandatory testing may be appropriate. An example would be after a nurse or doctor has suffered a needle stick, scalpel wound, or blood splash in connection with treatment of an AIDS patient. Other examples include a chef or dentist whose symptoms suggest that he or she may have HIV. Finally, testing of all applicants for a sensitive or high-risk job, such as blood bank laboratory technician, should be permitted. Stated differently, employers should have reasonable cause to require an applicant or employee to submit to the test. The reason may be exposure to HIV through an accident or the duties of a particular job. Our statutory and case laws should not deprive employers of the right to test for the presence of HIV after they have carefully analyzed the particular circumstances and have legitimate, sound reasons for requiring the test.

All of the above discussion is irrelevant to *voluntary* testing for HIV. There are many more circumstances when employees and others should be *encouraged* to be tested. Further, any positive test result—whether voluntary or mandatory—should be confirmed as previously explained.

Dealing with an Applicant Who Has AIDS

Perhaps it's a positive test result, or a report from a past employer or present employee who knows the applicant, or maybe the applicant volunteers his condition during the interview, but regardless of the source, the employer now knows these basic facts about an applicant: He is a white, forty-five-year-old male with ten years of experience in the job for which he is applying, who has AIDS! The personnel director, of course, is legally prohibited from giving any consideration to the applicant's race, sex, and age—must he or she also ignore the AIDS condition in deciding whether to hire the applicant? May the personnel officer at least consider his AIDS condition in determining where to place him?

The first inquiry is a legal one: Is there a law—federal, state, or local—that prohibits employers from refusing to hire applicants because of an AIDS condition? To answer this, it is necessary to examine the specific state and local laws in the particular jurisdiction. Also, ask whether the employer is a contrator with or recipient of funds from the federal government. If so, the Vocational Rehabilitation Act will probably classify the AIDS condition as a handicap with the result that refusing to hire may be a violation. Criteria for determining whether a particular employer is a contractor with the federal government within the definition of that act are outlined in Appendix D, document 1.

Assuming that simply being positive for HIV antibodies or having ARC without an impairment is legally found not to be a handicap, or that the employer is not a federal government contractor, and that no local laws prohibit the employer from rejecting an applicant with an AIDS condition, the next line of inquiry concerns a specific description of the condition at hand:

1. Does the applicant have AIDS? ARC? Or does he merely test positive for the virus, without any indication of AIDS?

2. What, if anything, has his doctor reported about the condition, including both its present status and chances of future development?

At this point, the risk and impact assessment set forth above would be appropriate. Bear in mind the cost and time required for training a newly hired employee for the job in question. For example, is this a janitorial job for which one can be trained and effectively performing the functions of the job in one day, or does the position involve three months of training on sophisticated equipment at a considerable cost to the employer, with the result that the new employee is not effectively performing the job until four to five months after being hired?

The questions relating to the physical and mental ability of the applicant to perform the job for which he has applied should also be heavily emphasized. If the applicant is presently impaired in a way that prevents him from fully and effectively satisfying the various duties connected to the job, the employer has a legitimate interest in not hiring him. Additionally, if the applicant is presently in remission, but has lengthy hospital stays in his recent past, with even longer incapacity expected in the near future because he is experiencing AIDS in its later stages, the employer should not be required to hire the applicant. Conversely, if the applicant simply tests positive for HIV but is free of any symptoms of ARC or AIDS, and presently possesses the ability to perform the duties in question, he should normally be hired. A more difficult situation arises with an applicant with ARC who has experienced serious illness in the recent past and can be expected to have extended absences in the near future as the syndrome progresses. A few non-AIDS medical condition court cases suggest that an employer cannot take into account expected deterioration in the future when deciding whether to hire an applicant. However, AIDS can be distinguished on the ground that, until a cure and effective treatment are found, deterioration and death are inevitable. It is suggested that the employer should not be required to hire an employee who, inevitably and in the near future, will experience absences, progressive deterioration of skills, and eventual death. Thus the employer would be heavily relying upon medical evidence of the applicant's ability (mental and physical) to perform the essential functions of the job in question during the next twelve months.

Dealing with an Employee Who Has AIDS

Employers' obligations toward employees with AIDS conditions extend considerably beyond whatever may exist for applicants. In these situations, the victim may have been on the payroll for several weeks and perhaps many years. Group medical, life, and perhaps disability insurance policies are currently covering the employee. Most likely, these group policies are the employee's only coverage. An employment relationship has been established with the victim, who may well have a satisfactory or even exceptional past record with the employer. An employee is considerably more than one of a large group of almost anonymous people who simply completed an employment application and took a physical examination. In light of these intangibles, a presumption should be established that the employee with an AIDS condition will not be terminated; instead, the employer will make every reasonable effort to accommodate the victim with a job (not necessarily the present one), and continue insurance policies in effect for the benefit of the employee and his or her family.

The framework for analysis previously set forth in this chapter should be applied to the particular facts of any employee with an AIDS condition. If no protective laws are either directly or indirectly applicable, the employer should nevertheless exercise extreme caution before taking any action in conflict with the position of the employee. If, for example, the employee has a positive test for the virus, but no impairment, he or she would normally be left in the present job, unless that position involved potential exposure of contaminated blood to others. (Laboratory technician in a blood bank, nurse in the operating room, or food handler are three positions in which an accidental cut or spill of infected blood could have an impact on others.) If some degree of impairment has occurred, or is expected to take place in the near future because AIDS has more fully developed, then the question should arise as to whether the employer can make a reasonable accommodation by assigning the employee to another position that he or she could physically and mentally perform with full effectiveness. Obviously, application of existing policies, such as medical leave of absence and disability, are also possible solutions.

Here are options for consideration that may well equate to a reasonable accommodation:

1. Transfer the employee to another job with duties that he or she can perform; this job may be in a more isolated location in the facility.

2. Have the employee work at home or at another location away from the facility.

3. Place the employee on paid leave of absence, with insurance coverage remaining in effect and premiums being paid as in the past.

4. Put the employee on unpaid leave of absence pursuant to regular policy that allows leave for personal and other reasons.

5. Inform the employee that he or she is on disability or medical leave of absence, pursuant to employer's policy.

A strong factor affecting the resolution of dilemmas involving employees is the particular job in question. Is the victim at a hospital, restaurant, or hotel, with constant exposure to hundreds of employees and members of the public during the course of employment, or is the victim in an isolated part of an office or warehouse, doing all or almost all of the work there? Is the position physically demanding—such as that of a machine operator, maintenance worker, or truck driver—or is the victim sitting on a stool at the end of an assembly line throughout the day?

Discharge should only be a last resort. If legally permitted and seriously considered, the employer should review all potentially applicable policies and practices to ensure that discharge is not inconsistent with the resolution of past employee medical problems.

Determining Whether an Employee with AIDS Can Perform the Job

Perhaps the most difficult factor in the risk and impact analysis is item 7: "What is the specific ability of the victim to perform the duties of the job in question, both presently and in the near future?" The word *ability* refers to both physical and mental capability.

The manager attempting to objectively analyze this factor should list each of the duties connected with the job in question and then determine the physical and mental requirements for satisfactorily performing each of the duties. Many AIDS victims have long periods when they feel physically fit and believe they are able to perform the duties of their former positions. Typically, these patients inform their doctors that they are feeling much better, and the doctors are pleased to give them a note or letter stating that they are fit for return to their jobs. And, in most cases, they will be *physically* capable of performing the various duties of their jobs, as verified by the doctors, but a serious and complex question is whether they are *mentally* able to perform the duties of their former positions.

As previously indicated, one of the sad facts about AIDS is the devastation frequently visited in the victim's brain, as well as in the immune system. A substantial percentage of AIDS patients show signs of brain disease or deterioration, including dementia. Specific symptoms are loss of memory, inability to make and effectuate decisions, and a feeling of indifference. Some doctors have noted definite psychosis. Hence, it may be that in some cases AIDS victms not only are incapable of performing at least a few of the duties of their particular jobs, but their attempts to do so may present a danger or hazard to fellow employees, customers, and equipment.

How can an employer determine whether a particular AIDS victim, reporting to work with a statement from his doctor that he is physically fit, has suffered mental deterioration that has severely impaired his ability to perform work? The answer is medical— including psychiatric—evaluations and documentation of those evaluations. Rather than relying upon the victim's personal physician, it may be appropriate for the employer to use or retain its own doctor who has experience in treating AIDS victims. The doctor should be given specific and detailed information concerning the duties of the job in question. For example, the possible consequences of mental deterioration in an AIDS victim who works as a janitor in an office are far different from those a computer operator, surgeon, or bank officer handling complex financial transactions. Tests can be administered to measure mental skills and abilities, and the results should be reported to the employer. Any oral information from the doctor concerning the results of examinations should be well documented. Whenever possible, a copy of written medical reports describing the evaluation, diagnosis, and conclusions of the doctor should be obtained and placed, along with other materials, in a secure file. The term "reasonable accommodation" means simply that the employer must make a reasonable attempt to accommodate the AIDS victim. If the employer arranges and pays for medical evaluations and is informed that the victim has suffered mental or physical deterioration to the point of being incapable of performing either his or her former job or any other job that is available, the employer has fulfilled its obligation.

It must be remembered that the employer retains the right to set and maintain standards of job performance. Any employee who can no longer meet those standards, regardless of past years of service and eligibility for handicapped status, may be removed from the job. Stated another way, any employee who can no longer perform the essential duties of his or her job due to deterioration of muscles or the brain caused by AIDS may be taken off the job, even if a law protecting the handicapped is applicable. This principle is especially critical to jobs requiring either sound, sharp exercise of mental judgment, such as doctors, lawyers, bankers, and computer operators (mental abilities), or constant vigorous exertion, such as pile driving, laying pipe offshore, and most construction jobs (physical abilities).

Written Policies on AIDS Problems

Almost every employer of an appreciable size has struggled with the question of whether a policy on AIDS in the workplace should be written, communicated to employees, and placed in a policy manual or employee handbook. Thus far the vast majority of employers have either decided against that approach or are continuing to take a wait-and-see attitude. Only a minority of companies have adopted written policies. Three separate management surveys in 1985 and 1986 revealed the percentages of employers having written policies were only 3, 4, and 5. While a 1987 survey by National Gay Rights Advocates concluded that 66 percent of the companies have policies of nondiscrimination against employees with AIDS, only 16.5 percent of the companies responded to the survey.

A distinct disadvantage to implementing a policy on AIDS in the workplace is the long list of unresolved questions. The law, currently in its embryonic stage, will develop over the years. As claims are filed, decisions rendered, and regulations implemented, the clouds will be removed and considerable light will be shed on the subject. Most employers fear that any particular matter they may set down in writing now will be contradicted by a statute, judge, or regulation at a later time. Further, many employers strongly believe that they are retaining flexibility and discretion in resolving these issues on a case-by-case rather than on a policy basis. Other employers believe existing policies on medical conditions or contagious diseases are applicable, and there is no need for a special policy on AIDS.

Examples of written policies on this subject appear in Appendix C, documents 1, 2, and 3. A special policy for AIDS at a hospital that allows almost all employees with HIV to work and rejects mandatory testing is in Appendix B, document 1. A more thorough policy for hospitals that demonstrates concern for preventing the spread of the virus and protecting fellow employees is given in Appendix B, document 5. An approach taken by some employers is to draft and implement a policy on infections or communicable diseases that expressly includes AIDS; see Appendix C, document 1. The rule would be posted on the bulletin board, published in the employee handbook, included in a listing of employment rules, and otherwise communicated to all personnel. The policy, on the other hand, would only be placed in the personnel policy manual and studied by managers and supervisors. A similar approach is to have a policy on life-threatening illnesses, including AIDS; see Appendix B, document 4. Some companies wish to require employees with AIDS to report that condition and obtain medical evaluations of their condition and ability to perform work; see Appendix C, document 2. Sample provisions for employee handbooks are in Appendix C, document 4.

Levi Strauss & Co., Bank of America, and other employers in California believe companies should play a broad role of educating the public, serving as a bridge between the community and its resources, and supporting employees with AIDS conditions. See Appendix C, document 3, for the policy of Bank of America. IBM and TIME are examples of companies that treat AIDS like any other illness. Thus, they apply their regular sick leave and medical policies to these situations. Westinghouse classifies AIDS like any other disability. While employee victims are appreciative of this approach, it fails to recognize that AIDS conditions are quite unlike other illnesses. HIV is infectious, and all those affected with AIDS eventually die. These two undisputed facts suggest that a special problem like AIDS should be approached in a special way.

A unique aspect of AIDS in the workplace is the danger to the victim of continuing to work and being exposed to opportunistic infections that his or her immune system is unable to repel. Having a person with an AIDS condition continue working is almost always more dangerous for him or her than fellow employees, patients, customers, or the public. A checklist of steps to take concerning an employee with HIV, ARC, or AIDS continuing to work is in Appendix C, document 5.

In conclusion, the preferable approach is to eschew a written policy and carefully examine and analyze each AIDS problem when it arises. Then, applying the risk and impact criteria delinated above, solve the problem. Each problem and its resolution should be carefully documented, with all documents placed in a special AIDS file. This will both promote consistency in the handling of AIDS cases in different departments and locations and provide valuable documentation in the event of legal challenge.

Special Problems and Solutions Involving AIDS in the Employment Arena

The remainder of this chapter presents a series of practical problems facing employers on the issue of AIDS in the workplace. With the small amount of law on this subject, it is impossible to render hard and fast answers to the various questions. The proposed responses are heavily based upon the approaches of judges and arbitrators in analogous situations, existing statutes and cases involving AIDS, and the application of the risk and impact criteria set forth earlier. It must be remembered that the one constant thing about labor laws is that they are always changing, and it is important to first determine if a new federal, state, or local statute or case disposes of the question before utilizing the risk and impact analysis.

Problem 1

Henry, a thirty-four-year-old computer operator at a large toy distribution center with an excellent record of performance during his five years of employment, didn't divulge to his employer that he has the HIV virus. Soon after his roommate developed AIDS, Henry tested positive. During the eighteen months after the test he felt fine, until a mild cough became a serious pain in his chest. His doctor diagnosed both pneumonia and AIDS. After two weeks of rest, Henry returns to work with a statement from his doctor that he is physically and mentally able to perform his duties. It is September, and the computer manager, who has been reprimanded by his supervisor for falling behind in processing orders, needs a reliable operator who will be available for overtime and weekend work until the Christmas rush is over in December. Should Henry be reinstated?

Solution. Unless the manager obtains another doctor's statement disputing the claim that Henry is mentally and physically fit, he should be reinstated, regardless of whether a state or local law is applicable. This is not a situation in which customers may boycott, sales plummet, or profits dry up because a computer operator at a distant warehouse has AIDS. Further, other computer operators should not refuse to work, as the chances that Henry will infect others are remote at best. It is disturbing that Henry failed to report his virus condition when he learned of it, but even if the company has a policy requiring employees to inform it of communicable diseases (such a policy, well communicated to employees, is an excellent idea), refusal to reinstate would be a rather severe penalty (a reprimand would be more appropriate). The computer manager has reason to anticipate that Henry may be absent several times, but predicted attendance problems should not be grounds to refuse reinstatement. It would be prudent, however, for the manager to recruit and perhaps hire another computer operator on a temporary basis for the Christmas rush. If needed, this person would be available to convert to regular status in the event of prolonged absences by Henry.

Problem 2

Max's Mobile Homes, located in a rural area of Nebraska, is suffering from a severe downturn in sales. In an effort to reduce its costs, several insurance companies were asked to submit bids on the group medical policy. A bid 30 percent below the others contained a provision that specifically excludes from coverage any costs related to AIDS. Should Max accept the lowest bid?

Solution. Does Nebraska (or the relevant state) have a statute regulating this matter? If not, the exclusion would be legal. But is it consistent with sound employee relations? Is the principle of discriminating against AIDS victims ethical?

    While Max's effort to economize is admirable, he should explore other directions. As a practical matter, he could probably sign the contract and the issue would never arise because the chances of an employee in rural Nebraska developing ARC or AIDS are quite low. Nevertheless, the principle of discrimination against potential AIDS victims simply to curb costs is repugnant to business ethics.

Problem 3

Ford's Family Restaurants owns and operates over 100 units through the Midwest. There is substantial interchange of employees at each restaurant from job to job, depending on attendance; thus, one of the employees may work as a waiter, cashier, assistant to the cook, or clean-up in any one week. Mr. Ford tells his corporate personnel manager that having an AIDS victim on his payroll would be disastrous, and asks if he could test all applicants for the AIDS virus and exclude those who are positive.

Solution. Any Ford restaurant in an area that has a state or local law prohibiting either AIDS testing or discrimination against applicants because they have the virus would, of course, have to comply. The remaining restaurants would not be affected by federal laws because Mr. Ford doesn't deal with the federal government and is not a contractor with the United States. Hence, there is virtually no risk of a violation or penalty if the policy is effectuated. Further, the possible impact of not testing and excluding AIDS victims could be considerable: a perception by the public that they could be infected by a kitchen worker or waitress with AIDS could result in a boycott and financial difficulty, or there is the possibility of trouble with employees not wanting to work closely with the victim. Given the particular facts of a small restaurant—where no available job is isolated from others, and where food is handled and served—and the genuine danger of economic harm, it is reasonable to conclude that Ford may effectuate his policies of testing and exclusion where not proscribed by law.

Problem 4

A shipbuilder for the U.S. Navy employs over 2,000 workers at a large facility outside a major metropolitan area. A male welder, one of approximately twenty employees rumored to be homosexual, is arrested for propositioning an undercover policeman for sex. Furious about the newspaper and television stories that identify the welder's employer, the president of the company orders his personnel manager to fire all homosexuals at the facility, including the welder, and to place on the proverbial pink slip "prevention of AIDS."

Solution. The order is an unfortunate, knee-jerk reaction to poor publicity; it won't solve any problems and probably will cause more problems. But is it illegal? Since the employer is obviously a federal contractor within the meaning of the Vocational Rehabilitation Act of 1973, and AIDS is a handicap within the meaning of the act, the risk of implementing the order is high. The company's defense would be homosexuals without AIDS are not handicapped, but the OFCCP may take the position that gays perceived to have AIDS are protected. Moreover, the penalty—assuming there is a violation—is enormous: backpay and reinstatement for the discharged gay employees and disbarment of the employer from future government contracts. While the actual number of companies blacklisted from additional contracts over the years is small, the outrageous facts in this case are likely to stimulate the government to request maximum penalties. The personnel manager should screw up his courage, look his boss in the eye, educate him on the transmission of AIDS, and persuade him to rescind the directive. After all, there is not a scintilla of evidence that any of the gay employees have AIDS or ARC, or are even capable of transmitting the virus! Finally, employees should not be discharged simply for being arrested, since the criminal case may be dismissed, undercutting the reason for the discharge.

Problem 5

Presbyterian Hospital is located in a metropolitan area with a substantial gay community and a serious drug problem. The administrators are worried that an employee may inadvertently infect others with the virus or that an expatient or employee with AIDS may file a lawsuit claiming that it was contracted at the hospital. Accordingly, the decision is made to require all personnel involved with patient care or the handling of blood to submit to an AIDS test. Any who test positive will be transferred to other positions without loss of pay or benefits.

Solution. This is a well thought out, reasonable response to a very real potential problem. Nursing and other patient care personnel could be infected through needle sticks, blood splashes, or other means. While current studies suggest that the risk of transmission is low, they acknowledge that there is some risk; however, the studies are incomplete. Admission of AIDS patients to hospitals, on the rise in recent years, will soon skyrocket. As more and more employees are involved in treating these victims, the risk of infection increases. Opponents of the tests may argue that the probability of a patient transmitting the virus to an employee during treatment is extremely low; but accidents involving punctures from contaminated needles and splashing of infected blood have occurred in many hospitals in the past, and there will be more in the future. Until the medical community has definite proof that transmission of HIV from patient to employee—other than through sexual relations or shared needles—is impossible, hospitals should possess the right to periodically test employees involved in treating AIDS patients.

There is another legitimate concern on the part of hospitals: frivolous lawsuits by people who develop AIDS and then sue a hospital at which they had been treated in the past, claiming they contracted the virus there. Technically, the burden would be on the plaintiff to establish a causative connection between his or her experience in the hospital and the virus. But assume the plaintiff testifies that he or she has neither had a sexual experience with a homosexual nor shared needles with anyone else, and that the male nurse at the hospital had homosexual tendencies. Suppose further that, in an attempt to develop evidence to support a motion for summary judgment, the hospital tests the male nurse—and the result is *positive!* Now the hospital has a difficult case to defend. And all lawsuits—serious and frivolous—are expensive and time consuming.

Suppose Presbyterian Hospital effectuates its policy of requiring patient care employees to be tested periodically. Thereafter, the same type of suit is filed. The hospital simply provides records of past negative test results proving that none of the nurses who treated the plaintiff had the virus—and thus were incapable of transmitting the infection. Case closed. Another positive aspect of the policy, of course, is that any patient care personnel who test positive at any time would be immediately removed from their positions and transferred to other slots.

The policy is justified, and the adverse impact on employees who test positive is minimal. Thus, the testing policy should be approved. Obviously, though, it cannot be applied in areas with laws or ordinances prohibiting tests or discrimination involving AIDS.

Problem 6

Methodist Hospital has long had a policy requiring employees to report needle sticks and other accidents that could involve infected blood. During one particular month, a large number of AIDS patients were admitted, and three nurses reported separate accidents involving needles previously used for AIDS victims. Methodist requested them to submit to tests for HIV once a month for twelve months; two complied, but the third refused, saying she didn't want to know if she had the virus because there was nothing that could be done, and she would thereafter worry about developing AIDS. Can or should the hospital compel her to submit to the tests? How? Would it be illegal or improper to discharge her for refusing to be tested?

Solution. Methodist should order her to be tested. Many hospitals only request personnel in these circumstances to be tested. If, as here, an exposed employee rejects the request, he or she will continue in the normal job, possibly infecting others every week. Assume that the employee refusing to be tested is a registered nurse in the operating room. The potential medical and legal ramifications are enormous. While arguments may be made on each side of the testing issue, it is not unreasonable for hospitals to require employees reporting exposure to the AIDS virus to be tested for it. Those refusing should be counseled on the many reasons why it is best for them and the hospital. Those who continue to refuse would be subject to discharge. Again, this response is inapplicable in any area with laws that prohibit mandatory testing.

Problem 7

A bottling plant sends all applicants who receive initial approval to a clinic for a thorough physical examination. Although he was never asked to test for AIDS, Dr. Jones does an AIDS test on George, who "fit the homosexual stereotype," because he assumed the company would want that information. The test is positive, but there is no indication of ARC or AIDS. Should the employer hire George into the job for which he applied—electrician?

Solution. If the state or city has a law prohibiting testing, the company is probably in violation because, regardless of authorization, Dr. Jones is its agent. Assuming no law is applicable, the salient facts are: 1) George only has the virus; he may never develop AIDS; 2) the job at issue does not present opportunities for infecting the public or other employees; and 3) George is perfectly capable of performing all duties and no impairment is expected in the near future. Thus, the risk of negative economic impact on the employer is near zero, and the act of depriving George of a well paid job simply because he is carrying the AIDS virus would be improper.

Problem 8

Jason, who works as a quality control inspector at a manufacturing facility with over 2,000 employees, has been absent twenty of the last twenty-five working days. When he reports back to work after a one-week absence, his time card has been replaced by a note to report immediately to the office of the department head. Jason walks into the office and quickly, before the manager can say anything to him, informs him that a doctor has diagnosed his medical problems as caused by AIDS. The manager, obviously surprised, says that documentation of that will be necessary and asks Jason to return to his office later that afternoon.

When Jason returns, he hands the manager a note from his doctor, dated three months earlier, confirming his AIDS condition. Also present in the office are the personnel manager, the plant manager, and Jason's immediate supervisor. The department head glances at the note, looks at Jason, and tells him that he is being terminated for excessive absenteeism. Jason protests, saying that he needs his job and that the continuing insurance coverage is very important to him and his mother, who is on welfare. When the manager says there is nothing else to discuss, hands Jason his final check, and instructs him to leave the plant, Jason threatens to secure an attorney and file a lawsuit. Should the company reconsider the matter? What claims could Jason file? What are the defenses to each?

Solution. If the company had notified Jason of his termination for excessive absenteeism prior to being informed of Jason's AIDS condition, it would have had an excellent defense. However, the fact that the termination is being communicated and implemented only a few hours after learning of his AIDS condition presents serious problems. Through his attorney, Jason can argue that he was terminated because he has AIDS even though at the time he reported for work and was informed of his termination he was physically and mentally capable of carrying out all the duties of his position. The applicable local, state, or federal law protecting the handicap could be relied upon. The company's defense would probably be that the department head made the decision to terminate Jason for excessive absenteeism prior to his conversation with Jason; in support of that testimony, the company would point to the fact that the time card was removed and replaced by an instruction to report to the office. However, there was nothing on the note about termination. Unless the company has other documentation confirming that the decision was made before it learned of Jason's AIDS condition, the facts would be in favor of Jason's claim.

Further, Jason's attorney may consider libel, slander, defamation of character, and invasion of privacy claims based upon the apparent action of the department head in communicating Jason's AIDS condition to other managers, and perhaps to rank-and-file employees or other people in the community. The defense, of course, would be that the only communication of this information was to members of management with direct responsibility for Jason and his job.

The primary questions to be answered by a court would be what actually motivated the company to terminate Jason, and was his AIDS condition unnecessarily communicated to other people. The company could, with only a small amount of accommodation, either transfer Jason to another position in a large manufacturing facility or leave him in the old job. Further, even an unpaid medical leave of absence, which would allow his insurance to remain in effect, would be far superior to a discharge. Based upon the facts in this particular case, the company should reconsider its decision.

Problem 9

Eddie Johnson is upset and worried because his male roommate and sex partner has just learned that he is positive for HIV virus. Eddie asked his supervisor at the cafeteria where he works as a server behind the line whether that means he will develop AIDS.

He constantly talked about his roommate's situation with other employees, both during breaks while sitting at a vacant table in the public area and when business was slow during work time. When Eddie recognized a doctor and his family coming down the cafeteria line, he told the doctor about his roommate and asked about the chances of contracting the virus or AIDS from his roommate. Other employees, worried about Eddie infecting them, have asked the manager what he is going to do to resolve the situation and hinted at a walkout or other protest. The manager would like to take some action, but he is concerned about violating the state law protecting the handicapped or causing some other legal problem. What, if anything, can the manager do?

Solution. Employees with AIDS, the HIV virus, or those perceived to be candidates for AIDS are not immune from counseling and disciplinary action. In this situation, Eddie requires a stern reprimand and warning, not because he may develop AIDS from his roommate, but, rather, because he is upsetting fellow employees and very possibly irritating customers by constantly discussing his roommate's condition while he is supposed to be working. It would be most appropriate—and legal—for the manager to inform Eddie that he should not discuss his roommate's AIDS condition with customers at any time, and there is no reason for him to discuss that subject with employees while he is supposed to be working. The legitimate, business-related reasons for these instructions should be communicated, and Eddie's conduct thereafter should be monitored. Hopefully, the problem will be corrected and the matter resolved. If, however, Eddie persists in these communications in a disruptive manner that threatens the success of the business, he should be further disciplined. Eventually, if Eddie refuses to repent after repeated counseling sessions, discharge may be in order, not because Eddie may one day contract AIDS but because Eddie refuses to follow reasonable and legitimate management directives. All counseling sessions, warnings, and reprimands should be well documented.

Problem 10

A dentist employs five hygienists, a receptionist, and a bookkeeper in a suite at a medical building. He has long suspected that Shirley, one of his hygienists, is on drugs. One of the other hygienists informs him surreptitiously that Shirley's husband is bisexual and a frequent user of intravenous drugs. The dentist is concerned that, if this is true, Shirley may be a carrier of AIDS who could be infecting patients. Can the dentist legally insist that Shirley submit to a test for the antibodies to the AIDS virus? If she refuses, can he discharge her? If she submits to the test and the result is positive, would he have the legal right to discharge her? Is she is positive, does he have an obligation to inform his patients whose teeth have been cleaned by Shirley of the result of her AIDS test?

Solution. The first question to ask is what law, if any, could be applied to this situation. Certainly, the dentist is not a contractor with the federal government; thus, the Vocational Rehabilitation Act of 1973 would be inapplicable. Further, most state handicap laws only apply to employers with fifteen or more employees. Hence, it may be that neither state nor federal laws could be relied upon by Shirley, her husband, or her attorney. Care must be taken, of course, that no local laws on the subject of AIDS would prevent testing or discharge.

Assuming the investigation concludes that no laws are applicable, it seems most reasonable for the dentist to: 1) ask Shirley whether she has ever been tested for the AIDS virus; 2) instruct her that he would like to have her submit to the test as a condition of her employment; 3) give her, if she initially refuses, a careful explanation of the legitimate reasons for his concern, assuring her that the content of their conversations on this topic and the test result are most confidential; and 4) allow her ample time to consider the matter, but ultimately insist that she either submit to the test, at his expense, or face termination. If she should test positive, he should first consider if there is another job, such as receptionist, to which he could transfer her. If this is totally impractical, he should conclude that an accommodation is not reasonable and either place her on extended, unpaid medical leave of absence or effectuate the termination.

The question of whether the dentist should inform Shirley's patients that she tested positive is not easy. Since the dentist is removing Shirley from the job, there obviously is some concern about a hygienist infecting patients. Is this concern sufficient to trigger an alarming communication to fifty or more patients, most of whom will never return to the dentist and some of whom may file lawsuits? Investigation of medical studies and conferrals with doctors would be in order here. Has it been definitely established that HIV can be transmitted from hygienist to patient during routine cleaning procedures? Is there a clear and present danger to the patients? This case is seemingly different from that of blood banks, with knowledge of contaminated blood, that trace past recipients. Here the probability of transmitted infection in the past appears low. Still, the dentist may feel ethically obligated to send a factual letter to patients treated by Shirley, informing them of her positive condition and offering to pay for HIV testing of them. If, of course, the dentist learns that one of Shirley's past patients has contracted the virus, then tracing and notifying would be most appropriate.

7
Prevention of AIDS-Related Claims

A major goal of any employee relations program is prevention of labor crises. Whether the potential problem involves the union, charges with the EEOC, or an OSHA investigation, sophisticated employers work hard to establish and administer personnel programs designed to prevent or at least minimize the damage and disruption often associated with legal claims. They realize that employers with effective, successful employee relations programs are more likely to have low employee turnover and absenteeism, high productivity, excellent quality, and few legal claims. Conversely, companies with poorly conceived and loosely administered programs have a higher probability of problems with turnover, quality, attendance, and unions, as well as more lawsuits and claims with governmental agencies.

A lawsuit involving AIDS has the potential for being particularly disruptive. The costs of lost time and attorneys' fees, and the possibility of monetary damages, are present in almost every legal case. With AIDS, however, would come the added dimension of extensive publicity, which could be especially detrimental to retail concerns, restaurants, hotels, or health care facilities. Futher ramifications include customer boycotts, employee refusals to work with the victim, and continued coverage by the press. Normally, labor law matters are handled almost exclusively by the legal and human resource departments, but an employer with an AIDS case will also require a public relations agent and marketing manager.

Here is a checklist of items to consider for preventing the filing of AIDS-related claims against an employer:

1. *Education of All Personnel.*
   Educate employees on the medical facts concerning AIDS. Bring in a medical doctor, nurse, or other expert to your facility for the purpose of explaining, in basic language, facts and figures about AIDS and its transmission. Emphasis should be placed on the fact that it cannot be casually communicated. Be blunt in describing how it can and is transmitted. Make presentations pertinent to the particular type of facility and business in question. Use charts, graphs, and other visual aids, including films, to increase the effectiveness of the program. Allow ample time for questions and comments by employees. Consider meeting in small groups of ten to fifteen, which will faciliate discussion, as opposed to lecturing a large group of fifty or more employees. Follow up these meetings with letters to their homes, notices on the bulletin board, and distribution of pamphlets summarizing the points and principles explained during the meeting.

   The efforts at educating personnel should be particularly thorough and frequent at health care and food handling facilities. More detailed presentations, use of examples, and opportunities for discussion are appropriate here.

2. *Training of Managers and Supervisors.*
   All supervisors, superintendents, managers, and officers should receive special training, in addition to the edcuation described above, on the handling of AIDS-related matters. If the company has a written policy, copies of that policy should be distributed, and its contents and the procedures for implementing it should be discussed in detail. Various hypothetical situations should be presented and managers tested on how they should respond. If a case-by-case approach is utilized, managers and supervisors should be drilled on the need to coordinate all decisions and actions on the subject with a central person or department, as opposed to unilaterally making decisions. They should be carefully instructed to immediately report all AIDS-related situations to the personnel department or central person, and to refrain from initiating any action on their own. Managers and su-

pervisors are agents of the employer; the employer is therefore legally responsible for all their actions on the job, including those which are ill-conceived or contrary to policy and past practice.

One of the problems with the subject of AIDS in the workplace is the rumors that are usually rampant. Supervisors should be instructed to defuse instead of repeat rumors and to be sources of factual information among their employees.

3. *Confidentiality of Records and Information on Applicants and Employees with the AIDS Virus.*
   It is critical for all personnel—exempt and nonexempt, manager and staff employee—to keep communications (written and oral) with applicants and employees on this subject absolutely confidential. Access to personnel files or medical records with data on AIDS should be severely restricted to those managers and staff members with an absolute need to utilize the records. As part of their training, all managers, officers, and supervisors should be instructed to refrain from discussing AIDS matters involving employees with other employees, family, friends, or any member of the public. Numerous state court claims could be filed, including slander, libel, defamation of character, negligent hiring, and negligent testing. Rules should be drafted and publicized which classify breach of confidentiality of records as misconduct triggering discipline.

4. *Designate Coordinator or Department for Central Review.*
   A particular person or department should be selected to coordinate all matters involving AIDS in the workplace. While this usually would be the personnel office, any responsible manager could do the job. No decisions involving an applicant or employee with AIDS, ARC, or the virus could be implemented without his or her input or review. This person should confer with legal counsel to ensure compliance with any applicable laws on the subject. It's highly important for the coordinator to always be up to date concerning local and state laws on this subject in each area where the em-

ployer does business. This central person should plan the educational and training sessions described above for managers and employees in each facility.

It is critical to achieve *consistency* in the handling of these matters and to avoid situations whereby different supervisors apply different criteria to reach different results with basically the same set of facts. If there is ever a lack of uniformity inside the company, it should be because one facility has departed from past practice to comply with local statute or ordinance.

5. *Follow Policy or Practice.*

   While some employers will want written policies disseminated to employees in handbooks and on bulletin boards, most companies are opting to resolve AIDS employment matters on a case-by-case basis. With the latter approach, it is especially important to uniformly follow the established practice or at least to avoid inconsistencies. To achieve consistency, the coordinator should maintan a file on the subject, document how each case is handled, and consult that file before implementing decisions in new cases. Sample policies and provisions for employee handbooks are contained in Appendix C, document 4.

6. *Establish Procedures for Internally Resolving AIDS Problems and Complaints.*

   Employees who file claims with governmental agencies or retain counsel to consider lawsuits against their employer often do so out of a feeling of frustration over the lack of anyone within the company who will listen to them or give consideration to their complaint. An approach for avoiding this undesirable result is to establish and implement a definite procedure that employees can be taught to use to voice their complaints, problems, ideas, and suggestions. It should be a major goal to identify and resolve employee problems on an *internal* basis, as opposed to unwittingly pushing personnel to the government or a union. This concept is especially important with AIDS, which can present a host of problems when submitted in the form of a grievance, charge, or lawsuit.

The procedure must be somewhat specific and have teeth to it. It is expecting too much merely to inform employees that the company has an "open door policy" and to rely upon them to utilize it. Such an approach will almost surely result in disappointment for both the employee and employer. At the other extreme, a formal step-by-step grievance procedure can be forbidding, impersonal, and discouraging. What would be appropriate is a definite procedure—set forth in the employee handbook, on the bulletin board, and communicated to employees from time to time during regular meetings—which would encourage employees first to consult their supervisor but which would also present outlets for employees frustrated that their supervisor is not taking effective action. Employers with a personnel department will want to place the director prominently in line for the frustrated employee to consult. Supervisors must be trained to accept instead of resent employees going around them from time to time to voice a complaint.

Finally, Appendix B and C contain checklists to assist employers in preventing AIDS-related problems: 1) Appendix C, document 5, gives steps for an employer to take concerning an employee with an AIDS condition who continues to work; 2) Appendix B, document 11, presents steps for health care facilities to take in attempting to prevent problems associated with AIDS; and 3) Appendix B, document 7, lists items to be communicated by a manager of a health care facility to employee exposed to the HIV virus through an AIDS patient.

8
Employer Defenses against AIDS-Related Claims

At times, regardless of the sincerity of the commitment of an employer to prevent claims, lawsuits are filed and processed. Whenever a formal claim is lodged, the immediate and overall goal of the employer, thrust into a defensive position, is to secure its dismissal. The applicant, employee, or former employee has formally accused the employer of illegal conduct and has requested a costly remedy, such as compensatory damages, punitive damages, and reinstatement. Depending on the particular law, other possible remedies include debarment from consideration for future contracts with the federal government, a fine, and imprisonment. The employer is exposed to risk of substantial liabililty. Resulting publicity could be harmful. While mediation and settlement efforts may occur, the bottom-line objective is to prevail. In these circumstances, the employer should exploit every conceivable defense that is legitimately available to it, procedural or substantive.

The following checklist of twenty-five different employer defenses to claims involving AIDS in the workplace should be strongly considered for applicability:

1. No federal law expressly prohibits the discrimination that is alleged in the complaint or petition.

2. No state law expressly prohibits the discrimination that is alleged in the complaint or petition.

3. No local law expressly prohibits the discimination that is alleged in the complaint or petition.

4. The court or administrative agency lacks jurisdiction over

the claimant or plaintiff, who therefore has no standing to bring the claim.

5. The court or administrative agency has no jurisdiction over the subject matter described in the complaint or petition; the law or statute set forth in the complaint has no real application to what happened to the claimant.

6. AIDS, ARC, or HIV is not a handicap, so the law protecting the handicapped set forth in the complaint has no application. (The U.S. Supreme Court ruled in *Arline* that AIDS itself is a handicap within the meaning of the Vocational Rehabilitation Act of 1973, but it specifically left open the question of whether a person with HIV is handicapped; further, state courts and legislatures will be struggling with the entire question with respect to their own laws protecting the handicapped.)

7. In the complaint, the plaintiff claims to be a carrier of the HIV virus, but nowhere is it claimed that he or she is physically or mentally impaired or even that he or she has ARC or AIDS. Since the law was designed to protect victims of AIDS who are impaired, the plaintiff does not have a justiciable claim.

8. The plaintiff's claim, when boiled down, is simply that he or she is a homosexual or drug user, and is perceived as a *potential* victim of AIDS. However, the only people protected by the law at issue are those who have actually contracted AIDS; hence, the suit must be dismissed.

9. The plaintiff was *physically* unable to perform the essential duties or functions of his or her job, or the job for which he or she applied.

10. The plaintiff was *mentally* unable to perform the essential duties or functions of his or her job, or the job for which he or she applied.

11. The employer cannot reasonably accommodate the plaintiff.

12. The employer made reasonable attempts to accommodate

the plaintiff by offering a transfer to another position, but the plaintiff refused and voluntarily quit.

13. There is a real and substantial risk of infecting other employees, customers, patients, or members of the public if the plaintiff were allowed to work in the position at issue.

14. The employer has a legal and moral obligation to protect the health and safety of employees in the workplace who would be jeopardized if the claimant were allowed to work in the position desired.

15. There is a serious potential loss of customers and revenue if the claimant were allowed to work in the position at issue.

16. The employer's heatlh insurance costs would substantially increase if it did what the plaintiff wants.

17. The employer would be unreasonably subjecting itself to legal claims by *patients* or *customers* if it allowed the plaintiff to work in the position at issue.

18. The employer would be unreasonably subjecting itself to legal claims by *employees* if it allowed the plaintiff to work in the position at issue.

19. The plaintiff has filed a grievance under the current collective bargaining agreement that his or her union is processing toward arbitration. The subject matter of the grievance is very similar to that of the legal claim, and the court or commission should dismiss the legal claim and defer to the arbitrator. Further, by first filing the grievance through the union, the plaintiff made a binding election of remedies.

20. The plaintiff has failed to attempt to use the employer's written procedure for resolving employee complaints and problems. This claim should be dismissed and the court or commission should defer to the internal procedures for filing and processing complaints.

21. A complaint raising the same AIDS-in-employment issue was previously filed by the plaintiff in state or city court. To

avoid duplication of effort and possibly inconsistent results, the present court should dismiss the lawsuit and defer to the other jurisdiction. Also, when the plaintiff filed
first with the other court or commission, he or she made
a binding election of remedies.

22. The employer discussed the plaintiff's attendance problem
    and decided to discharge him or her for excessive absen-
    teeism before it learned that the plaintiff was suffering from
    AIDS. At the time the decision to discharge was made, the
    employer lacked knowledge of the AIDS condition.

23. The employer acknowledges that the plaintiff, a victim of
    AIDS, was discharged, but avers and explains that its de-
    cision was not motivated by the knowledge that the plain-
    tiff had AIDS. Instead, the reason that the plaintiff was
    discharged was poor performance, for which he or she was
    counseled and reprimanded several times.

24. The plaintiff was not discharged—he or she clearly noti-
    fied the relevant manager of the decision to quit. The em-
    ployer then processed the termination as voluntary. The
    plaintiff was not pressured or coerced into leaving but sim-
    ply decided to leave, voluntarily.

25. The lawsuit is barred by a settlement of these claims that
    was voluntarily negotiated by the plaintiff and the em-
    ployer. After the plaintiff submitted medical confirmation
    of the AIDS condition to the personnel manager, there was
    a series of meetings during which various options were
    discussed. Eventually, the plaintiff and the personnel man-
    ager reached agreement on these terms: payment of vaca-
    tion and severance pay to the plaintiff; a six-month unpaid
    leave of absence during which the plaintiff would continue
    to be covered under the group medical policy; and termi-
    nation of all benefits, payments, and employment status
    after expiration of the six-month leave. The employer ful-
    filled its obligations, and the plaintiff should be prevented
    from processing this suit when he or she has obtained past
    settlement and satisfaction.

Conclusion

F rom the perspective of the individual with AIDS, the syndrome is incurable, physically incapacitating, mentally debilitating, and —finally—lethal. In struggling through the final months of their lives, these victims—too often very young—require compassion and sensitivity. Discharge from employment and loss of insurance coverage should be avoided, and instead, the employer should extend efforts to provide emotional support and financial assistance.

There are, however, limits to what can be expected of employers in these situations. Because of the infectious nature of HIV, certain employers have obligations to and concerns for customers, patients, fellow employees, and the public. At times, the best interests of the infected employee are at odds with those of others. It must also be remembered that AIDS is an epidemic, and the number of people, including heterosexuals, infected with HIV, ARC, and AIDS is greatly expanding each year. In these circumstances, steps to protect the public safety are very much in order, even if they flatten a few individual rights.

In drafting legislation at the various levels of government and in deciding AIDS-in-employment issues submitted to them, legislators and judges should grant employers considerably more flexibility and latitude in dealing with applicants as opposed to employees. Also, the exact industry and type of job should be analyzed and across-the-board rules for all employers avoided. The focus should be on the legitimacy and reasonableness of the action taken by the employer in the particular circumstances surrounding it. Here are some specific suggestions:

1. Employers hiring food service and health care personnel should be able to ask applicants on an application form or in an interview whether they have either HIV or AIDS. The superior approach would be to inquire whether they have any communicable diseases, including tuberculosis, hepatitis, HIV, and AIDS. These employers should also possess the right to require AIDS testing for applicants directly involved with food handling and patient care. Mass, mandatory screening is *not* being advocated: testing is appropriate only for high-risk jobs in which the opportunities for transmitting the virus to customers, patients, fellow employees or the public are greater than normal.

2. Applicants with positive HIV results should not be uniformly rejected. As indicated, many will never develop ARC or AIDS. Employers with high risk positions should utilize the test to assist in *placement only*.

3. Health care and food service employers should be permitted to propound a rule requiring a report from employees if either they or members of their immediate families contract contagious diseases. Examples of infectious diseases—including HIV, ARC, and AIDS—should be listed and communicated to employees. Those who fail to report should be subject to disciplinary action up to and including discharge—not for having AIDS, but because they violated the rule mandating disclosure. The legitimate reason for the rule, of course, is to protect the health and safety of the workplace. Specific procedures for ensuring the confidentiality of those reports and records is critical. Employers in other industries, however, may decide such a rule is inappropriate for them.

4. Health care employers should be able to require an employee exposed to the HIV virus through needle stick, blood spill, or other means to submit to testing for HIV antibodies. Any employees who refuse to cooperate should be subject to discharge for failing to comply with the employer's policy.

5. Employers should bend over backward to avoid discharging an employee with AIDS. As indicated, the type of job, the risk of infection, and the physical and mental ability of the employee to perform must all be analyzed. Hopefully, the employee can be retained in his or her regular job or accommodated with a transfer. If not, a vigorous attempt should be made to allow the employee to perform work at home or at another location. And the last resort should be a leave of absence that allows him or her to be covered under the medical insurance plan. Even after expiration of the leave, assuming the employer's policy has a maximum duration, the employee-victim's medical bills could be covered under COBRA for another eighteen months.

Until medical and legal aspects involving AIDS are more fully developed, most employers should not have a specific policy on handling AIDS problems. Those who feel the need for one should adopt a policy on infectious diseases that would encompass HIV, ARC, and AIDS. A possible exception to this general rule is hospitals, which have special problems with transmitting HIV and are vulnerable to suits by patients or employees who later contract it. Regardless of a written policy, it is critical for employers to thoroughly and accurately document their *practices* and to achieve strong consistency in their approaches to AIDS-related problems.

It's deeply disappointing that, thus far, the Federal Government has not done more to combat AIDS. Research for cure and treatment could certainly benefit from additional dollars, but it is in the area of education that the Reagan administration has fallen so sharply short. Here are specific programs that should be adopted or expanded:

1. Radio and television advertisements designed to alert the public to the problem, inform them on how to avoid spreading it, urge voluntary testing in certain circumstances, and educate them on workplace issues. Networks should be given incentives to devote the time, or at least discount the price, to the federal government.

2. A significant number of federally owned or subsidized test-

ing centers, located in the undereducated and poorer sections of large cities, designed to be efficient to voluntarily and anonymously use. These centers should have trained counselors on the premises available for dispensing advice and condoms without charge.

3. Grants to hospitals regularly treating AIDS patients for improving infection control procedures and educating personnel.

4. Special subsidies to organizations establishing hospices exclusively for AIDS patients.

5. Educational materials on AIDS in general and how it is spread in specific for distribution to employers, with emphasis on the low probability of infecting others in the workplace. Designate public health doctors, nurses, and officials as *AIDS Information Officers* to solicit invitations to speak to groups of employees and distribute the materials— this is especially important in large cities and in both the health care and food service industries.

6. Model infectious disease programs and policies for various federally operated facilities, including health care and food service. Document their impact, and report the results—with recommendations—to employers across the country.

Appendix A
U.S. Government
Guidelines on AIDS

Document 1

Summary of Recommendations by the U.S. Public Health Service

A. Recommendations to Prevent the Spread of AIDS

1. Do not have sexual contact with persons known or suspected of having AIDS.

2. Do not have sex with multiple partners, or with persons who have had multiple partners.

3. Persons who are at increased risk for having AIDS should not donate blood.

4. Physicians should order blood transfusions for patients only when medically necessary. Health workers should use extreme care when handling or disposing of hypodermic needles.

5. Don't abuse intravenous drugs. If you use intravenous drugs, then don't share needles or syringes (boiling does not guarantee sterility).

6. Don't have sex with people who abuse intravenous drugs.

B. Special Recommendations for Persons Who Have Tested Positive for HTLV-III for the Purpose of Preventing the Spread of AIDS

1. A regular medical evaluation and follow-up is advised for persons with positive test results.

2. Persons with positive blood test may pass the disease on to others and should not donate blood, plasma, body organs, other tissue, or sperm. They should take precautions against exchanging body fluids during sexual activity.

3. There is a risk of infecting others by sexual intercourse, sharing of needles, and possibly exposure of others to saliva through oral genital contact or intimate kissing. The effectiveness of condoms in preventing infection with HTLV-III is not proved, but their consistent use may reduce transmission, since exchange of body fluids is known to increase risk.

4. Toothbrushes, razors, or other implements that could become contaminated with blood should not be shared.

5. A woman whose sex partner is antibody-positive is at increased risk of acquiring AIDS. If she becomes pregnant, their children are also at increased risk of acquiring AIDS.

Document 2

Statement by the Acting Assistant Secretary for Health

STATEMENT
BY
JAMES O. MASON, M.D., Dr.P.H.
ACTING ASSISTANT SECRETARY FOR HEALTH
U.S. PUBLIC HEALTH SERVICE

November 14, 1985

Today we are making available to you the Public Health Service's new guidelines on AIDS in the workplace. These guidelines, which are aimed at protecting the public health, are being published in tomorrow's Morbidity and Mortality Weekly Report.

The guidelines are directed to:

● *Health care workers*—a broad category that includes health professionals; laboratory and blood bank technologists and technicians; emergency personnel; morticians; housekeepers; laundry workers; and others whose work involves contact with AIDS patients, their blood or other body fluids, or corpses.

● *Personal service workers*—those whose occupations involve close personal contact with clients; for example, hairdressers, barbers, cosmetologists, manicurists and pedicurists, massage therapists, and others.

● *Food service workers*—a category included because of public concern that HTLV-III/LAV, the "AIDS virus," may be transmitted in food and beverages handled by infected persons. (This concern, while understandable, is wholly unfounded.)

● *Other workers*—persons in work settings such as offices, schools, factories, and construction sites, where there is no known risk of AIDS virus transmission.

Before discussing the guidelines we are releasing today in greater detail, I would like to stress that they represent no change in the basic message about AIDS that the Public Health Service has been conveying all along—that AIDS is a bloodborne, sexually transmitted disease that is *not* spread by casual contact.

Don't misunderstand me—AIDS is frightening. And we are in the midst of an epidemic of fear, which is both good and bad. Two kinds of fear are at work here. One is reasonable fear among people whose behavior may put them at risk for AIDS. For those people, fear may accomplish what knowledge alone will not— fear may cause people to change the behavior that puts them at risk.

On the other hand, fear among people who are not at risk is unwarranted and counterproductive. People who are frightened of friends, coworkers, and family members who may be at risk of AIDS are suffering unwarranted fear, and that fear doesn't produce any worthwhile outcomes. This is the fear we need to do away with.

Now, let me briefly outline some of the points the guidelines cover.

The longest section of the guidelines deals with *health care workers* and recommends precautions appropriate to prevent transmission of all bloodborne infectious diseases, including HTLV-III/LAV infection and hepatitis B. These precautions are spelled out in detail in the MMWR article in your press kit. They take into account the possibility of transmission of infection from patient to health care worker and from health care worker to patient, and they should be enforced routinely. They include recommendations for managing parenteral and mucous membrane exposures to blood or other body fluids; precautions to be taken with needles and sharp instruments; appropriate use of gloves and other protective garments; use of equipment to minimize the need for mouth-to-mouth resuscitation; sterilization and disinfection procedures; housekeeping procedures; and disposal of infective body wastes. Precautions for people caring for AIDS patients at home and for providers of pre-hospital emergency care are also included.

The section dealing with *personal service workers*—to which I again refer you for additional details—emphasizes that we have no evidence of any instances of transmission of the AIDS virus between these workers and their clients, or from client to client. Nevertheless, a risk would exist in situations where there is trauma to an uninfected person that would give the virus a portal of entry, combined with access of blood or serous fluid from an infected person to the open tissue, as could occur in the case of a cut. There would also be a risk of transmission from client to client if instruments contaminated with blood were not sterilized or disinfected between clients.

Personal service workers whose services require needles or other instruments that penetrate the skin should follow precautions recommended in the guidelines for health care workers. Instruments used to pierce the skin—for example, tattooing and acupuncture needles and ear-piercing devices—should be used once and disposed of, or should be thoroughly cleaned and disinfected, using the procedures the guidelines recommend.

Any personal service worker (and any health care worker) who has exudative lesions or weeping dermatitis—regardless of that person's status with respect to infection with the AIDS virus—should refrain from direct contact with clients until the condition clears.

With respect to *food service workers*—for example, cooks, caterers, waiters, bartenders, and airline attendants—all evidence from epidemiologic and laboratory studies indicates that bloodborne and sexually transmitted infections such as AIDS are not transmitted in connection with the preparation or serving of food or beverages. There have been no documented instances of transmission of either hepatitis B or AIDS in this manner.

The guidelines state that food service workers should follow established standards and practices of good personal hygiene and food sanitation. Food service workers should not prepare or serve food when they have exudative lesions or weeping dermatitis, and they should take care to avoid injury to their hands when preparing food. If such injury should occur, food contaminated with blood should be discarded. Of course, this recommendation should be followed anyway, just for aesthetic reasons.

Food service workers known to be infected with the AIDS virus need not be restricted from work unless they show evidence of another infection, condition, or illness for which there should be such a restriction.

The guidelines for *other workers* emphasize that AIDS is not spread by the kind of nonsexual, person-to-person contact that occurs among workers, clients, and consumers in such settings as offices, schools, factories, and construction sites. Workers known to be infected with the AIDS virus should not be restricted from work on this account, nor should they be restricted from using telephones, office equipment, toilets, showers, eating facilities, and water fountains. In the case of accidents in the work setting, equipment that is contaminated with blood or other body fluids from any worker, known to be infected or not, should be cleaned with soap and water or a detergent. A disinfectant or a fresh solution of household bleach, as described in the guidelines, should be used to wipe the area after cleaning.

We ask your help in dispelling unwarranted public fears by continuing to emphasize that AIDS is *not* easy to catch and is *not* spread by casual contact. Again, I repeat what I have said many times before: Personal choices made by each individual with respect to responsible sexual behavior and nonuse of intravenous drugs are the best guarantees of protection from the AIDS virus.

Document 3

CDC Recommendations for Preventing AIDS Transmission in the Workplace

Summary:
Recommendations for Preventing Transmission of Infection with Human T-Lymphotropic Virus Type III/ Lymphadenopathy-Associated Virus in the Workplace

The information and recommendations contained in this document have been developed with particular emphasis on health-care workers and others in related occupations in which exposure might occur to blood from persons infected with HTLV-III/LAV, the "AIDS virus." Because of public concern about the purported risk of transmission of HTLV-III/LAV by persons providing personal services and those preparing and serving food and beverages, this document also addresses personal-service and food-service workers. Finally, it addresses "other workers"— persons in settings, such as offices, schools, factories, and construction sites, where there is no known risk of AIDS virus transmission.

Because AIDS is a bloodborne, sexually transmitted disease that is not spread by casual contact, this document does *not* recommend routine HTLV-III/LAV antibody screening for the groups addressed. Because AIDS is not transmitted through preparation or serving of food and beverages, these recommendations state that food-service workers known to be infected with AIDS should not be restricted from work unless they have another infection or illness for which such restriction would be warranted.

This document contains detailed recommendations for precautions appropriate to prevent transmission of all bloodborne infectious diseases to people exposed—in the course of their duties—to blood from persons who may be infected with HTLV-III/LAV. They emphasize that health-care workers should take all possible precautions to prevent needlestick injury. The recommendations are based on the well-documented modes of HTLV-III/LAV transmission and incorporate a "worst case" scenario, the hepatitis B model of transmission. Because the hepatitis B virus is also bloodborne and is both hardier and more infectious than HTLV-III/LAV, recommendations that would prevent transmission of hepatitis B will also prevent transmission of AIDS.

Formulation of specific recommendations for health-care workers who perform invasive procedures is in progress.

Recommendations for Preventing Transmission of Infection with Human T-Lymphotropic Virus Type III/ Lymphadenopathy-Associated Virus in the Workplace

Persons at increased risk of acquiring infection with human T-lymphotropic virus type III/lymphadenopathy-associated virus (HTLV-III/LAV), the virus that causes acquired immunodeficiency syndrome (AIDS), include homosexual and bisexual men, intravenous (IV) drug abusers, persons transfused with contaminated blood or blood products, heterosexual contacts of persons with HTLV-III/LAV infection, and children born to infected mothers. HTLV-III/LAV is transmitted through sexual contact, parenteral exposure to infected blood or blood components, and perinatal transmission from mother to neonate. HTLV-III/LAV has been isolated from blood, semen, saliva, tears, breast milk, and urine and is likely to be isolated from some other body fluids, secretions, and excretions, but epidemiologic evidence has implicated only blood and semen in transmission. Studies of nonsexual household contacts of AIDS patients indicate that casual contact with saliva and tears does not result in transmission of infection. Spread of infection to household contacts of infected persons has not been detected when the household contacts have not been sex partners or have not been infants of infected mothers. The kind of nonsexual person-to-person contact that generally occurs among workers and clients or consumers in the workplace does not pose a risk for transmission of HTLV-III/LAV.

As in the development of any such recommendations, the paramount consideration is the protection of the public's health. The following recommendations have been developed for all workers, particularly workers in occupations in which exposure might occur to blood from individuals infected with HTLV-III/LAV. These recommendations reinforce and supplement the specific recommendations that were published earlier for clinical and laboratory staffs and for dental-care personnel and persons performing necropsies and morticians' services. Because of public concern about the purported risk of transmission of HTLV-III/LAV by persons providing personal services and by food and beverages, these recommendations contain information and recommendations for personal-service and food-service workers. Finally, these recommendations address workplaces in general where there is no known risk of transmission of HTLV-III/LAV (e.g., offices, schools, factories, construction sites). Formulation of specific recommendations for health-care workers (HCWs) who perform invasive procedures (e.g., surgeons, dentists) is in progress. Separate recommendations are also being developed to prevent HTLV-III/LAV transmission in prisons, other correctional facilities, and institutions housing individuals who may exhibit uncontrollable behavior (e.g., custodial institutions) and in the perinatal setting. In addition, separate recommendations have already been developed for children in schools and day-care centers.

HTLV-III/LAV-infected individuals include those with AIDS; those diagnosed by their physician(s) as having other illnesses due to infection with HTLV-III/LAV; and those who have virologic or serologic evidence of infection with HTLV-III/LAV but who are not ill.

These recommendations are based on the well-documented modes of HTLV-III/LAV transmission identified in epidemiologic studies and on comparison with the hepatitis B experience. Other recommendations are based on the hepatitis B model of transmission.

Comparison with the Hepatitis B Virus Experience

The epidemiology of HTLV-III/LAV infection is similar to that of hepatitis B virus (HBV) infection, and much that has been learned over the last 15 years related to the risk of acquiring hepatitis B in the workplace can be applied to understanding the risk of HTLV-III/LAV transmission in the health-care and other occupational settings. Both viruses are transmitted through sexual contact, parenteral exposure to contaminated blood or blood products, and perinatal transmission from infected mothers to their offspring. Thus, some of the same major groups at high risk for HBV infection (e.g., homosexual men, IV drug abusers, persons with hemophilia, infants born to infected mothers) are also the groups at highest risk for HTLV-III/LAV infection. Neither HBV nor HTLV-III/LAV has been shown to be transmitted by casual contact in the workplace, contaminated food or water, or airborne or fecal-oral routes.

HBV infection is an occupational risk for HCWs, but this risk is related to degree of contact with blood or contaminated needles. HCWs who do not have contact with blood or needles contaminated with blood are not at risk for acquiring HBV infection in the workplace.

In the health-care setting, HBV transmission has not been documented between hospitalized patients, except in hemodialysis units, where blood contamination of the environment has been extensive or where HBV-positive blood from one patient has been transferred to another patient through contamination of instruments. Evidence of HBV transmission from HCWs to patients has been rare and limited to situations in which the HCWs exhibited high concentrations of virus in their blood (at least 100,000,000 infectious virus particles per ml of serum), and the HCWs sustained a puncture wound while performing traumatic procedures on patients or had exudative or weeping lesions that allowed virus to contaminate instruments or open wounds of patients.

Current evidence indicates that, despite epidemiologic similarities of HBV and HTLV-III/LAV infection, the risk for HBV transmission in health-care settings far exceeds that for HTLV-III/LAV transmission. The risk of acquiring HBV infection following a needlestick from an HBV carrier ranges from 6% to 30%, far in excess of the risk of HTLV-III/LAV infection following a needlestick involving a source patient infected with HTLV-III/LAV, which is less than 1%. In addition, all HCWs who have been shown to transmit HBV infection in health-care settings have belonged to the subset of chronic HBV carriers who, when tested, have exhibited evidence of exceptionally high concentrations of virus (at least 100,000,000 infectious virus particles per ml) in their blood. Chronic carriers who have substantially lower concentrations of virus in their blood have not been implicated in transmission in the health-care setting. The HBV model thus represents a "worst case" condition in regard to transmission in health-care and other related settings. Therefore, recommendations for the control of HBV infection should, if followed, also effectively prevent spread of HTLV-III/LAV. Whether additional measures are indicated for those HCWs who perform invasive procedures will be addressed in the recommendations currently being developed.

Routine screening of all patients or HCWs for evidence of HBV infection has never been recommended. Control of HBV transmission in the health-care setting has emphasized the implementation of recommendations for the appropriate handling of blood, other body fluids, and items soiled with blood or other body fluids.

Transmission from Patients to Health-Care Workers

HCWs include, but are not limited to, nurses, physicians, dentists and other dental workers, optometrists, podiatrists, chiropractors, laboratory and blood bank technologists and technicians, phlebotomists, dialysis personnel, paramedics, emergency medical technicians, medical examiners, morticians, housekeepers, laundry workers, and others whose work involves contact with patients, their blood or other body fluids, or corpses.

Recommendations for HCWs emphasize precautions appropriate for preventing transmission of bloodborne infectious diseases, including HTLV-III/LAV and HBV infections. Thus, these precautions should be enforced routinely, as should other standard infection-control precautions, regardless of whether HCWs or patients are known to be infected with HTLV-III/LAV or HBV. In addition to being informed of these precautions, all HCWs, including students and housestaff, should be educated regarding the epidemiology, modes of transmission, and prevention of HTLV-III/LAV infection.

Risk of HCWs acquiring HTLV-III/LAV in the workplace. Using the HBV model, the highest risk for transmission of HTLV-III/LAV in the workplace would involve parenteral exposure to a needle or other sharp instrument contaminated with blood of an infected patient. The risk to HCWs of acquiring HTLV-III/LAV infection in the workplace has been evaluated in several studies. In five separate studies, a total of 1,498 HCWs have been tested for antibody to HTLV-III/LAV. In these studies, 666 (44.5%) of the HCWs had direct parenteral (needlestick or cut) or mucous membrane exposure to patients with AIDS or HTLV-III/LAV infection. Most of these exposures were to blood rather than to other body fluids. None of the HCWs whose initial serologic tests were negative developed subsequent evidence of HTLV-III/LAV infection following their exposures. Twenty-six HCWs in these five studies were seropositive when first tested; all but three of these persons belonged to groups recognized to be at increased risk for AIDS. Since one was tested anonymously, epidemiologic information was available on only two of these three seropositive HCWs. Although these two HCWs were reported as probable occupationally related HTLV-III/LAV infection, neither had a preexposure nor an early postexposure serum sample available to help determine the onset of infection. One case reported from England describes a nurse who seroconverted following an accidental parenteral exposure to a needle contaminated with blood from an AIDS patient.

In spite of the extremely low risk of transmission of HTLV-III/LAV infection, even when needlestick injuries occur, more emphasis must be given to precautions targeted to prevent needlestick injuries in HCWs caring for any patient, since such injuries continue to occur even during the care of patients who are known to be infected with HTLV-III/LAV.

Precautions to prevent acquisition of HTLV-III/LAV infection by HCWs in the workplace. These precautions represent prudent practices that apply to preventing transmission of HTLV-III/LAV and other bloodborne infections and should be used routinely.

1. Sharp items (needles, scalpel blades, and other sharp instruments) should be considered as potentially infective and be handled with extraordinary care to prevent accidental injuries.

2. Disposable syringes and needles, scalpel blades, and other sharp items should be placed into puncture-resistant containers located as close as practical to the area in which they were used. To prevent needlestick injuries, needles should not be recapped, purposefully bent, broken, removed from disposable syringes, or otherwise manipulated by hand.

3. When the possibility of exposure to blood or other body fluids exists, routinely recommended precautions should be followed. The anticipated exposure may require gloves alone, as in handling items soiled with blood or equipment contaminated with blood or other body fluids, or may also require gowns, masks, and eye-coverings when performing procedures involving more extensive contact with blood or potentially infective body fluids, as in some dental or endoscopic procedures or postmortem examinations. Hands should be washed thoroughly and immediately if they accidentally become contaminated with blood.

4. To minimize the need for emergency mouth-to-mouth resuscitation, mouth pieces, resuscitation bags, or other ventilation devices should be strategically located and available for use in areas where the need for resuscitation is predictable.

5. Pregnant HCWs are not known to be at greater risk of contracting HTLV-III/LAV infections than HCWs who are not pregnant; however, if a HCW develops HTLV-III/LAV infection during pregnancy, the infant is at increased risk of infection resulting from perinatal transmission. Because of this risk, pregnant HCWs should be especially familiar with precautions for the preventing HTLV-III/LAV transmission.

Precautions for HCWs during home care of persons infected with HTLV-III/ LAV. Persons infected with HTLV-III/LAV can be safely cared for in home environments. Studies of family members of patients infected with HTLV-III/LAV have found no evidence of HTLV-III/LAV transmission to adults who were not sexual contacts of the infected patients or to children who were not at risk for perinatal transmission. HCWs providing home care face the same risk of transmission of infection as HCWs in hospitals and other health-care settings, especially if there are needlesticks or other parenteral or mucous membrane exposures to blood or other body fluids.

When providing health-care service in the home to persons infected with HTLV-III/LAV, measures similar to those used in hospitals are appropriate. As in the hospital, needles should not be recapped, purposefully bent, broken, removed from disposable syringes, or otherwise manipulated by hand. Needles and other sharp items should be placed into puncture-resistant containers and disposed of in accordance with local regulations for solid waste. Blood and other body fluids can be flushed down the toilet. Other items for disposal that are contaminated with blood or other body fluids that cannot be flushed down the toilet should be wrapped securely in a plastic bag that is impervious and sturdy (not easily penetrated). It should be placed in a second bag before being discarded in a manner consistent with local regulations for solid waste disposal. Spills of blood or other body fluids should be cleaned up with soap and water or a household detergent. As in the hospital, individuals cleaning up such spills should wear disposable gloves. A disinfectant solution or a freshly prepared solution of sodium hypochlorite (household bleach, see below) should be used to wipe the area after cleaning.

Precautions for providers of prehospital emergency health care. Providers of prehospital emergency health care include the following: paramedics, emergency medical technicians, law enforcement personnel, firefighters, lifeguards, and others whose job might require them to provide first-response medical care. The risk of transmission of infection, including HTLV-III/LAV infection, from infected persons to providers of prehospital emergency health care should be no higher than that for HCWs providing emergency care in the hospital if appropriate precautions are taken to prevent exposure to blood or other body fluids.

Providers of prehospital emergency health care should follow the precautions outlined above for other HCWs. No transmission of HBV infection during mouth-to-mouth resuscitation has been documented. However, because of the theoretical risk of salivary transmission of HTLV-III/LAV during mouth-to-mouth resuscitation, special attention should be given to the use of disposable airway equipment or resuscitation bags and the wearing of gloves when in contact with blood or other body fluids. Resuscitation equipment and devices known or suspected to be contaminated with blood or other body fluids should be used once and disposed of or be thoroughly cleaned and disinfected after each use.

Management of parenteral and mucous membrane exposures of HCWs. If a HCW has a parenteral (e.g., needlestick or cut) or mucous membrane (e.g., splash to the eye or mouth) exposure to blood or other body fluids, the source patient should be assessed clinically and epidemiologically to determine the likelihood of HTLV-III/LAV infection. If the assessment suggests that infection may exist, the patient should be informed of the incident and requested to consent to serologic testing for evidence of HTLV-III/LAV infection. If the source patient has AIDS or other evidence of HTLV-III/LAV infection, declines testing, or has a positive test, the HCW should be evaluated clinically and serologically for evidence of HTLV-III/LAV infection as soon as possible after the exposure, and, if seronegative, retested after 6 weeks and on a periodic basis thereafter (e.g., 3, 6 and 12 months following exposure) to determine if transmission has occurred. During this follow-up period, especially the first 6–12 weeks, when most infected persons are expected to seroconvert, exposed HCWs should receive counseling about the risk of infection and follow U.S. Public Health Service (PHS) recommendations for preventing transmission of AIDS. If the source patient is seronegative and has no other evidence of HTLV-III/LAV infection, no further follow-up of the HCW is necessary. If the source patient cannot be identified, decisions regarding appropriate follow-up should be individualized based on the type of exposure and the likelihood that the source patient was infected.

Serologic testing of patients. Routine serologic testing of all patients for antibody to HTLV-III/LAV is not recommended to prevent transmission of HTLV-III/LAV infection in the workplace. Results of such testing are unlikely to further reduce the risk of transmission, which, even with documented needlesticks, is already extremely low. Furthermore, the risk of needlestick and other parenteral exposures could be reduced by emphasizing and more consistently implementing routinely recommended infection-control precautions (e.g., not recapping needles). Moreover, results of routine serologic testing would not be available for emergency cases and patients with short lengths of stay, and additional tests to determine whether a positive test was a true or false positive would be required in populations with a low prevalence of infection. However, this recommendation is based only on considerations of occupational risks and should not be construed as a recommendation against other uses of the serologic test, such as for diagnosis or to facilitate medical management of patients. Since the experience with infected patients varies substantially among hospitals (75% of all AIDS cases have been reported by only 280 of the more than 6,000 acute-care hospitals in the United States), some hospitals in certain geographic areas may deem it appropriate to initiate serologic testing of patients.

Transmission from Health-Care Workers to Patients

Risk of transmission of HTLV-III/LAV infection from HCWs to patients. Although there is no evidence that HCWs infected with HTLV-III/LAV have transmitted infection to patients, a risk of transmission of HTLV-III/LAV infection from HCWs to patients would exist in situations where there is both (1) a high degree of trauma to the patient that would provide a portal of entry for the virus (e.g., during invasive procedures) and (2) access of blood or serous fluid from the infected HCW to the open tissue of a patient, as could occur if the HCW sustains a needlestick or scalpel injury during an invasive procedure. HCWs known to be infected with HTLV-III/LAV who do not perform invasive procedures need not be restricted from work unless they have evidence of other infection or illness for which any HCW should be restricted. Whether additional restrictions are indicated for HCWs who perform invasive procedures is currently being considered.

Precautions to prevent transmission of HTLV-III/LAV infection from HCWs to patients. These precautions apply to all HCWs, regardless of whether they perform invasive procedures: (1) All HCWs should wear gloves for direct contact with mucous membranes or nonintact skin of all patients and (2) HCWs who have exudative lesions or weeping dermatitis should refrain from all direct patient care and from handling patient-care equipment until the condition resolves.

Management of parenteral and mucous membrane exposures of patients. If a patient has a parenteral or mucous membrane exposure to blood or other body fluids of a HCW, the patient should be informed of the incident and the same procedure outlined above for exposures of HCWs to patients should be followed for both the source HCW and the potentially exposed patient. Management of this type of exposure will be addressed in more detail in the recommendations for HCWs who perform invasive procedures.

Serologic testing of HCWs. Routine serologic testing of HCWs who do not perform invasive procedures (including providers of home and prehospital emergency care) is not recommended to prevent transmission of HTLV-III/LAV infection. The risk of transmission is extremely low and can be further minimized when routinely recommended infection-control precautions are followed. However, serologic testing should be available to HCWs who may wish to know their HTLV-III/LAV infection status. Whether indications exist for serologic testing of HCWs who perform invasive procedures is currently being considered.

Risk of occupational acquisition of other infectious diseases by HCWs infected with HTLV-III/LAV. HCWs who are known to be infected with HTLV-III/LAV and who have defective immune systems are at increased risk of acquiring or experiencing serious complications of other infectious diseases. Of particular concern is the risk of severe infection following exposure to patients with infectious diseases that are easily transmitted if appropriate precautions are not taken (e.g., tuberculosis). HCWs infected with HTLV-III/LAV should be counseled about the potential risk associated with taking care of patients with transmissible infections and should continue to follow existing recommendations for infection control to minimize their risk of exposure to other infectious agents. The HCWs' personal physician(s), in conjunction with their institutions' personnel health services or medical directors, should determine on an individual basis whether the infected HCWs can adequately and safely perform patient-care duties and suggest changes in work assignments, if indicated. In making this determination, recommendations of the Immunization Practices Advisory Committee and institutional policies concerning requirements for vaccinating HCWs with live-virus vaccines should also be considered.

Sterilization, Disinfection, Housekeeping, and Waste Disposal to Prevent Transmission of HTLV-III/LAV

Sterilization and disinfection procedures currently recommended for use in health-care and dental facilities are adequate to sterilize or disinfect instruments, devices, or other items contaminated with the blood or other body fluids from individuals infected with HTLV-III/LAV. Instruments or other nondisposable items that enter normally sterile tissue or the vascular system or through which blood flows should be sterilized before reuse. Surgical instruments used on all patients should be decontaminated after use rather than just rinsed with water. Decontamination can be accomplished by machine or by hand cleaning by trained personnel wearing appropriate protective attire and using appropriate chemical germicides. Instruments or other nondisposable items that touch intact mucous membranes should receive high-level disinfection.

Several liquid chemical germicides commonly used in laboratories and health-care facilities have been shown to kill HTLV-III/LAV at concentrations much lower than are used in practice. When decontaminating instruments or medical devices, chemical germicides that are registered with and approved by the U.S. Environmental Protection Agency (EPA) as "sterilants" can be used either for sterilization or for high-level disinfection depending on contact time; germicides that are approved for use as "hospital disinfectants" and are mycobactericidal when used at appropriate dilutions can also be used for high-level disinfection of devices and instruments. Germicides that are mycobactericidal are preferred because mycobacteria represent one of the most resistant groups of microorganisms; therefore, germicides that are effective against mycobacteria are also effective against other bacterial and viral pathogens. When chemical germicides are used, instruments or devices to be sterilized or disinfected should be thoroughly cleaned before exposure to the germicide, and the manufacturer's instructions for use of the germicide should be followed.

Laundry and dishwashing cycles commonly used in hospitals are adequate to decontaminate linens, dishes, glassware, and utensils. When cleaning environmental surfaces, housekeeping procedures commonly used in hospitals are adequate; surfaces exposed to blood and body fluids should be cleaned with a detergent followed by decontamination using an EPA-approved hospital disinfectant that is mycobactericidal. Individuals cleaning up such spills should wear disposable gloves. Information on specific label claims of commercial germicides can be obtained by writing to the Disinfectants Branch, Office of Pesticides, Environmental Protection Agency, 401 M Street, S.W., Washington, D.C., 20460.

In addition to hospital disinfectants, a freshly prepared solution of sodium hypochlorite (household bleach) is an inexpensive and very effective germicide. Concentrations ranging from 5,000 ppm (a 1:10 dilution of household bleach) to 500 ppm (a 1:100 dilution) sodium hypochlorite are effective, depending on the amount of organic material (e.g., blood, mucus, etc.) present on the surface to be cleaned and disinfected.

Sharp items should be considered as potentially infective and should be handled and disposed of with extraordinary care to prevent accidental injuries. Other potentially infective waste should be contained and transported in clearly identified impervious plastic bags. If the outside of the bag is contaminated with blood or other body fluids, a second outer bag should be used. Recommended practices for disposal of infective waste are adequate for disposal of waste contaminated by HTLV-III/LAV. Blood and other body fluids may be carefully poured down a drain connected to a sanitary sewer.

Considerations Relevant to Other Workers

Personal-service workers (PSWs). PSWs are defined as individuals whose occupations involve close personal contact with clients (e.g., hairdressers, barbers, estheticians, cosmetologists, manicurists, pedicurists, massage therapists). PSWs whose services (tattooing, ear piercing, acupuncture, etc.) require needles or other instruments that penetrate the skin should follow precautions indicated for HCWs. Although there is no evidence of transmission of HTLV-III/LAV from clients to PSWs, from PSWs to clients, or between clients of PSWs, a risk of transmission would exist from PSWs to clients and vice versa in situations where there is both (1) trauma to one of the individuals that would provide a portal of entry for the virus and (2) access of blood or serous fluid from one infected person to the open tissue of the other, as could occur if either sustained a cut. A risk of transmission from client to client exists when instruments contaminated with blood are not sterilized or disinfected between clients. However, HBV transmission has been documented only rarely in acupuncture, ear piercing, and tattoo establishments and never in other personal-service settings, indicating that any risk for HTLV-III/LAV transmission in personal-service settings must be extremely low.

All PSWs should be educated about transmission of bloodborne infections, including HTLV-III/LAV and HBV. Such education should emphasize principles of good hygiene, antisepsis, and disinfection. This education can be accomplished by national or state professional organizations, with assistance from state and local health departments, using lectures at meetings or self-instructional materials. Licensure requirements should include evidence of such education. Instruments that are intended to penetrate the skin (e.g., tattooing and acupuncture needles, ear piercing devices) should be used once and disposed of or be thoroughly cleaned and sterilized after each use using procedures recommended for use in health-care institutions. Instruments not intended to penetrate the skin but which may become contaminated with blood (e.g., razors), should be used for only one client and be disposed of or thoroughly cleaned and disinfected after use using procedures recommended for use in health-care institutions. Any PSW with exudative lesions or weeping dermatitis, regardless of HTLV-III/LAV infection status, should refrain from direct contact with clients until the condition resolves. PSWs known to be infected with HTLV-III/LAV need not be restricted from work unless they have evidence of other infections or illnesses for which any PSW should also be restricted.

Routine serologic testing of PSWs for antibody to HTLV-III/LAV is not recommended to prevent transmission from PSWs to clients.

Food-service workers (FSWs). FSWs are defined as individuals whose occupations involve the preparation or serving of food or beverages (e.g., cooks, caterers, servers, waiters, bartenders, airline attendants). All epidemiologic and laboratory evidence indicates that bloodborne and sexually transmitted infections are not transmitted during the preparation or serving of food or beverages, and no instances of HBV or HTLV-III/LAV transmission have been documented in this setting.

All FSWs should follow recommended standards and practices of good personal hygiene and food sanitation. All FSWs should exercise care to avoid injury to hands when preparing food. Should such an injury occur, both aesthetic and sanitary considerations would dictate that food contaminated with blood be discarded. FSWs known to be infected with HTLV-III/LAV need not be restricted from work unless they have evidence of other infection or illness for which any FSW should also be restricted.

Routine serologic testing of FSWs for antibody to HTLV-III/LAV is not recommended to prevent disease transmission from FSWs to consumers.

Other workers sharing the same work environment. No known risk of transmission to co-workers, clients, or consumers exists from HTLV-III/LAV-infected workers in other settings (e.g., offices, schools, factories, construction sites). This infection is spread by sexual contact with infected persons, injection of contaminated blood or blood products, and by perinatal transmission. Workers known to be infected with HTLV-III/LAV should not be restricted from work solely based on this finding. Moreover, they should not be restricted from using telephones, office equipment, toilets, showers, eating facilities, and water fountains. Equipment contaminated with blood or other body fluids of any worker, regardless of HTLV-III/LAV infection status, should be cleaned with soap and water or a detergent. A disinfectant solution or a fresh solution of sodium hypochlorite (household bleach, see above) should be used to wipe the area after cleaning.

Other Issues in the Workplace

The information and recommendations contained in this document do not address all the potential issues that may have to be considered when making specific employment decisions for persons with HTLV-III/LAV infection. The diagnosis of HTLV-III/LAV infection may evoke unwarranted fear and suspicion in some co-workers. Other issues that may be considered include the need for confidentiality, applicable federal, state, or local laws governing occupational safety and health, civil rights of employees, workers' compensation laws, provisions of collective bargaining agreements, confidentiality of medical records, informed consent, employee and patient privacy rights, and employee right-to-know statutes.

Development of These Recommendations

The information and recommendations contained in these recommendations were developed and compiled by CDC and other PHS agencies in consultation with individuals representing various organizations. The following organizations were represented: Association of State and Territorial Health Officials, Conference of State and Territorial Epidemiologists, Association of State and Territorial Public Health Laboratory Directors, National Association of County Health Officials, American Hospital Association, United States Conference of Local Health Officers, Association for Practitioners in Infection Control, Society of Hospital Epidemiologists of America, American Dental Association, American Medical Association, American Nurses' Association, American Association of Medical Colleges, American Association of Dental Schools, National Institutes of Health, Food and Drug Administration, Food Research Institute, National Restaurant

Association, National Hairdressers and Cosmetologists Association, National Gay Task Force, National Funeral Directors and Morticians Association, American Association of Physicians for Human Rights, and National Association of Emergency Medical Technicians. The consultants also included a labor union representative, an attorney, a corporate medical director, and a pathologist. However, these recommendations may not reflect the views of individual consultants or the organizations they represented.

Appendix B
Health Care Materials: Policies, Forms, Guidelines, and Checklists

Document 1

Sample Policy: Employees Infected with HIV

ABC HOSPITAL

PERSONNEL POLICIES

SUBJECT: HUMAN T-LYMPHOTROPIC VIRUS TYPE III/
LYMPHADENOPATHY-ASSOCIATED VIRUS (ACQUIRED
IMMUNE DEFICIENCY SYNDROME)

Policy:

A. Health Care Workers Infected with HTLV-III/LAV

1. Health Care Workers (HCWs) known to be infected with HTLV-III/LAV who do not perform invasive procedures need not be restricted from work unless they have evidence of other infection or illness for which any HCW should be restricted. HCWs infected with HTLV-III/LAV will not be allowed to perform invasive procedures.

2. Each HCW infected with HTLV-III/LAV shall be permitted to work once it is determined in consultation with the Employee Health Nurse and the HCW's private physician that:

   a. The employee is free from any other infection or illness for which restriction is indicated.

   b. The employee is not duly susceptible to infections he/she might come in contact with in the line of his/her work.

3. Work duties shall be evaluated according to an ongoing clinical evaluation of the infected HCW's medical condition.

B. HCWs Working with HTLV-III/LAV Infected Patients or Employees

1. Pregnant employees shall not engage in the direct care of patients infected with HTLV-III/LAV because of the possible risk of acquiring cytomegalovirus.

2. HCWs refusing to perform his/her work duties involving the care of an HTLV-III/LAV infected patient shall be disciplined.

3. HCWs refusing to work with another employee with HTLV-III/LAV infection shall be disciplined.

4. Food service workers known to be infected with HTLV-III/LAV need not be restricted from work unless they have evidence of other infection or illness for which any food service worker should also be restricted.

C. Serologic Testing of Employees

1. Routine serologic testing of HCWs is not provided.

2. Serologic testing is available to HCWs who wish to know their HTLV-III/LAV status at the County Local Health District.

3. HCWs who have sustained a parenteral or mucous membrane exposure to blood or body fluids shall follow the protocol established for parenteral and mucous membrane exposures of HCWs.

Document 2

Sample Policy: Caring for the AIDS Patient

I. POLICY:

AIDS (Acquired Immunodeficiency Syndrome) is a serious disease caused by HIV, the Human Immunodeficiency Virus, sometimes referred to as HTLV-III/LAV. The disease is characterized by damage to the immune system which renders the patient susceptible to opportunistic infection.

AIDS is not a casually spread disease. It is transmitted by sexual contact or blood to blood exposure. Personnel working at _____ General Hospital may, in the course of their duties, render care to AIDS patients. AIDS patients will be rendered the same high quality care as is given to all patients. All hospital services shall be available to patients diagnosed or suspected of having AIDS.

It will be the responsibility of the attending physician to notify appropriate nursing personnel and the Infection Control Department when there is serious consideration of AIDS, ARC (AIDS Related Complex) or HIV virus infection as a diagnosis, so that proper precautions may be initiated.

II. DEPARTMENTS AFFECTED:

All

III. PROCEDURE:

1. Patients diagnosed with AIDS, ARC or a positive HTLV-III antibody test will be assigned to a private room.

2. Patients with known or suspect AIDS/ARC or positive anti-HTLV III serologic test shall be placed on Blood/Body Fluid Precautions. If the patient is admitted with such a diagnosis and appropriate isolation orders are not written, the nurse caring for the patient shall contact the attending physician and obtain the order for isolation. Blood/Body Fluid Precautions should be initiated immediately and maintained throughout the patient's hospitalization unless AIDS, ARC or HIV/HTLV-III/LAV infection is excluded as a possible diagnosis.

   The nurse taking the order for isolation shall notify the Infection Control Department when she has completed initiation of the isolation protocol or if she does not receive the requested order.

   Unless exposure to blood/body fluids is anticipated, gowns, gloves, etc., need not be worn to enter the room for such procedures as obtaining vital signs. Visitors to the patient need not wear isolation garb unless there is concern for exposure to blood/body fluids, i.e., patient is vomiting, bleeding, etc.

The use of gloves, gowns, etc., is recommended only if contact with blood/body fluids or secretions is anticipated in rendering care to the patient (i.e., starting an invasive line, insertion of a catheter or dressing change, emptying bedpans/urinals).

Wash hands following contact with the patient.

For additional information relating to isolation precautions, refer to the Hospital Isolation Manual.

3. Pulmonary resuscitation equipment, e.g., an ambu-bag and oral airway, should be immediately available for use with the patient should the need arise.

4. When requesting services from ancillary departments (i.e., Lab, X-Ray, Respiratory Care, etc.), indicate on the requisition that the patient is on Blood/Body Fluid Precautions. It is important for other departments to be aware there is a need for proper precautions when rendering care to the patient.

5. All non-disposable materials/supplies/equipment which are contaminated with blood or body fluids shall be red bagged and labeled with Blood/Body Fluid Precautions tag prior to being sent to Central Services for disinfection or sterilization. Disposable items contaminated with blood or body fluids will be placed in red bags and disposed as infectious waste.

6. A needle disposable box will be placed in the patient room. Needles are NOT to be recapped, purposely bent/broken or removed from syringe prior to placing in the needle box. Needle injuries most frequently occur during these activities. The foam filled needle protector will be utilized to prevent recapping.

7. The patient need not be restricted to his/her room and may walk about the unit, if physically capable of doing so. Blood/Body Fluid Precautions do not require a patient to remain in the room at all times.

8. The use of protective eye wear, such as goggles in connection with masks, is recommended in situations in which splatter of blood/body fluids or body secretions is possible. This is particularly recommended in the performance of procedures such as endotracheal intubation, bronchoscopy or GI endoscopy. The need for eye cover precautions during other procedures should be judgeds on an individual basis.

9. Soiled linens and other laundry shall be placed in the isolation linen bags.

10. Blood/body fluid spills should be cleaned up promptly with a solution of diluted bleach which is prepared daily. A fresh container of this solution should be obtained from Environmental services each day as long as the patient is on the nursing unit.

11. Pregnant personnel are at no increased risk of acquiring AIDS while rendering care to the AIDS patient. Many AIDS patients do, however, excrete CMV (Cytomegalovirus). CMV may pose a risk to the unborn fetus, if the mother should become infected. For this reason, nursing personnel

who are pregnant will not be assigned to care for the AIDS patient. If under emergent circumstances, reassignment cannot be arranged, pregnant personnel caring for the AIDS patient should scrupulously adhere to Blood/Body Fluid Precautions. This is especially important in respect to urine, where the CMV virus is concentrated.

12. Any personnel sustaining either needle injury or exposure to blood/body fluids should report this to Employee Health as soon as possible.

13. UNDER NO CIRCUMSTANCES SHOULD THE PATIENT'S DIAGNOSIS OR SUSPECTED DIAGNOSIS BE DISCUSSED WITH VISITORS OR THOSE NOT DIRECTLY INVOLVED IN THE CARE OF THE PATIENT. ANCILLARY DEPARTMENT PERSONNEL NEED ONLY BE INFORMED THAT THE PATIENT IS ON BLOOD/BODY FLUID PRECAUTIONS.

THE TERM "AIDS" IS NOT TO BE PLACED ON THE PATIENT'S DOOR, ISOLATION SIGN, CHART COVER, NOR ENTERED ON REQUESTS TO ANCILLARY DEPARTMENTS.

MAINTAINING PATIENT CONFIDENTIALITY IS OF CRITICAL IMPORTANCE!

Approved by Infection Control Committee 11-26-86
Approved by Medical Executive Committee 12-9-86

Document 3

Sample Policy: Hospital Personnel Infected with HIV-Human Immuno-Deficiency Virus

I. POLICY:

Hospital personnel diagnosed with AIDS, AIDS related complex (ARC) or a positive anti-HTLV III shall adhere to the protocols established in this policy. The health of the employee is of foremost concern. Individuals infected with HIV are at risk from opportunistic infection and it may be necessary to restrict contact with patients known to have communicable disease. Patient contact may be restricted for certain occupations due to risk of transmission to the patient.

II. DEPARTMENTS AFFECTED:

All

III. GUIDELINES:

1. Personnel who are aware they have been diagnosed with AIDS, ARC or a positive anti-HTLV III shall report this to the Employee Health Department. ALL RECORDS IN EMPLOYEE HEALTH ARE KEPT IN STRICTEST CONFIDENCE AND ARE ONLY AVAILABLE ON A NEED TO KNOW BASIS.

2. The medical director of Employee Health will meet with the employee and in joint consultation with the attending physician appraise the current health status. At that time, the medical director will assess the duties of the employee in relation to risk of transmission to patients or co-workers and will counsel the employee concerning precautions which are applicable to the area where employed.

   Personnel known to be infected with HIV present a difficult issue that requires special consideration on an individual basis. Additional precautions or restrictions of duties, when invasive procedures are performed, may be in order. The employee will also be advised of the need for avoiding contact with patients known to be infected with easily communicated diseases. It may be necessary to contact the employee's department director to facilitate reassignment of duties which may include a non-patient contact role.

   A record of the meeting, detailing precautions and other pertinent topics discussed, will be documented by the medical director of Employee Health. The documentation shall include acknowledgment of the discussion by the employee and authorization to permit the employee's private physician to communicate with the medical director of Employee Health regarding the employee's health status.

A copy of the document will be given to the employee and a copy will be placed in the employee's file in employee Health.

The work duties of the employee will be evaluated as part of an ongoing medical evaluation by the employee's private physician in conjunction with Employee Health.

3. The Infection Control coordinator and the employee's department director shall be notified of the employee's diagnosis by the Employee Health supervisor.

4. It shall be the responsibility of the individual department director to reassign (if possible) the employee to non-patient contact or otherwise modify the employee's duties if indicated by the medical director of Employee Health.

5. On a semi-annual basis the employee must obtain documentation, from his/her personal physician, indicating current health status as well as the employee's ability to continue working. Examination by the medical director of Employee Health may be required at this time. Precautionary procedures applicable to his/her work assignment will again be addressed at this time and will be documented. A copy will be given to the employee and a copy will be placed in the employee's employee health record.

6. AIDS is a reportable disease by state law, requiring confidential notification to the State Public Health Department, AIDS Surveillance Unit. The Infection Control Department will be responsible for completion of reportable disease notification related to diagnosed cases of AIDS, in consultation with the employee's personal physician.

ARC (AIDS related complex) or a positive HTLV-III antibody alone is not reportable to Public Health.

The Center for Disease Control "Guidelines for health care workers infected with HTLV-III/LAV" will be utilized for determining precautionary procedures for employees as well as decisions concerning patient contact by the employee.

This policy represents the most current available information relative to AIDS in the workplace. As new data becomes available, this policy is subject to revision, modification, or change.

Approved by Infection Control Committee 11-26-86
Approved by Medical Executive Committee 12-9-86

Document 4

Sample Policy: Assisting Employees with Life-Threatening Illness

HOSPITAL PERSONNEL POLICY GUIDELINES

Subject   : Assisting Employees with Life Threatening Illness

Applies to :

Number:	Issued:	Page 1

I. *Policy*

―――― Hospital recognizes that employees with life threatening illnesses may wish to continue to engage in as many of their normal pursuits as their condition allows, including work. As long as these employees are able to meet acceptable performance and attendance standards, and medical evidence indicates that their conditions are not a threat to themselves or others, managers should be sensitive to their conditions and attempt to accommodate them. Life threatening illnesses are defined to include cancer, heart disease, chronic pulmonary disease, and AIDS (with AIDS including employees with AIDS, ARC and the HTLV-III virus).

At the same time, ―――― Hospital seeks to provide a safe environment for all employees, visitors, and patients. Therefore, precautions should be taken to ensure that an employee's condition does not present a health and/or safety threat to others. Consistent with this concern, the following guidelines will be used to address the handling of employees with life threatening illnesses.

II. *Guidelines*

A. Notification Requirements for Employees Diagnosed as Having a Life Threatening Illness

1) Employees who are diagnosed as having any type of life threatening illness must immediately inform the Employee Health Department Manager.

2) The medical records and conditions of our employees are strictly confidential and the discussion or mishandling of such information is strictly prohibited.

3) Whenever such notification is given, the Employee Health Department Manager will consult with the Medical Director, Infection Control Department and the Vice President of Human Resources. Together they will assess all circumstances, including the ability of the employee to

perform his/her duties, the potential harm to employees, visitors, and patients, and then recommend the proper course of action.

B. Procedure for Handling Employees Diagnosed of Life Threatening Illness

1) A thorough and complete assessment will be made on a case by case basis. In making this assessment, ———— will use all resources available, including, but not limited to, Medical Staff, Employee Relations Staff, and Legal Staff. The assessment will be done in a strictly confidential manner to ensure protection for the employee involved.

2) Whenever practical, the employee shall be accommodated with assignment to his regular job or another position without loss of pay or benefits. All employees diagnosed with a life threatening illness will be required to make periodic health monitoring visits to the Employee Health Department and submit to required medical tests. The frequency of these visits and the type of tests will be determined by the Employee Health Physician.

3) In cases where assignment to regular or alternative jobs at ———— is not appropriate, the employee will be either given work to perform at home or a location other than the Hospital or placed on leave of absence.

C. Guidelines for Managers of Employees Diagnosed of Life Threatening Illnesses

1) Remember that an employee's health condition is personal and confidential, and reasonable precautions should be taken to protect information regarding an employee's health condition.

2) Contact the Director of Personnel if you believe that you or other employees need information about terminal illness, or if you need further guidance in managing a situation that involves an employee with a life threatening illness.

3) Contact the Employee Health Department Manager if you have any concern about the possible contagious nature of an employee's illness.

4) If warranted, make reasonable accommodation for employees with life threatening illnesses consistent with the business needs of the department.

5) Be sensitive and responsive to co-workers' concerns, and emphasize employee education available through the Employee Health Department.

6) Do not give special consideration beyond normal transfer requests for employees who feel threatened by a co-worker's life threatening illness.

7) In the event that co-workers refuse to work with or around an employee with a life threatening illness, contact the Director of Personnel immediately. Normally, education of those employees concerning the facts about the illness and how to prevent its transmission, will be accomplished.————medical personnel should be used to communicate facts to these employees and answer their questions.

Document 5

Sample Policy: Dealing with Applicants and Employees Having HIV, ARC, and AIDS

XYZ HOSPITAL

PERSONNEL POLICY ON AIDS

January, 1987

I. *Objectives*

Objectives of this policy are to prevent the transmission of AIDS in our facilities, protect hospital employees and patients from contracting the virus, and treat employees with HIV, ARC or AIDS in a dignified, humane manner that recognizes, to the extent practicable, their individual concerns for privacy, confidentiality, and continued insurance coverage.

II. *AIDS Virus*

A. *Applicants*

(1) The personnel director shall work with department managers in developing a listing of "AIDS High Risk" positions which shall include surgeons, operating and emergency room nurses, and other personnel directly involved with invasive procedures and handling blood.

(2) All applicants for AIDS High Risk positions who are otherwise qualified and being seriously considered for a job shall be given the ELISA test that screens for antibodies to HIV *before* being hired or ordered to begin work. Any who test positive shall be given the same test a second time. Any who test positive again shall be administered the Western Blot test. Any who are positive for all three tests shall not be placed in a job on the list, but may be considered for openings in other areas. If there are no openings for which the applicant is qualified, he shall not be hired.

(3) Applicants for positions not on the list of AIDS High Risk positions shall *not* be tested.

(4) Before being tested, applicants shall sign a form giving their authorization for AIDS tests and waiving any claim they may have connected to the tests. Both the executed, dated, and witnessed form and documents relating to the tests must be retained in secure files.

(5) Any applicant for a job on the list who refuses either to submit to the tests or sign the form shall not be considered for employment.

(6) The result of any AIDS test shall be communicated to both the applicant and the personnel department.

B. *Employees*

(1) During new employee orientation, employees shall be told it is a condition of their employment that they agree to submit to AIDS tests when requested, and reminded that when they applied for a position they signed a statement saying they would cooperate.

(2) Only those employees performing work in the jobs listed as "AIDS High Risk" shall be tested. This applies to any employee in one of those jobs at any time, regardless of full-time or part-time or temporary, or a transfer as opposed to being hired into the position. No personnel in other positions shall be tested.

(3) While the Hospital reserves the right to test employees in the High Risk jobs, exercise of this right shall be restrained. Normally, testing will not be necessary absent direct exposure to HIV (see next paragraph) or special circumstances.

(4) A Rule shall be published which requires employees to report to their department head any accident or incident which could possibly involve their being exposed to the HIV virus. Examples of exposure include needle sticks, splashes of contaminated fluids—mucous membranes—to eyes, mouth or other openings, and spills of infected blood. A written report shall be compiled, signed by the employee, and a copy sent to the personnel department. Failure of an employee to make the report shall result in disciplinary action.

(5) Whenever the Hospital becomes aware of any employee becoming exposed to HIV (see above paragraph)—whether through a report or other means—that employee will be required to submit to a series of tests for the AIDS virus. The tests shall be performed immediately after the exposure and again at 1, 3, 6, 9, and 12 months following the exposure.

(6) If the employee tests positive on ELISA, the same test shall be administered again. If positive both times, the Western Blot shall be used. If all three tests are positive, the employee shall be removed from a job on the High Risk list. He could be transferred to another position without loss of pay, placed on leave of absence (with or without pay) or discharged, depending on availability of jobs, and his physical and mental ability to perform work.

(7) Any applicant who refuses to be tested shall be discharged for failing to cooperate with previously announced and communicated policy.

(8) The result of all AIDS tests shall be communicated to the employee and the personnel department.

III. *ARC and AIDS*

A. When the Hospital is informed that an employee has ARC or AIDS, the personnel director shall (a) review documentation on his medical condition, arranging for a physical or mental examination if appropriate; (b) determine if he has been performing all the duties of his job in a satisfactory manner; (c) confer with the employee, soliciting his feelings about continuing to work (bear in mind that the risk of a hospital employee with AIDS contracting a fatal disease while continuing to work is far greater than fellow employees being infected with HIV by him); (d) review the availability of other jobs that he may be qualified for and capable of performing; and (e) recommend to the Administrator whether to leave him in his regular job, transfer him to another position, assign him work to perform at home or some other location, place him on leave of absence, or discharge him. The decision shall be based upon analysis of factors, including continued mental and physical ability of the employee to perform the work in question and the availability of jobs for which he is both qualified and capable.

B. Employees with ARC or AIDS who continue working must submit to medical examinations by Hospital physicians as often as required. The physicians shall be informed of the duties of the jobs in question and asked whether the victim is fully capable of effectively and safely discharging all of those duties.

C. Employees with ARC or AIDS who are suffering some physical or mental impairments due to their condition shall be allowed to continue on the payroll as long as they can be reasonably accommodated.

D. Counseling shall be provided at Hospital expense for all employees suffering from ARC or AIDS. The counseling shall include advice and instruction on procedures to take to avoid spreading the infection both inside and outside the hospital. Specifically, instructions on wearing gloves and adhering carefully to all safety procedures must be given.

IV. *Confidentiality*

All tests for HIV and medical or personnel records concerning an applicant or employee must be maintained in secure, sealed files, with limited access. The tests results or medical condition cannot be discussed with other employees or the public.

V. *The Law*

Legal counsel shall be consulted about every AIDS or HIV situation before a decision is implemented to ensure compliance with any applicable federal, state, or local law.

VI. *Education*

A. Doctors and nursing personnel heavily experienced in communicable diseases shall conduct educational sessions with all Hospital employees on a periodic basis. Factual information on transmission and prevention of HIV shall be presented.

B. The personnel department shall remind employees of Hospital rules and policies regarding AIDS during employee meetings.

C. All managers and supervisors shall attend special training sessions on administration of this policy.

Document 6

Personnel Postexposure Policy and Procedures

AIDS FOLLOW-UP, POST-EXPOSURE POLICY AND PROCEDURES

March, 1986

DISTRIBUTION: All Departments

FORMULATED BY: Infection Control

PURPOSE: Appropriately render serological and clinical follow-up when exposed to a known AIDS or HTLV-III positive source via parenteral or mucous membrane exposure

APPLIES TO: All Personnel

ATTACHMENTS: See Algorithm AIDS Exposure Protocol and Health History Criteria

EQUIPMENT: None

POLICY: All Personnel involved in a needle puncture or mucous membrane exposure with a known AIDS or positive HTLV-III source will be offered serologic and clinical follow-up.

RESPONSIBILITY: Human Resources/Risk Management/Infection Control/ Emergency Care Unit/Lab

PROCEDURE: Define: Exposure to a known AIDS and/or HTLV-III positive patient shall include parenteral (e.g., needlestick or cut) and/or mucous membrane exposure (e.g., splash to eye or mouth) or significant contact with blood or other body fluids. Patients with no prior HTLV-III testing, but who are considered at high risk for AIDS or suspected cases should be referred to Infection Control/Risk Management for discussion with source's (patient's) attending physician.

1. The exposed health care worker should complete an employee incident report form and report to the Emergency Care Unit.

2. The exposed health care worker should be evaluated by:
   A. Routine Hepatitis protocol
   B. HTLV-III antibody testing

3. The HTLV-III blood samples drawn from the health care worker will be stored for future use and/or testing. The Blood Bank protocol for freezing should be followed. The sample should remain frozen indefinitely.

4. The source patient with the diagnosis of AIDS should be evaluated, utilizing the Hepatitis protocol.

5. The incident report should be forwarded to Risk Management immediately. The Infection Control Officer should be notified of the incident by calling————. A message may be left with the Nursing Service Office.

6. The exposed health care worker's history shall be taken by an RN (Risk Manager or Infection Control Officer or their designate) as soon as possible after the exposure, with special attention to the attached criteria. Clinical evaluation will be done via the contracted Employee Health Physician. The Risk Management Department Secretary will arrange an appointment time. The evaluating physician is requested to note both positive and negative findings in relation to each of the criteria.

7. If the health care worker is sero-negative, he should be retested at 6 weeks, and therefter at 3, 6, and 12 months following exposure. If health care worker sero-converts, he will be referred to a physician. The physician will be requested to evaluate, counsel and follow-up at the physician's discretion.

8. The Infection Control Officer will be available to answer questions posed by the health care worker.

9. The exposed health care worker has the option of refusing the above protocol; however, such refusal shall be in totality and no partial protocol will be offered/received.

Document 7

Checklist of Items To Be Communicated to Employees Exposed to the HIV Virus through an AIDS Patient

Because of your exposure to the HIV virus through an AIDS patient (by needle stick, splash from mucus membranes to the eyes or mouth, or exposure to blood or other body fluids), you should know certain facts of this disease as they concern you:

1. A study called HTLV-III is done immediately on you, the employee. This test will tell whether your body has the AIDS virus in it—not whether you have the disease.

2. The HTLV-III test is done on you again at six weeks, three, six, nine and twelve months. If all of these are negative, you should have little to fear.

3. Until the twelve-month study is done, you are cautioned to avoid pregnancy, since it is known that the AIDS virus can pass to the unborn baby.

4. You are to avoid donation of plasma, blood, body organs, and sperm.

5. You are cautioned to avoid exchanging body fluids during sexual activity, deep "French kissing," and oral-genital contact.

6. You must know that the vast majority of employees exposed to AIDS patients never develop the disease.

7. You must know that there is often a long incubation period (time between exposure and development of the disease), possibly as long as three years.

8. For all practical purposes, if your test is negative after the twelfth month of testing, it is *highly* unlikely that you will come down with the disease.

I have read the above information, had it explained to me, and had the opportunity to ask questions.

Signed _____

Witness _____ Date _____

Document 8

Counseling Guidelines for Employees with HIV

Guidelines for persons in the workplace exhibiting any of the following:

A. Hepatitis B Antigenemia
B. Reactive HIV antibody
C. Inconclusive diagnostic testing for the above (A or B).

Care should be taken to avoid exposing your blood and/or body secretions with other people as long as any of the above conditions persist or as instructed by Infection Control/Employee Health.

The following guidelines are statements which are the expected standards you must adhere to as long as dictated.

Your Department Head, Employee Health Services, Infection Control and Human Resources are aware of your expected adherence, and these standards will be used to evaluate your continued employment status.

1. Avoid sustaining puncture wounds, abrasions or other nicks/scrapes to your skin surfaces, especially the hand surfaces. If this occurs, *immediately* notify your Supervisor and attempt to control bleeding yourself. Follow the standard Incident Report procedure and report to the Emergency Care Unit.

2. Wash your hands well before and after performing or assisting with invasive procedures or those procedures which require mucus membrane contact or contact with non-intact skin of patients. Gloves are not necessary unless the policy/procedure dictates the use of gloves.

3. Report any exudative lesions on your skin surfaces (especially the hands). Exudative lesions include, but are not limited to, fresh open wounds, exudative dermatitis, puncture wounds or cuts which may exude blood or other serous/sero-sanguineous/or purulent material. Report any lesion to your immediate Supervisor and to Employee Health or Infection Control *immediately*. If in doubt, call.

4. If exudative lesions are present, appropriate instructions will be given to you by Employee Health/Infection Control.

5. If while rendering patient care, your blood or other body fluids should enter or come in contact with the patient's mucus membranes or non-intact skin, (i.e. patient bites you, perform mouth to mouth resuscitation, etc.) notify your Supervisor and Employee Health or Infection Control *immediately*.

The above guidelines have been explained in language appropriate to the employee's level of understanding. _____

has verbalized understanding and is able to answer questions regarding the expected employee behavior.

Signature of Counsellors: _____

_____
Date

I have read the above guidelines and I understand the behavior expected of me. I have been given the opportunity to ask questions and have had my questions answered to my satisfaction.

I understand that any information regarding my health status will be held in confidence by my employer.

I have been given a copy of the above guidelines.

_____
Employee

_____
Date

Interim Policy Initiated
11/21/86
Revised 12/3/86

Document 9

Health Care Worker's Exposure to AIDS Follow-Up Forms

Employee Name: _____

Department: _____

<u>Recent Medical History</u>   Date: __/__/__

In the past six months, have any of these signs or symptoms been present as a chronic or persistent problem for at least 1 month? (Please specify all positive and negative info.)

Yes No

___ ___ Fever

___ ___ Night Sweats

___ ___ Malaise/fatigue

___ ___ Chronic Lymphadenopathy,—Sites Noted: _____

___ ___ Arthralgias/myalgias

___ ___ Weight loss, unexpected, 15 pounds or 10% normal body weight

___ ___ Chronic diarrhea ___ No pathogenic/cause identified
                         ___ Specific pathogenic/cause identified

___ ___   Persistent bone marrow dysfunction ___ Leukopenia ___ Lymphopenia
                                              ___ Thrombocytopenia

___ ___ Cough/Shortness of Breath

___ ___ Other (specify) _____

___ ___ None of above

PHYSICAL EXAMINATION   Date: __/__/__

Weight in pounds ____

Lymphadenopathy __ Yes __ No

               __ Cervical   __ Axillary   __ Inguinal

               __ Supraclavicular __ Epitrochlear __ Other

Oral Thrush   __ Yes __ No

Hepatomegaly   __ Yes __ No

Splenomegaly   __ Yes __ No

Other mucocutaneous ulceration

         Location: __ Oral Cavity   __ Pharynx   __ Genitalia

Skin Lesions   __ Yes __ No

         Location: _____

         Description: _____

Other Abnormalities: __ Yes __ No

         Description: _____

LABORATORY EXAMINATION

HTLV III Antibody __ Baseline results

                  __ Date

*See attached lab reports for periodic screening.

*Other diagnostic testing may be ordered at the discretion of the examining physician.

COMMENTS:

_____

_____

_____

_____   _____

Examining Physician   Date

*Retain copy for physician's files

DATE:

TO:

FROM: Risk Management Office

RE: Exposure/Needlestick of _____

In connection with your exposure/needlestick on _____ ,
the following is a timetable of the HTLV III testing follow-ups which <u>MUST</u> be
followed:

                    6 Week   _____
                    3 Month   _____
                    6 Month   _____
                    12 Month   _____

IT IS IMPERATIVE THAT ALL TESTING BE COMPLETED ON OR BEFORE
THE ABOVE LISTED DATES.

It is of primary importance to your health state that you follow the recommended
protocol. Failure to do so may be detrimental to your health.

A memorandum for each testing date will be available in the Risk Management
Office. Please contact Risk Management (   ) prior to each date to make arrangements for you to pick up the appropriate memorandum.

No testing will be performed by the Lab unless the memorandum is presented to
the Lab personnel.

Should you have any questions, please contact the Risk Management Office.

cc: Department Head— _____ Dept/Unit

NAME	HISTORY	PHYSICAL	6 WEEK HTLVIII D. Due/D. Done	3 MONTH HTLVIII D. Due/D. Done	6 MONTH HTLVIII D. Due/D. Done	12 MONTH HTLVIII D. Due/D. Done

Document 10

Recommendations of the Advisory Committee on Infections within Hospitals, American Hospital Association

Development of an AIDS Program in Hospitals

In some hospitals, the admission of an AIDS patient has been disruptive to normal hospital routine and has significantly impaired the ability of the hospital to function effectively. This has occurred primarily because of widespread anxiety and misunderstanding about management, with maintaining patient census, with physician willingness to use the hospital, and with public relations. The advisory committee believes that a hospital that anticipates these problems and plans for them can avoid most of them.

Every hospital should address the policy and management issues raised by treatment of patients with AIDS. This is particularly important for hospitals that thus far have had little or no experience with AIDS patients, since most hospitals that have treated large numbers of AIDS patients have already developed policies and procedures to deal with the numerous issues that AIDS brings to the hospital.

A Prospective AIDS Education Program

The hospital should recognize that the admission of an AIDS patient may cause substantial anxiety among some staff members and patients who are concerned about their personal safety. Moreover, a victim of AIDS is also anxious and is having to cope with a serious disease. AIDS victims have sometimes been shunned or abandoned by family or close friends, and they may feel similarly neglected or abused by hospital personnel unless special supportive steps are taken by hospital staff members. These nonmedical needs of both patients and staff may become so pressing that medical care of AIDS and other patients may be compromised.

Hospitals that have developed aggressive education and intervention programs for their staff, including the medical staff, have been successful in minimizing anxiety and disruption. Intensive efforts at education and crisis intervention by skilled, knowledgeable, and respected hospital personnel are perhaps the most useful activities to ensure that a hospital continues to function adequately when an AIDS patient is present. Several hospitals have developed special teams of personnel who are readily available to answer medical questions about AIDS, advise about appropriate practices, and provide support to personnel and patients. These teams usually include persons such as infection control nurse, a psychiatric social worker, a psychiatrist, a nursing administrator, and a patient advocate.

Widespread and open discussion of the issues raised by treating patients with AIDS appears to be beneficial, especially when that discussion occurs before a patient with AIDS is actually admitted. Some hospitals have made special efforts to involve persons from support services, such as housekeeping, dietary, laboratory, and radiology departments, in these discussions. Some hospitals have also found it useful to add hospital labor union representatives to these study groups.

When a broadly based group of hospital employees participates in discussions of what is known and what is not known, they are likely to respond appropriately when given the opportunity to care for a patient with AIDS.

The advisory committee recommends, therefore, that hospitals consider the formation of special AIDS coordinating group, which would have broad educational and supportive responsibilities within the hospital setting. The group should be broadly representative of the hospital community, and should not be limited to "experts," or to ranking administrative personnel. The group must have visible and aggressive support from both administration and experts. In small hospitals, the group might consist of only one or two individuals. The coordinating group should develop education programs directed toward all levels of hospital personnel, and the program should, if possible, be implemented before an AIDS patient is admitted. Representatives from the employee or staff groups to be educated should be involved in determining the content of the educational program. Occasionally, physicians caring for patients with AIDS may wish to employ extraordinary or overly stringent precautions. Such instances have been demoralizing, both to the patient and to hospital personnel, and disruptive to patient care. It is particularly harmful when a physician uses extraordinary precautions since that unnecessarily raises anxiety on the part of patients and other hospital personnel. The AIDS coordinating group is encouraged to work with the medical staff organization to ensure uniform and consistent application throughout the hospital of recommended AIDS precautions.

Public Relations

Public relations issues present both problems and opportunities. Some hospitals have found that the treatment of patients with AIDS has had adverse public relations consequences. On occasion, members of the press have placed disruptive and time-consuming demands upon hospital staff. On other occasions, patients or members of the medical staff have placed inappropriate demands on the hospital, such as by asking that AIDS patients not be treated in the institution. The hospital must not allow these disruptions to interfere with patient care. The use of an AIDS coordinating team, as previously recommended, is especially useful in dealing with disruptions by staff members and patients, since education will often allay inappropriate concerns. In many communities, contact with news media will present unique opportunities for hospitals to assume leadership roles in public education about AIDS.

In dealing with the press, careful and honest sharing of information will usually diminish adverse publicity, and promote public education. The hospital should establish several principles for dealing with the press. First, patient confidentiality and dignity must be preserved. Second, a knowledgeable and authoritative representative of the hospital must be the designated representative to the press, and other hospital staff members should be required to coordinate all press communications through that representative.

Personnel Management

Some health care personnel, including physicians, have been reluctant to provide hands-on care to AIDS patients. However, at this time there is no evidence that the risks in doing so are any greater than the risks associated with caring for any other sick persons. The advisory committee recommends that otherwise healthy health care personnel should not be excused on their own request from providing care to patients with AIDS; there is no scientific or ethical reason to do so. If an employee simply refuses to perform his or her duties in relation to caring for AIDS patients, the issue becomes a legal and administrative problem to be resolved on an individual basis. Hospitals are urged to solicit the advice of their legal counsel in such situations.

Health care personnel who believe they may be at increased risk because they are immunosuppressed or have other clinical conditions that may confer an increased risk of acquiring an infection should discuss their work responsibilities with the employee health service or with their own personal physician. If the physician determines that that person is indeed at any increased risk, or that there are certain work assignments that the employee should not accept in relation to the care of AIDS patients, a written recommendation should be provided to the employing department for appropriate action in accordance with that institution's personnel policies and procedures.

Pregnant Personnel

There is no increased risk to pregnant personnel from caring for uninfected AIDS patients. However, many patients with AIDS excrete large amounts of cytomegalovirus; hence, it is recommended that hospitals follow existing policies with regard to possible cytomegalovirus exposure to pregnant personnel, or the CDC *Guidelines for Infection Control in Hospital Personnel*.

Personnel with AIDS or Suspect AIDS

As previously indicated, a small number of cases of AIDS have been reported among health care personnel, although most of these have occurred in personnel belonging to the high-risk groups previously defined. These infrequent occurrences have, nevertheless, required hospitals to make some decisions with regard to direct patient care responsibilities for employees with AIDS. This is a difficult issue that requires special consideration on an individual basis. Factors to be considered include not only the health status of the employee with AIDS, but also the nature of the employee's patient care responsibilities. Employees with AIDS who carry out intimate or invasive patient care procedures may be of special concern.

Two approaches are possible.

A hospital might reassign asymptomatic employees with AIDS to non-patient care positions in order to protect patient from exposure to the putative AIDS agent or from opportunistic pathogens that might be carried by the symptomatic employee with AIDS and conversely, to protect the employee from nosocomial pathogens.

A hospital might arrange for a continuing evaluation of the employee with AIDS on an individual basis by the employee health service or the employee's personal physician. Patient care responsibilities might then be assigned, or not assigned, depending on such a continuing clinical evaluation of the individual employee's health status.

Similar considerations apply to physicians with AIDS. The hospital medical staff structure must be prepared to monitor and to deal with the possibility of excluding physicians from the hospital should it become apparent that there may be significant risks to either the physician or to patients. Hospitals who have employees or physicians with AIDS are urged to solicit advice from their legal counsel and the CDC.

Patient Care Precautions

1. A private room is not necessary unless the patient's hygiene is poor, or as may be mandated by the presence of other infections requiring a private room. A patient sharing a room with an AIDS patient should not be immunosuppressed or infected with potentially transmissible pathogens. It will frequently be necessary to care for AIDS patients, particularly those with *Pneumocystis carinii* pneumonia or other serious opportunistic infections, in intensive care units. Hospitals must use particular care not to deny AIDS patients the potential benefits of intensive care facilities, if medically indicated. If ICU care is required, an isolation room in the ICU is desirable; a bed in an open ICU may also be used, however, as long as the additional requirements of blood and body fluid precautions can be observed.

2. To obviate concerns about mouth-to-mouth respiration, portable cardiopulmonary resuscitation equipment, e.g., a disposable ambubag and oral airway, should be immediately available for use on AIDS patients.

3. Masks are not routinely necessary for the care of AIDS patients. The use of masks is recommended for health care personnel who have direct, sustained contact with a patient who is coughing extensively or a patient who is intubated and being suctioned.

4. The use of gowns is recommended only if soiling of clothing with blood or body fluids is anticipated.

5. The use of nonsterile gloves is recommended if contact with blood or body fluids, secretions, or excretions is anticipated. This recommendation is particularly important for personnel who have cuts or abrasions on their hands.

6. Hands must be washed routinely when caring for AIDS patients, especially if they are contaminated with blood, body fluids, secretions, or excretions. This precaution should be observed regardless of the use of gloves.

7. The use of protective eyewear, such as goggles, is recommended in situations in which splatter with blood, bloody secretions, or body fluids is possible. This is particularly recommended in the performance of procedures such as endotracheal intubation, bronchoscopy, or GI endoscopy. Precautions during other surgical procedures should be judged on an individual basis.

8. Needles and syringes should be disposable and should be disposed of in rigid, puncture-resistant containers. Needles should not be recapped and should not be purposely bent or broken by hand, since accidental needle puncture may occur. The use of needle-cutting devices is not recommended.

9. Extraordinary care should be taken to avoid accidental wounds from needles or other sharp instruments. Parenteral injections and blood drawing should

be planned to keep these procedures at a minimum; they should be carried out by experienced personnel.

10. Blood and other specimens should be labeled prominently with a warning such as "Blood/Body Fluid Precautions." The label should accompany the specimen through all phases of processing until ultimate disposal. If the outside of the specimen container is visibly contaminated with blood, it should be cleaned with a disinfectant, such as a freshly prepared (once daily) 1:10 dilution of 5.25 percent sodium hypochlorite (household bleach) with water. All blood specimens should be placed in a second container, such as an impervious bag, for transport. The container or bag should be examined carefully for leaks or cracks.

11. Soiled linens and other laundry should be bagged, appropriately labeled or color-coded, and processed according to the hospital's existing policy regarding linens from patients on isolation precautions.

12. Nondisposable articles contaminated with blood or body fluids should be bagged and labeled before being sent for decontamination and reprocessing. Disposable items should be incinerated or disposed of in accordance with the hospital's policies for disposal of infectious waste.

13. No special precautions for dishes are necessary; either reusable or disposable dishes may be used.

14. Patients with AIDS who are being transported require no special precautions other than blood/body fluid precautions. AIDS patients with infections requiring isolation precautions should be managed according to existing policy or the CDC *Guideline for Isolation Precautions in Hospitals* Personnel in the area to which the patient is to be taken should be notified of precautions to be used.

15. Decontamination of surgical equipment, endoscopes, and so forth, should be accomplished by the same sterilization procedures (for such equipment used on patients with AIDS) as those currently recommended for equipment used for patients with hepatitis B. If possible, surgical procedures on AIDS patients should be scheduled at the end of a day, to allow sterilization of endoscopes overnight (shorter-term procedures result in high level disinfection, rather than sterilization). Invasive patient care equipment should be disposable or should be sterilized. Lensed instruments should be sterilized with ethylene oxide. Ventilator tubing should be either disposable or sterilized before reuse. Instruments that come into contact with blood, secretions, excretions, or tissues, including laryngoscopes and endotracheal tubes, should be sterilized before reuse.

16. Blood spills should be cleaned up promptly with a solution of 5.25 percent sodium hypochlorite, diluted 1:10 water (prepared daily).

17. Patients with AIDS who may require hemodialysis or peritoneal dialysis should be managed in a manner comparable to patients who are known to be carriers of hepatitis B surface antigen (HB_sAg). Disposable components in dialysis equipment must not be reused.

18. Patients with AIDS who must undergo dental procedures should be managed just as patients known to be carriers of HB_sAg. The use of protective eyewear, masks, and nonsterile gloves is recommended. Dental instruments must, of course, be sterilized after such procedures.

Document 11

Checklist of Steps for Health Care Facilities Attempting to Prevent Problems Associated with AIDS

1. Review or survey the workplace for areas, procedures, and so on, that could potentially result in the HIV virus being transmitted to employees, patients, or members of the public while in the hospital or nursing home.

2. Train employees on the use of sharp instruments; have definite procedures for properly storing them; prohibit their handling by persons not using them in their jobs.

3. Establish procedures for treating and monitoring cuts, injuries, and so on, that penetrate the skin.

4. Insist on strict compliance with health requirements pertaining to the serving and handling of food.

5. Document all education and training in this area. Be able to prove that the employer took all reasonable steps to prevent the transmission of AIDS or another communicable disease in the workplace.

Document 12
List of Reportable Diseases

Reporting: In Louisiana, physicians are required by Sanitary Code regulation "to report to the State Health Officer, through the Health Unit of the parish or municipality wherein such physician practices, any case or suspected case of reportable disease which he is attending, or has examined, or for which such physician has prescribed. The report shall be made promptly at the time the physician first visits, examines or prescribes for the patient, and such report shall state the name, age, sex, race, usual residence, place where the patient is to be found, the nature of the disease and the date of onset." Confidential Case Report forms for the purpose of reporting are available from Parish Health Units. The current list of reportable diseases is as follows:

Amebiasis
Anthrax
Aseptic meningitis
Acquired Immune Deficiency
  Syndrome (AIDS)
Botulism*
Brucellosis
Chancroid
Cholera*
Diphtheria*
Encephalitis (specify primary or
  post-infectious)
Foodborne illness*
Gonorrhea
Granuloma Inguinale
Hepatitis, Viral (specify type)
Herpes, neonatal
Legionellosis
Leprosy
Leptospirosis
Lymphogranuloma Venereum
Malaria
Measles (rubeola)*
Meningitis, *Haemophilus*
Meningococcal Infection*
  (including meningitis)

Mumps
Mycobacteriosis, atypical
Pertussis (whooping cough)
Plague*
Poliomyelitis
Psittacosis
Rabies (animals & man)
Reyes Syndrome
Rocky Mountain Spotted Fever
Rubella (German measles)*
Rubella (congenital syndrome)
Salmonellosis
Severe under nutrition (severe
  anemia, failure to thrive)
Shigellosis
Syphilis
Tetanus
Trichinosis
Tuberculosis
Tularemia
Typhoid fever
Typhus fever, murine (fleaborne)
Yellow fever

*Report suspected cases immediately by telephone. In addition to the above, all cases of rare or exotic communicable disease and all outbreaks shall be reported.

A 43.11 card should be completed on all of the above and forwarded to the Division of Disease Control, Room 615, State Office Building, P.O. Box 60630, New Orleans, Louisiana 70160. Telephone: (504) 568-5005. Physicians practicing outside of Orleans Parish, submit the 43.11 card to the local parish health unit.

Appendix C
Employer Policies, Procedures, and Checklists

———

Document 1

Sample Policy: Infectious or Communicable Diseases

ABC COMPANY

RULE AND POLICY PERTAINING TO INFECTIOUS OR
COMMUNICABLE DISEASES

January, 1987

1. RULE

Employees must notify the [plant manager] if either they or members of their immediate family contract an infectious disease. All such communications shall be confidential. Examples of infectious diseases include hepatitis A and B, AIDS, AIDS virus (HTLV-III), tuberculosis, German measles (Rubella) and chicken pox. Employees who fail to notify the company, in violation of this rule, are subject to disciplinary action.

2. POLICY AND PROCEDURES FOR HANDLING INFECTIOUS OR COMMUNICABLE DISEASES

A. The employer recognizes its duty to protect and promote the health and safety of its employees at all work locations.

B. The health of the work force is threatened when either a fellow employee or a member of his immediate family contracts an infectious or communicable disease.

C. Employees are periodically informed and reminded of the Rule that they must notify the appropriate company representative if either they or members of their immediate family contract an infectious or communicable disease.

The communication of this Rule shall be by bulletin board announcement, employee handbook, and during employee meetings when employment rules and policies are reviewed. All such communications must be documented and maintained in a secure file (for example, note shall be made of the date and place of employee meetings when the subject is discussed, and copies of bulletin board announcements shall be placed in the appropriate file.

D. The definition of infectious or communicable disease includes hepatitis A and B, HTLV-III (the AIDS virus), AIDS, ARC, tuberculosis, German measles (Rubella), and chicken pox.

E. A central manager shall be designated to receive all reports from employees, confer with appropriate doctors, obtain pertinent medical documentation, and recommend whether any action should be taken by the employer. The manager is responsible for working with the affected employee to complete a written report of the disease which will be signed by both the employee and the manager, as well as dated. Possible courses of action include leaving the employee in his or her regular job, transferring him to a more isolated location, having him perform duties at home or at a location other than the facility, paid medical leave of absence, unpaid medical leave of absence, and discharge. The decision shall be based upon an analysis of all pertinent factors, including the ability (physical and mental) of the employee to perform all of the duties of the position and the availability of other jobs for which he is qualified and capable. Normally, attempts shall be made to reasonably accommodate employees with infectious diseases to the extent practicable.

F. If legally required, information on the infectious disease shall be communicated to the state or city health department. However, neither the manager coordinating the matter nor any supervisor or manager with knowledge of it shall communicate this information to rank-and-file employees, their families, or members of the public.

Document 2

Sample Policy: Special Corporate Policy on AIDS

1. All employees with any communicable disease, including an AIDS condition, must report that condition to the personnel office, where a special form will be completed and signed. The information will be retained in a special sealed file, and will be treated confidentially, with highly limited access.

2. Employees with communicable diseases will be considered for a leave of absence; the decision as to whether the leave is appropriate and, if so, whether it should be mandatory or voluntary, will be based upon discussions with the employee in question, his or her opinion and desire, and the employer's judgment as to what is best for fellow employees and the employer. Medical evaluations of the ability of the employee to perform the essential duties of his or her particular job, the threat to the health and safety, and other relevant data will be reviewed.

3. Any employee with an AIDS condition desiring to return from a leave of absence, whether paid or unpaid, must submit written statements from his or her physician, stating *both* that the employee can physically and mentally return to work and perform the essential duties of his or her job, *and* that the presence of the employee in the workplace is neither a threat to the health and safety of others (fellow employees, patients, customers, the public) or the employee. Further, the employer reserves the right to appoint a physician to examine the employee in question and submit a written medical evaluation of these factors.

4. Any employee with an AIDS condition returning to work following a medical leave of absence or any other type of absence must execute a release certifying that he or she understands the risks and dangers to his or her health associated with the return, and releasing the employer of all liability, assuming the risk with full knowledge of its implications.

Document 3

Policy of BankAmerica: Assisting Employees with Life-Threatening Illnesses

POLICY OF BANKAMERICA

1986

ASSISTING EMPLOYEES WITH LIFE-THREATENING ILLNESSES

a. Policy—BankAmerica recognizes that employees with life-threatening illnesses including but not limited to cancer, heart disease, and AIDS may wish to continue to engage in as many of their normal pursuits as their condition allows, including work. As long as these employees are able to meet acceptable performance standards, and medical evidence indicates that their conditions are not a threat to themselves or others, managers should be sensitive to their conditions and ensure that they are treated consistently with other employees. At the same time, BankAmerica seeks to provide a safe work environment for all employees and customers. Therefore, precautions should be taken to ensure that an employee's condition does not present a health and/or safety threat to other employees or customers.

b. Personnel Relations—Consistent with this concern for employees with life-threatening illnesses, BankAmerica offers the following range of resources available through Personnel Relations:

  1) Management and employee education and information on terminal illness and specific life-threatening illnesses.

  2) Referral to agencies and organizations that offer supportive services for life-threatening illnesses.

  3) Benefit consultation to assist employees in effectively managing health, leave, and other benefits.

c. Guidelines—When dealing with situations involving employees with life-threatening illnesses, managers should:

  1) Remember that an employee's health condition is personal and confidential, and reasonable precautions should be taken to protect information regarding an employee's health condition.

  2) Contact Personnel Relations if you believe that you or other employees need information about terminal illness, or a specific life-threatening illness, or if you need further guidance in managing a situation that involves an employee with a life-threatening illness.

  3) Contact Personnel Relations if you have any concern about the possible contagious nature of an employee's illness.

4) Contact Personnel Relations to determine if a statement should be obtained from the employee's attending physician that continued presence at work will pose no threat to the employee, co-workers or customers. BankAmerica reserves the right to require an examination by a medical doctor appointed by the company.

5) If warranted, make reasonable accommodation for employees with life-threatening illnesses consistent with the business needs of the division/unit.

6) Make a reasonable attempt to transfer employees with life-threatening illnesses who request a transfer and are experiencing undue emotional stress.

7) Be sensitive and responsive to co-workers' concerns, and emphasize employee education available through Personnel Relations.

8) Not give special consideration beyond normal transfer requests for employees who feel threatened by a co-worker's life-threatening illness.

9) Be sensitive to the fact that continued employment for an employee with a life-threatening illness may sometimes be therapeutically important in the remission or recovery process, or may help to prolong that employee's life.

10) Encourage employees to seek assistance from established community support groups for medical treatment and counseling services. Information on these can be requested through Personnel Relations or Corporate Health Programs #3666.

Document 4

Alternative Provisions for Employee Handbooks Concerning AIDS

1. *Life-Threatening Illnesses and Infectious Diseases:*

   All employees are required to report any life-threatening or infectious illness or disease they may contract to the Personnel Department as soon as they learn of it. Employees must complete and sign a form, and a doctor's statement describing their ability to perform the essential functions of the job in question and assessing the risk of infecting others in the workplace must be submitted.

2. *AIDS Conditions:*

   Any employee who has or develops the HIV virus, ARC, or AIDS must report his or her specific condition in writing to the Personnel Department. A medical evaluation will then be conducted to determine the ability and qualifications of the employee to perform the job in question, and the danger—if any—of infecting employees, customers, patients, or others. The employer shall comply with all applicable laws on this subject in discharging its obligations to both the employee and fellow employees.

3. *Consider Adding the Following to Either of the Above Provisions:*

   The employer shall maintain any and all forms and medical records and correspondence on this subject on a strictly confidential basis. Specifically, they shall be reviewed only by the personnel and facility managers, sealed in envelopes marked "confidential," and maintained in a special file cabinet with a secure lock.

Document 5

Checklist: Steps for an Employer To Take Concerning an Employee with an AIDS Condition Who Continues To Work

1. Have a conversation with him or her, in the presence of a witness, that makes the following points.

2. Advise and disclose to the employee that the AIDS condition makes him or her vulnerable to health hazards in the workplace, that he or she may contract an infectious disease from coworkers who are successfully fighting it off and perhaps do not even realize they have it.

3. Explain that a statement from the employee's doctor certifying that he or she is released to work in the specific job in question is necessary before he or she can continue working.

4. Consider having the employer's physician examine the person with the AIDS condition and advise him or her of the possibility of picking up an opportunistic disease from coworkers, customers, patients, or others in the workplace.

5. Secure a release from the employee, executed before a notary public, certifying that the employee has had the risk of secondary infections explained to him or her and has voluntarily and knowingly agreed to assume that risk in continuing to work.

6. Carefully document all of these conversations.

Appendix D
Legal Documents
Pertaining to AIDS

Document 1

Checklist for Determining Whether an Employer Is a Federal Government Contractor

1. The company has 50 or more employees; *and*

   a. has a contract of $50,000 or more; *or*

   b. has government bills of lading which in any twelve-month period total or can reasonably be expected to total $50,000 or more; *or*

   c. the company serves as a depository of government funds in any amount; *or*

   d. the company is a financial institution which is an issuing and paying agent for U.S. Savings Bonds and Savings Notes in any amount.

2. The foregoing requirements are also applicable to *subcontractors* of covered companies.

3. The regulations define government contract as:

   . . . any agreement or modification thereof between any contracting agency and any person for the furnishing of supplies or services or for the use of real or personal property, *including lease arrangements*. The term "services" as used in this section includes, but is not limited to the following services: utility, construction, transportation, research, insurance, and fund depository. (Emphasis supplied.)

4. The $50,000/50 employee standard would apply to any of the foregoing agreements.

Document 2

Section 503 of the Vocational Rehabilitation Act of 1973

EMPLOYMENT UNDER FEDERAL CONTRACTS

Sec.503. (a) Any contract in excess of $2,500 entered into by any Federal department or agency for the procurement of personal property and nonpersonal services (including construction) for the United States shall contain a provision requiring that, in employing persons to carry out such contract the party contracting with the United States shall take affirmative action to employ and advance in employment qualified handicapped individuals as defined in section 7(8) of this title. The provisions of this section shall apply to any subcontract in excess of $2,500 entered into by a prime contractor in carrying out any contract for the procurement of personal property and nonpersonal services (including construction) for the United States. The President shall implement the provisions of this section by promulgating regulations within ninety days after September 26, 1973. [As last amended by P.L. 99-506, effective October 21, 1986.]

(b) If any handicapped individual beleives any contractor has failed or refuses to comply with the provisions of his contract with the United States, relating to employment of handicapped individuals, such individual may file a complaint with the Department of Labor. The Department shall promptly investigate such complaint and shall take such action thereon as the facts and circumstances warrant, consistent with the terms of such contract and the laws and regulations applicable thereto.

(c) The requirements of this section may be waived, in whole in part, by the President with respect to a particular contract or subcontract, in accordance with guidelines set forth in regulations which he shall prescribe, when he determines that special circumstances in the national interest so require and states in writing his reasons for such determination. (29 U.S.C. §793)

Document 3

Section 504 of the Vocational Rehabilitation Act of 1973

NONDISCRIMINATION UNDER FEDERAL GRANTS AND PROGRAMS

Sec.504. No otherwise qualified handicapped individual in the United States as defined in section 7(8), shall solely by reason of his handicap, be excluded from the participation in, be denied the benefits of, or be subjected to discrimination under any program or activity conducted by any Executive agency or by the United States Postal Service. The head of each such agency shall promulgate such regulations as may be necessary to carry out the amendments to this section made by the Rehabilitation, Comprehensive Services, and Developmental Disabilities Act of 1978. Copies of any proposed regulation shall be submitted to appropriate authorizing committees of the Congress, and such regulation may take effect no earlier than the thirtieth day after the date on which such regulation is so submitted to such committees. (29 U.S.C. §794) [As last amended by P.L. 99-506, effective Oct. 21, 1986]

Document 4

Federal Court Complaint Alleging Illegal Discrimination against an Employee in an AIDS Testing Situation

UNITED STATES DISTRICT COURT

EASTERN DISTRICT OF LOUISIANA

Plaintiff _____

—against—

BOARD OF COMMISSIONERS OF HOSPITAL _____

Defendants

COMPLAINT

I. JURISDICTION AND VENUE

1. This Court has jurisdiction of this matter pursuant to 29 U.S.C. 794 (the Rehabilitation Act of 1973 as amended, Section 504), 28 U.S.C. 1331, 28 U.S.C. 1343(3) and the Fourteenth Amendment to the Constitution of the United States for violations under color of state law of rights, privileges and immunities protected under the United States Constitution and federal law (including the abovementioned statutes and 42 U.S.C. 1983).

2. Pendent jurisdiction is alleged for those matters cognizable under the laws of the state of Louisiana, including R.S. 46:2251 et seq. (Civil Rights for Handicapped Persons), and the Declaration of Rights of the Louisiana Constitution, including, among others, the rights to due process and equal protection of the laws, the right to individual dignity (including the right against discrimination because of physical condition), and the right to privacy.

3. Venue is proper pursuant to 28 U.S.C. 1391(b) and 29 U.S.C. 1132. The cause of action arose in _____ Parish, Louisiana, located in the Eastern District of Louisiana.

II. PARTIES

4. Plaintiff _____ is a resident and citizen of the United States and the State of Louisiana.

5. Defendant BOARD OF COMMISSIONERS OF HOSPITAL SERVICE DISTRICT _____ (the Commissioners) is a governmental entity created under the Louisiana Hospital Service District Law of 1950, as amended. The Commissioners are appointed by the _____ Parish Police Jury pursuant to LSA R.S. 46:1052 and are charged with the governance of the _____ Medical Center, as well as the making, altering and promulgating of rules and regulations governing the conduct of the Medical Center.

6. Defendants are the incumbent members of the Board of Commissioners, and were so at all pertinent times. They are sued in their official capacities.

7. Defendant _____ is the executive director of the _____ Medical Center, appointed by the Board of Commissioners. He is charged with administering the Medical Center and carrying out the policies of the Board. He is sued in his individual and official capacity.

8. Defendants _____ and _____ are, respectively, the Director of Nursing and the Infection Control Nurse of the _____ Medical Center. They are sued individually and in their official capacity.

9. Defendant _____ is the Director of Human Resources for the Hospital. He is sued in his individual and official capacity.

III. FACTS

10. Plaintiff _____ was employed by the defendant _____ MEDICAL CENTER as a staff Licensed Practical Nurse from June, 1978 to April, 1986.

11. In the latter part of March, 1986, plaintiff's friend and roommate was admitted to _____ Medical Center for what was later diagnosed as a complication of Acquired Immune Deficiency Syndrome (AIDS). The friend remained at that facility until April 10, 1986, when he was transferred to a private hospital in New Orleans because of a rapid deterioration in his health. He died on April 21, 1986 of a secondary infection incident to AIDS.

12. On April 10, 1986, the day his friend was transferred, plaintiff _____ was telephoned at home and asked to come in to meet with Defendant _____ , the Infection Control Nurse for the defendant MEDICAL CENTER.

13. At their meeting, held the same day, defendant _____ spoke with plaintiff about AIDS and her knowledge that plaintiff and his friend were roommates. She asked plaintiff to take blood tests which would determine whether plaintiff had been exposed to the virus believed to cause AIDS.

14. On information and belief, there were at that time two separate tests designed to test exposure to the virus believed to cause AIDS. Those tests are (1) the enzyme-linked immunosorbent assay ("ELISA") and (2) the Western blot assay.

15. Defendant _____ wanted _____ to take both tests mentioned in paragraph 16 above.

16. On the following day, defendant _____ telephoned plaintiff and asked him for the results of his tests. Plaintiff stated that he did not have the results and that, even if he had them, he would not submit them to her.

17. On information and belief, Defendant _____ spoke with Defendant _____ , Director of Nursing, and related to her the substance of her conversation with plaintiff.

18. After speaking with Defendant _____ , Defendant _____ again telephoned plaintiff and instructed him that he would not be allowed to return to work unless he submitted the results of the tests.

19. On April 11, 12 and 13, plaintiff did not work for medical reasons unrelated to AIDS (an infectious cyst). He informed the hospital of his medical problem and was released by his doctor to return to work on April 14.

20. Plaintiff was next scheduled to work on April 16. Shortly prior to his

scheduled work period, plaintiff was contacted by defendant _____ and again instructed not to return to work until he submitted results of the tests.

21. Plaintiff confirmed with the evening house supervisor that he would not report for work on April 16 and 17. Plaintiff was scheduled off for April 18, 19 and 20.

22. On April 21, plaintiff spoke with the nursing staff coordinator and was again told he would not be allowed to report for work until he submitted the results of the tests. He replied he would not submit the results and was told not to report on April 21 or 22.

23. Plaintiff was scheduled off for April 23 and 24.

24. On April 25, plaintiff was again told by the nursing staff coordinator he would not be allowed to work until he submitted the results of his tests. He was not allowed to work as scheduled April 25, 26 and 27.

25. Plaintiff was scheduled off for April 28 and 29, but was requested to meet with Defendant _____ , Director of Human Resources.

26. Plaintiff met with Defendant _____ on April 29 and was told he was being terminated for failure to report for work April 25, 26 and 27.

27. On information and belief, had plaintiff submitted test results which showed that he had been exposed to the virus believed to cause AIDS, he would have been terminated by the defendants.

28. Plaintiff, since his termination on April 29, has actively pursued employment in _____ and _____ and has attempted to minimize damages.

29. Plaintiff, in his employment with the defendants, because of a previous exposure to hepatitis, employed barrier precautions in all his work-related duties for at least the last five years and continues to do so. The defendants were aware that the plaintiff was employing such precautions.

30. Plaintiff, in his employment with the defendants, performed no invasive procedures.

31. Plaintiff was and remains physically and mentally capable to perform the duties of his job and did not and does not evidence any signs or symptoms of AIDS or AIDS-related illnesses. He offered to continue to perform the duties of his job on a number of occasions, but was not allowed to do so.

32. Plaintiff is in all respects fully qualified for his position with the defendants.

33. On information and belief, the reasons for the termination of plaintiff by defendant _____ were one or more of the following:

(A) A fear that plaintiff had or would develop AIDS or AIDS-related complex (ARC, a less severe form of AIDS).

(B) A perception that plaintiff had been exposed to or infected with the virus that is believed to cause AIDS.

(C) A perception that because of plaintiff's exposure as set forth in (B) above, he was contagious.

(D) Plaintiff's refusal to submit the results of tests to determine whether or not he had been exposed to the virus believed to cause AIDS.

34. On information and belief, plaintiff was regarded by the defendants as having an impairment under 45 C.F.R. 84.3(j)(2)(iv) and 45 C.F.R. Pt. 84, App. A at 311.

35. The MEDICAL CENTER is a recipient of federal financial assistance as defined in the Rehabilitation Act of 1973, as amended and is an employer as defined in the Louisiana Civil Rights for Handicapped Persons Act.

36. The actions of the employees of the Medical Center in refusing to allow plaintiff to return to work and in terminating him were under color of state law and in compliance with the official policies or customs of the Board of Commissioners, executive director _____ and/or other persons with policy-making authority.

37. Plaintiff gave written notice to the defendants of the fact he intended to bring this action at least thirty days prior to the filing of this litigation, but has been unable to resolve this matter with the defendants.

38. The actions of the defendants set forth above were taken in reckless and callous indifference to the plaintiff's federally protected rights.

IV. CAUSES OF ACTION

39. The termination of plaintiff is a violation of the Rehabilitation Act of 1973, as amended, Section 504, 29 U.S.C. 794, because it constituted discrimination against a handicapped person or a person regarded as having a handicap who is otherwise qualified to perform the essential functions of his job as a staff licensed practical nurse.

40. The termination of plaintiff is a violation of the Louisiana Civil Rights for Handicapped Persons Act, R.S. 46:2251, et seq., because it constituted discrimination against a handicapped person or a person regarded as having a handicap who is otherwise qualified to perform the essential functions of his job as a staff licensed practical nurse.

41. The termination of plaintiff by the defendants is a violation of his federal constitutional and statutory rights under color of state law under 42 U.S.C. 1983.

42. The termination of plaintiff by the defendants acting under color of state law is a violation of his rights to due process of law and equal protection of the law under the Fourteenth Amendment to the United States Constitution.

43. The termination of plaintiff by the defendants is a violation of his rights under the Declaration of Rights of the Louisiana Constitution.

V. PRAYER

WHEREFORE, plaintiff prays for the following relief:

1. Compensatory damages dating from April 10, 1986, jointly, severally and *in solido* against the defendants;

2. Punitive damages in an amount to be determined by the court after full hearing on the merits;

3. Declaratory and injunctive relief declaring the actions of the defendants to be illegal and reinstating him in his job with all the rights, privileges and seniority to which he would have been entitled had his service not been illegally interrupted by the defendants;

4. Hospitalization, disability, death and retirement benefits and any other fringe benefits to which plaintiff would have been entitled;

5. Attorney's fees and costs;

6. Interest from the date of judicial demand; and

7. Such other relief as may appear necessary and proper.

Dated: September 29, 1986

Respectfully submitted,

AMERICAN CIVIL LIBERTIES   LAMBDA LEGAL DEFENSE AND
  UNION OF LOUISIANA   EDUCATION FUND

THE ADVOCACY CENTER FOR
  THE ELDERLY AND DISABLED

BY: _____
                                                        , Trial Attorney
                                            for Plaintiffs

Please Serve:

(1) Board of Commissioners of
                Medical Center

(2) _____ , Executive Director

(3) _____ , R.N., Infections Con-
    trol

(4) _____ , R.N., Director of Nursing

(5) _____ , Director of Human Services

At:
    _____ Medical Center
    _____
    Louisiana

Document 5

State Court Lawsuit Requesting Damages for Discharge after the Plaintiff was Diagnosed as Having AIDS

CIVIL DISTRICT COURT FOR THE PARISH OF ORLEANS
STATE OF LOUISIANA
DIVISION " " DOCKET NO. _____
WILLIAM _____
VERSUS
_____ HOTEL

FILED: _____   DEPUTY CLERK: _____

PETITION

The petition of William _____ , domiciled in the Parish of Orleans, State of Louisiana, respectfully represents that:

1.

Defendent, _____ Hotel, is a Delaware corporation domiciled and doing business in the Parish of Orleans, State of Louisiana, which has fifteen or more employees.

2.

Defendant is indebted to plaintiff for monetary and equitable relief pursuant to the Louisiana Civil Rights for Handicapped Persons Act, LSA-R.S. 46:2251 et seq., and under Louisiana tort law, LSA-C.C. Article 2315 for the following reasons.

3.

Plaintiff was hired by defendant as a room service waiter on March 26, 1985.

4.

Plaintiff successfully completed his probationary period with defendant.

5.

During the course of his employment with defendant, plaintiff was promoted from the day shift to the night shift, to be effective August 29, 1985.

6.

Room service waiters employed by defendant on the night shift earn, on average, more than room service waiters on the day shift.

7.

At defendant's request, as a condition of continued employment, plaintiff had a medical examination at his expense on or about August 25, 1985 to determine whether he was in good health, and specifically whether he suffered from Acquired Immune Deficiency Syndrome ("A.I.D.S.").

8.

Plaintiff furnished defendant a copy of the results of his medical examination on or about August 27, 1985 which indicated that he was in good health, and had no symptoms of Acquired Immune Deficiency Syndrome ("A.I.D.S.") or A.I.D.S.-related complex.

9.

When plaintiff arrived at work with the defendant on August 29, 1985, the cashiers who were employed by the defendant were wearing white gloves.

10.

On August 29, 1985 when plaintiff asked the cashiers, referred to in paragraph 9, why they were white wearing gloves, they responded "to avoid the plague".

11.

The cashiers referred to in paragraphs 9 and 10 were regular employees of defendant on August 29, 1985.

12.

Plaintiff was terminated from his position by defendant on August 29, 1985.

13.

The reason provided in writing by defendant to the plaintiff for plaintiff's termination was that plaintiff was "unable to function in department under present conditions."

14.

The real reason for plaintiff's termination was that defendant was aware that plaintiff was regarded by defendant's employees as having an impairment which substantially limits his life activities, solely because a friend of plaintiff's had been diagnosed as having Acquired Immune Deficiency Syndrome ("A.I.D.S.").

15.

At the time of his termination, plaintiff was in good medical condition and did not suffer from any physical and physiological disorder or condition which would have impaired his ability to perform any functions of his former job. He did not have A.I.D.S., nor A.I.D.S.-related complex, nor any secondary infections which are indications of A.I.D.S.

16.

Plaintiff was and is qualified to perform all functions of his former job with defendant.

17.

The actions of defendant in tolerating harassment of plaintiff by employees of the defendant due to a perceived handicapping condition and in terminating plaintiff because of his perceived handicap, despite his continued ability to perform the functions of his former job, constitute a violation of the Louisiana Civil Rights for Handicapped Persons Act, LSA-R.S. 46:2251 et seq.

18.

The actions of defendant in knowingly terminating plaintiff and tolerating harassment of plaintiff by employees of the defendant in violation of his civil rights constitute intentional or reckless infliction of emotional distress in violation of LSA-C.C. Article 2315 and LSA-R.S. 46:2251 et seq. These actions have caused and continue to cause plaintiff psychological injury, embarrassment and humiliation.

19.

Plaintiff itemizes the damages that he has sustained due to defendant's action as follows:

a) Back pay.. $12,000.00

b) Compensatory damages .... $ 2,000.00

c) Psychological injury, embarrassment
   and humiliation .... $ 5,000.00

d) Punitive damages.. <u>$38,000.00</u>

TOTAL.. $57,000.00

20.

Plaintiff has given defendant timely written notice of the discrimination alleged herein, and has made a good faith effort to resolve this dispute, to no avail.

WHEREFORE, plaintiff prays that after due proceedings there be judgment in his favor and against defendant as follows:

a) Declaring that the actions of defendant complained of herein violate plaintiff's rights as secured by the Louisiana Civil Rights for Handicapped Persons Act, LSA-R.S. 46:2251 et seq. and by Louisiana tort law, LSA-C.C. Article 2315;

b) Awarding plaintiff reinstatement with full back pay and benefits, remedial seniority, compensatory damages, damages for psychological injury, embarrassment and humiliation, and punitive damages, totalling $57,000.00 plus compounded interest from date of demand;

c) Awarding plaintiff attorney's fees and costs of litigation;

d) Awarding plaintiff any/and all such further relief as may be necessary and proper.

Respectfully submitted,

_____

Document 6

State Court Complaint by ACLU against Employer for Firing Employee with AIDS

CIVIL DISTRICT COURT FOR THE PARISH OF ORLEANS
STATE OF LOUISIANA
DIVISION " "
BOB _____
versus
CHANNEL _____ , INC.

COMPLAINT

I. JURISDICTION

1. This Court has jurisdiction over this matter pursuant to R.S. 46:2256, which provides that a person who is aggrieved under the Civil Rights Act for Handicapped Persons may file a complaint in the appropriate civil district court within one hundred eighty days from the date of discovery of a discriminatory act.

2. Plaintiff _____ was terminated from his employment with Defendant Channel _____ , Inc, on July 7, 1985 in Orleans Parish in violation of LSA. R.S. 46:2251 et seq.

II. PARTIES

3. Plaintiff Bob _____ is a citizen of the State of Louisiana of the full age of majority, residing in Orleans Parish. He formerly was employed by the defendants, Channel _____ , Inc.

4. Plaintiff _____ has been diagnosed to have Acquired Immune Deficiency Syndrome (A.I.D.S.), which is an impairment which substantially limits his major life activities.

5. Alternatively, plaintiff _____ is regarded by the defendant as having such an impairment.

6. Plaintiff _____ is an otherwise qualified handicapped person who can perform the essential functions of his former employment with the defendant.

7. Defendant Channel _____ , Inc. (Defendant Channel) is a Louisiana corporation employing fifteen or more employees.

III. FACTS

8. Plaintiff _____ was hired by defendant Channel _____ in December, 1984 for the position of Accounts Payable clerk.

9. On February 1, 1985, plaintiff _____ was promoted on the basis of merit to the position of Credit Manager.

10. During the month of February, 1985, plaintiff _____ was diagnosed as having A.I.D.S.-related complex (ARC). ARC is a set of symptoms which some-

times is a precursor to A.I.D.S. In other people, ARC apparently does not progress to a full case of A.I.D.S. as defined by the Centers for Disease Control.

11. A.I.D.S. is a medical syndrome which is an acquired immune deficiency. The syndrome is usually defined as the occurrence of secondary infections which are otherwise relatively rare. The two major secondary infections which are indications of A.I.D.S. are a certain form of pneumonia and Karposi's Sarcoma, a cancer.

12. Over 13,000 cases of A.I.D.S. have been reported by the Centers for Disease Control as of September 1, 1985, using its strict definition. Of these, almost 150 have been reported in Louisiana.

13. Of these reported cases, approximately fifty percent are dead. The longest that a person with A.I.D.S. has survived to date is approximately three years.

14. A.I.D.S. is not transmitted by casual non-intimate contact. Transmission requires sexual contact or the sharing of needles with an infected person. The virus which is believed to cause A.I.D.S., HTLV-III, is extremely labile (fragile) and can be killed with a weak bleach solution. There is not a single known case of transmission of A.I.D.S. by casual contact.

15. In early May, plaintiff _____ approached his supervisor and told him that he had ARC. With _____ 's permission, the management approached his doctor concerning the details of the illness.

16. In early June, plaintiff _____ developed pneumocystis pneumonia and was hospitalized. Because of the pneumonia, plaintiff _____ was diagnosed as having A.I.D.S.

17. Plaintiff _____ had a good attendance record at work prior to his development of pneumocystis pneumonia.

18. Upon his hospitalization, plaintiff _____ told the management of Channel _____ that he had been diagnosed as having A.I.D.S. On information and belief, the management discussed plaintiff _____ 's condition with personal physician, Dr. _____ .

19. After his discharge from the hospital, plaintiff _____ was terminated from his position by the defendant on July 7, 1985. Although the reason given for his termination by the management was the handling of four particular accounts, plaintiff _____ had not been assigned two of the accounts and had turned the other two over to a collection agency prior to his hospitalization.

20. On information and belief, the real reason for the termination was plaintiff _____'s handicapping condition, Acquired Immune Deficiency Syndrome.

21. Counsel for plaintiff addressed a letter to the management of defendant on August 2, 1985. _____ , Vice President of defendant in a telephone conversation with plaintiff's counsel refused to meet to discuss the situation.

22. Plaintiff has, through counsel, made a good faith effort to resolve the dispute prior to instituting this action.

23. Plaintiff _____ remains willing and able to work at the current time. He can perform the essential functions of his former job in its entirety with no accommodation.

IV. CAUSE OF ACTION

24. The actions of the defendant in terminating the plaintiff because of his handicap despite his continued ability to perform the essential functions of his former job is a violation of the Civil Rights Act for Handicapped Persons, R.S. 46:2251 et seq.

V. EQUITY

25. There is an actual controversy between parties having adverse legal interests. Plaintiff has no adequate remedy at law.

VI. PRAYER

WHEREFORE, plaintiff prays as follows:

1. For judgment in his favor and against the defendant for compensatory damages, attorney's fees and costs, as provided in R.S. 46:2256,
2. For declaratory and injunctive relief to make him whole,
3. For such other relief as may be necessary and proper.

Dated: December 20, 1985.

Respectfully submitted,

_____

American Civil Liberties Union
  of Louisiana
840 Gov. Nicholls
New Orleans, LA 70116
(504) 524-2487
Attorney for Plaintiff

PLEASE SERVE:

CHANNEL _____ , INC.
  through their registered agent
  for the service of process:

New Orleans, Louisiana 70112

Document 7

Letter from Plaintiff Attorney to a Hospital, Threatening To File Suit in an AIDS Situation

R. JAMES KELLOGG
———————————————— ATTORNEY AT LAW ————————————————

840 GOVERNOR NICHOLLS
NEW ORLEANS, LOUISIANA 70116
TELEPHONE (504) 524-2487

CERTIFIED RETURN RECEIPT REQUESTED

August 28, 1986

Mr. _____
Director of Human Services
_____ Medical Center
_____ Louisiana

Re:

Dear Mr. _____ :

I represent _____ concerning the termination of his employment with the _____ Medical Center. Please be advised, in accordance with the Louisiana Civil Rights for Handicapped Persons Act, R.S. 40:2251, et seq., that _____ intends to pursue court action against you in thirty days if we are unable to resolve this dispute. The details of the discrimination are as follows:

Mr. _____ was employed as a staff Licensed Practical Nurse with _____ Medical Center from June, 1978 to April, 1986. In late March, 1986, Mr. _____ 's friend and roommate was admitted to the _____ Medical Center. Before he was transferred to a hospital in New Orleans as his condition worsened, Mr. _____ 's friend was diagnosed as having Acquired Immune Deficiency Syndrome (AIDS).

On April 10, Mr. _____ met with _____ , Infection Control Nurse for the Medical Center, at her request. Ms. _____ spoke with him about AIDS and her knowledge that he and his friend were roommates. She instructed him to take a blood test designed to determine if a person has been exposed to the virus which is thought to cause AIDS and give her the results.

On April 11, Ms. _____ called Mr. _____ for the results of his test and, after conferring with _____ , the Director of Nursing, told Mr.
_____ he could not return to work without the test results.

On each occasion he was scheduled to work between April 10 and April 30, Mr. _____ , on the advice of counsel, telephoned the Medical Center and was on each occasion informed he could not return to work without the test results.

On April 30, Mr. _____ was terminated from employment. He has looked for comparable employment in the _____ and New Orleans area but has not been able to secure such employment.

It is our position that the termination of Mr. _____ is a violation of the Louisiana Civil Rights for Handicapped Persons Act, R.S. 46:2251 et seq., the Federal Rehabilitation Act of 1973, as amended 29 U.S.C. 794 and the Federal Employee Retirement Income Security Act, 29 U.S.C. 1000 et seq. It is our intention to file suit against you and other possible defendants in the United States District Court for the Eastern District of Louisiana at the expiration of thirty days from your receipt of this letter unless the matter is resolved amicably. The suit will include, but not be limited to, claims for compensatory damages, attorney's fees, costs and any other relief deemed appropriate, including reinstatement.

I call upon you to make a good faith effort, in accordance with R.S. 46:2256, to resolve this dispute before court action is commenced.

I would appreciate hearing from your attorney at the earliest opportunity.

Sincerely,

R. James Kellog

cc:
Ruth Colker, Louisiana ACLU
Nan Hunter, Staff Attorney, National ACLU
Abby Rubenfeld, Lambda Legal Defense and Education Fund, Inc.

Document 8

Sample Complaint To Be Filed in Federal Court by an Employee with an AIDS Condition against His Union and Employer

IN THE UNITED STATES DISTRICT COURT FOR THE
MIDDLE DISTRICT OF ____(State)____
_____ DIVISION

JOHN DOE,

      Plaintiff,

vs.

CMS CORPORATION AND RETAIL
AND OFFICE WORKERS UNION
AND ITS LOCAL NO. 14,

      Defendants.

CIVIL ACTION NO. _____

COMPLAINT

I.

Jurisdiction

Jurisdiction is based upon the existence of a federal question, Section 301 of the Labor Management Relations Act, 29 U.S.C. §185, and various decisions of the United States Supreme Court setting forth the statutory duty of the Labor Union to represent its members fairly and the opportunity of employees to file suit against their employers and unions for certain violations.

II.

Parties

The plaintiff is a citizen of the State of _____ and resides in _____ , _____ . He was a member of the Defendant Union for five years prior to his discharge. He was also employed by Defendant Company for five years prior to his termination. Further, he was a member of the bargaining unit covered under a collective bargaining agreement between the Defendant CMS Corporation and the Defendant Union.

The Defendant, CMS Corporation, is a corporation organized and existing in the State of _____ , with a place of business located in _____ , _____ , where it operates a manufacturing facility.

The Defendant Union, with headquarters in Washington, D.C., has a local with an office in _____ , _____ . It is organized and functioning as a labor union under federal labor laws.

Count I.

(1) Plaintiff, for a period of five years prior to the date this Complaint was filed, was employed by the Defendant Company and a member of the Defendant Union.

(2) In January, 1986, Plaintiff felt ill, was forced to miss work, and sought medical treatment. As a result of a medical examination and various tests, Plaintiff was informed that he was in an early stage of AIDS.

(3) In late January, 1986, Plaintiff returned to work with a letter from his doctor stating that while he was suffering from AIDS, he was physically and mentally able to perform all of the duties of his job, and he was released to return to work. Plaintiff presented this letter to the personnel director, who immediately sent him home. The next day a letter from the personnel manager was hand-delivered to Plaintiff's house, which informed Plaintiff that he was being involuntarily placed on a thirty-day leave of absence. At the expiration of the thirty-day period, he received another letter from the personnel director, certified mail, return receipt requested, stating that he was being terminated because of the risk of infecting other employees.

(4) The day after receiving his letter of termination, Plaintiff went to the office of his local union, where he explained to the receptionist what had happened, showed her the letter of termination, and asked to see the business agent. Despite waiting at the office of the local union for three hours, he was never given the opportunity to speak with either the business agent or any other official of the union. Instead, he was handed a grievance form by the receptionist.

(5) Plaintiff completed the grievance form, as best he could, without any assistance from union officials. The next day he returned to the office of the local union and once again asked to speak to the business agent. Again, the business agent failed to confer with Plaintiff despite Plaintiff waiting for over an hour.

(6) Approximately two weeks later, Plaintiff received another letter from the Company stating that his grievance was being denied because it was incomplete, not in compliance with procedural requirements, and lacking in merit.

(7) Plaintiff made repeated attempts to call the local union office for the purpose of discussing the grievance. His call was not returned until the next day. The union business agent gave an unsatisfactory explanation for the Union's failure to successfully process the grievance.

(8) Plaintiff was terminated by the Company for reasons other than "just cause" as required by the collective bargaining agreement. More specifically, Plaintiff was terminated because he has AIDS, a medical condition over which he has no control. Plaintiff compiled an excellent work record and never violated any rule or policy. The Company is in violation of the collective bargaining agreement in deciding to terminate Plaintiff.

(9) The Union is in breach of its duty to fairly and vigorously represent Plaintiff and protect his interests. Specifically, Defendant Union and its representatives failed to meet with Plaintiff, failed to properly represent him, failed to assist him in drafting and processing his grievance, and failed to secure his reinstatement with back pay. Instead, through negligence and collusion with the Company, the Union arranged or condoned his termination.

(10) As a proximate result of the improper and illegal actions of both Defendant Company and Defendant Union in violating provisions of the collective bargaining agreement and in failing and refusing to render proper representation

to Plaintiff, Plaintiff has suffered irreparable damages, including lost income in the form of wages; lost benefits, including holiday pay; vacation pay; insurance; and pension contributions; and suffered mental anguish, loss of reputation, and emotional trauma.

Count II.

(1) Plaintiff hereby incorporates by reference all factual allegations contained in all paragraphs contained in Count I of this Complaint.

WHEREFORE, Plaintiff demands judgment against Defendant Company in the amount of $500,000, plus interest, costs, and attorney's fees. Further, Plaintiff requests an Order directing Defendant Company to immediately reinstate Plaintiff to his former position and to instruct all employees to work and cooperate with Plaintiff without harassment or ridicule.

Count III.

(1) Plaintiff hereby incorporates by reference all factual allegations contained in all paragraphs contained in Count I of this Complaint.

WHEREFORE, Plaintiff demands judgment against Defendant Union, both the International and its Local No. 14, in the sum of $250,000, plus interest, costs, and attorney's fees. Further, Plaintiff requests an Order compelling Defendant Union to properly, thoroughly, and vigorously represent Plaintiff in any further grievances that may be filed that relate, directly or indirectly, to his AIDS condition.

Respectfully submitted this ____ day of March, 1986.

_____
(Name, Address, and Telephone
Number of Attorney for
Plaintiff)

Document 9

Sample Unfair Labor Practice Charge To Be Filed with the NLRB by an Employee with AIDS against His Union

FORM EXEMPT UNDER 44 U.S.C. 3512

FORM NLRB 508 (8-53)	UNITED STATES OF AMERICA NATIONAL LABOR RELATIONS BOARD **CHARGE AGAINST LABOR ORGANIZATION OR ITS AGENTS**	**DO NOT WRITE IN THIS SPACE**	
		Case	Date Filed

INSTRUCTIONS: File an original and 3 copies of this charge and an additional copy for each organization, each local, and each individual named in item 1 with the NLRB Regional Director of the region in which the alleged unfair labor practice occurred or is occurring.

1. LABOR ORGANIZATION OR ITS AGENTS AGAINST WHICH CHARGE IS BROUGHT

a. Name RETAIL AND OFFICE WORKERS UNION, LOCAL NO. 14	b. Union Representative to contact John Smith

c. Telephone No. 123-1000	d. Address *(street, city, state and ZIP code)* 456 A Street, Indianapolis, Indiana

e. The above-named organization(s) or its agents has *(have)* engaged in and is *(are)* engaging in unfair labor practices within the meaning of section 8(b), subsection(s) *(list subsections)* _____ of the National Labor Relations Act, and these unfair labor practices are unfair practices affecting commerce within the meaning of the Act

2 Basis of the Charge *(be specific as to facts, names, addresses, plants involved, dates, places, etc.)*

The union has arbitrarily and unreasonably failed to process my grievance
involving the company's decision to terminate me because I have AIDS.
This action and inaction on the part of the union constitutes an unfair
labor practice within the meaning of the National Labor Relations Act.

3. Name of Employer John Doe Corporation	4. Telephone No. 789-2000

5. Location of plant involved *(street, city, state and ZIP code)* #1 Highway, Indianapolis, Indiana	6. Employer representative to contact Jack Jones

7. Type of establishment *(factory, mine, wholesaler, etc.)* factory	8. Identify principal product or service	9. Number of workers employed

10. Full name of party filing charge

John Johnson

11. Address of party filing charge *(street, city, state and ZIP code)* 1986 7th Street, Indianapolis, Indiana	12. Telephone No. 444-5555

13. DECLARATION

I declare that I have read the above charge and that the statements therein are true to the best of my knowledge and belief.

By _____
   (signature of representative or person making charge)   *(title or office, if any)*

Address _____
                                  (Telephone No.)   *(date)*

WILLFUL FALSE STATEMENTS ON THIS CHARGE CAN BE PUNISHED BY FINE AND IMPRISONMENT (U. S. CODE, TITLE 18, SECTION 1001)

Document 10

Labor Arbitration Award: Employee Fired for Refusing To Have Contact with a Person with AIDS

IN THE MATTER OF THE ARBITRATION BETWEEN

THE AMERICAN FEDERATION
OF STATE, COUNTY AND
MUNICIPAL EMPLOYEES,
COUNCIL 6,

CASE NO. 85M-XVI-600-3183

Union,

and

THE STATE OF MINNESOTA,
DEPARTMENT OF
CORRECTIONS,

DECISION AND AWARD
OF
ARBITRATOR

Employer.

APPEARANCES

For the Union:

Paul Larson
Business Representative
American Federation of State,
   County and Municipal
   Employees, Council 6
265 Lafayette Road South
St. Paul, MN 55107-1683

For the Employer:

Craig M. Ayers
Assistant State Negotiator
Claudia H. Dieter
Labor Relations Representative
State of Minnesota
Department of Employee Relations
Third Floor
Space Center Building
444 Lafayette Road
St. Paul, MN 55101

On October 23, 1985, in St. Paul, Minnesota, a hearing was held before Thomas P. Gallagher, Arbitrator, during which evidence was received concerning a grievance brought by the Union against the Employer. The grievance alleges that the Employer violated the labor agreement between the parties when it discharged the grievant, Andrew J. Triemert, Jr. Post-hearing briefs were received on November 18, 1985.

FACTS

The Department of Corrections of the State of Minnesota (hereafter, the "Employer") operates several prison facilities, one of which is located at Stillwater, Minnesota. That facility is a maximum security prison—the Employer's primary facility for the imprisonment of adult males who have been convicted of felonies. About 1200 prisoners are housed there.

The Union represents the security staff ("guards") employed at Stillwater Prison. At the time of his discharge on August 16, 1985, the grievant was a member of that staff. He was classified as a "Correctional Counselor III"—a leadworker position, also called "Sergeant" by the parties. He had been employed on the security staff of the Prison for about six years, starting in the entry classification, "Correctional Counselor I."

The inmates at Stillwater Prison reside in four cell blocks—A Hall, B Hall, C Hall and D Hall. The cell blocks are divided further into smaller units. D Hall has three units. Prisoners who are in protective custody reside in one of them, and in another, those who are taking college credits. Newly incarcerated prisoners are housed in the third unit in D Hall—the Receiving and Orientation Unit (called by the parties, the "R & O Unit"). They remain in the R & O Unit for about six weeks. During that time, they are segregated from the rest of the Prison population as they are being introduced to life in the Prison, leaving the R & O Unit after the first three weeks and then only for meals and recreation.

During the morning of August 8, 1985, a physician from the St. Paul-Ramsey General Hospital (the hospital used by the Employer to attend inmates of the Prison) informed the Prison's administrative staff that an inmate who had been housed in the R & O Unit since July 11, 1985, had been diagnosed as having contracted the virus that causes Acquired Immune Deficiency Syndrome ("AIDS"). The inmate did not exhibit the symptoms of AIDS itself—failure of substantial weakening of the immune system—but he was experiencing the lesser, non-fatal symptoms—fever and swelling of glands—that are caused by the same virus and are known as "AIDS Related Complex" (also called "ARC" or "Pre-AIDS").

The Warden of the Prison, Robert A. Erickson, became aware that rumors about the case were circulating among the inmates. Because he was concerned that the inmates and staff of the Prison might react emotionally to the rumors, he decided to issue two memoranda—one to the inmates and one to the staff.

At about 11:45 a.m., on August 8, 1985, he had the following memorandum distributed to all inmates:

> Within the last few days our medical staff here and at Ramsey have diagnosed an inmate as having what is known as pre-AIDS. Dr. DeLaRosa has told me that this means only that the man is pre-disposed to develop AIDS, and that at this time *he does not have AIDS.* Dr. DeLaRosa also stated that there is no danger of contagion, but as an added precaution, we will place the inmate in isolation in the Health Services Unit at Oak Park Heights until his release on August 26, 1985.
>
> By now most of you are aware of the AIDS epidemic that is spreading in certain segments of the civilian population. Specifically, individuals at risk are homosexual and bisexual men and intravenous drug users (mainliners).
>
> Fortunately, AIDS can be prevented from being an epidemic if the population understands their responsibility and practices some simple preventative measures:
>
> 1. *Abstain from all homosexual activity!* Because with penile penetration there is damage to rectal tissue, which causes bleeding, potentially transmitting the disease.

2. *Do not use drugs, especially IV drugs.* AIDS is spread in the same way that Serum Hepatitis is. Needles from syringes and the needles used for tatooing have been responsible for most of the hepatitis contracted in correctional institutions.

3. *Do not share your personal items, i.e., toothbrushes, drags off cigarettes, etc. with anyone!*

No one really knows all the ways AIDS is transmitted, so be careful. Wash your hands regularly and practice good hygiene.

. . . . (Emphasis in the original.)

At about 1:30 p.m., on August 8, 1985, Warden Erickson had the following memorandum distributed to the Prison's staff:

AIDS has become a rather scary problem, and rightly so. We all hear the same information from the media, that the problem will become a lot worse before it gets better. It presents a special problem for prisons where the chances of the disease spreading is increased due to homosexual activity, one of the known ways it spreads. Within the last few days our medical staff here and at Ramsey have diagnosed an inmate as having what is called pre-AIDS. Dr. DeLaRosa has told me that this means only that the man is pre-disposed to develop AIDS, and that at this time *he does not have AIDS.* Dr. DeLaRosa also stated that there is no danger of contagion, but as an added precaution, we will place the inmate in isolation in the Health Services Unit at Oak Park Heights until his release on August 26, 1985.

There is no doubt that as time passes, we will be seeing more cases of this type and also of AIDS itself. Staff who must work with such cases will be kept fully informed and will be advised of necessary precautions. (Emphasis in the original.)

The grievant's assignment on August 8, 1985, was to the third shift—from 2:30 p.m. to 10:30 p.m. He did not receive a copy of Warden Erickson's memorandum to the staff, but at the start of his shift when he arrived at B Hall-East, where he was assigned to work, four inmates who had just returned from work showed him the memorandum that Erickson had distributed to the inmates. According to the grievant's testimony, they asked the grievant "what he was going to do about it."

The grievant read the Warden's memorandum and went to see his immediate supervisor, Lieutenant Marvin R. Merth. The grievant expressed his concern about the risk of AIDS contamination during the conduct of "pat searches." When conducting a pat search, a guard must run his hands over the clothing of the inmate being searched and attempt to feel for any weapons or contraband that the inmate may try to conceal. Although the Union offered some evidence challenging the regularity of the requirement, the Employer established that it routinely requires the security staff to pat search inmates as they enter the cell blocks where they reside upon returning from work, from meals and from other activities that take place away from the cell blocks.

The grievant asked Merth if it were not possible to use metal detectors as a substitute for pat searches. Merth told the grievant that there was nothing to worry about and that he had been pat searching inmates all day. The grievant could observe the other guards on duty at the entrance to B Hall and saw that they were not conducting pat searches as the inmates returned from work.

At about the time the shift began, Warden Erickson directed that the Registered Nurses employed at the Prison give instruction to the staff about AIDS, and at about 2:35 p.m., one of the nurses, Scott Bennett, went to B Hall and talked with the staff for about ten minutes. The grievant was present during that meeting. Erickson then directed that the inmates be locked in their cells so that the staff could be assembled in the Chapel for training by the nurses.

The grievant attended the twenty-minute training session in the Chapel. Bennett showed the staff a four-page newsletter about AIDS published by the Minnesota Department of Health. He used the newsletter in his lecture to point out the risks of contracting AIDS and the precautions recommended for avoidance of the disease. He told the staff that the inmate who had been diagnosed as having ARC had been segregated in the R & O Unit, and that he was no longer an inmate at the Prison.

Bennett pointed out that people of both sexes and of all ages had contracted the disease, but that it was concentrated in certain high risk groups—notably, homosexuals and those who have had an exchange of blood. He explained that the disease is not transmitted through casual contact, but by an exchange of body fluids—semen and blood, and possibly saliva. Copies of the newsletter were placed at the front of the Chapel, but the grievant testified that he did not receive one. The grievant asked Bennett, "how can it be guaranteed that I'm not going to contract this disease and take it home?" Bennett responded that he should avoid sexual contact and the use of intravenous needles. Another member of the staff asked whether the staff should use gloves in dealing with inmates and Bennett responded that gloves were unnecessary—that they were not even used by the nurses in the Health Service except when examining the genitals or rectum.

At the end of the meeting, Warden Erickson stood up and asked if there were anyone present who was not willing to do his job. No one responded. The grievant worked the balance of his shift on August 8, 1985, without incident.

Warden Erickson ordered the training of the guards about AIDS in part because he had heard from his supervisory staff that some guards had expressed concern that pat searching inmates might create a health risk. On the evening of August 8, 1985, Warden Erickson instructed his Associate Warden that he was authorized to suspend for the evening the requirement that guards conduct pat searches, if they objected to conducting them. Erickson testified that no such objection was made. The grievant testified that neither he nor any of the guards on duty in B Hall were conducting pat searches that evening.

On Friday, August 9, 1985, the grievant arrived at the Prison at about 2:10 p.m., twenty minutes before the start of his shift. A few minutes later, he went to Merth's office and asked him if it would be necessary to conduct pat searches. He told Merth that he was "scared to death of this virus," and he again suggested the use of metal detectors. The grievant also suggested that a general lock-up be imposed so that, with the elimination of inmate circulation within the Prison, the need to search would be eliminated.

Merth told the grievant that he had to conduct pat searches. The grievant said that he feared for his life and that Merth would have to give him a direct order to pat search the inmates. Merth ordered him to do so, but the grievant said he could not. Merth asked the grievant if he understood the consequences of his refusal, and the grievant said he did. Merth asked the grievant if he had "listened to the nurses," and the grievant said that he had, but that he did not believe their explanation. Merth testified that he was surprised by the grievant's refusal because he "had always been a pretty good Sergeant."

Merth asked the grievant to accompany him to the office of Lieutenant Andrew G. Fink, who was then the Watch Lieutenant—the officer in charge of the Prison during the evening shift. There, they met with Fink and with the Union Steward, Sergeant Terry Lusk. The grievant and Lusk conferred briefly outside the office and then met with Merth and Fink. Merth explained to Fink the circumstances of the grievant's refusal to conduct pat searches, and Merth and the grievant had substantially the same conversation they had had in Merth's office. Merth repeated his order to the grievant to conduct the searches. The grievant said, "I'm not going to do it; I fear for my life." The grievant did not ask for any protective equipment. Shortly after the meeting in Fink's office, Warden Erickson was informed of the grievant's refusal to pat search inmates. He suspended the grievant and sent him home, instructing him to return on Monday, August 12, 1985, for a meeting about the matter.

Fink testified that the other guards who were on duty during the evening shift of August 9, 1985, conducted pat searches without objection. He noticed that one was not doing a thorough job, but Fink told him he had to do the search correctly, and he complied.

On Sunday, August 11, 1985, Warden Erickson learned that the inmates were planning a mass sick call for the next morning. He decided to order a "lock up" of the institution, and did so with the following memorandum to all inmates:

> As I have indicated to you in my last memo, I had no intentions of locking up unless something happened that made it necessary. I think now that there is enough apprehension about AIDS among both the inmates and staff, that a lock-up is necessary while we work out some procedures, and make further information available to everybody.
>
> As our Doctor indicated to the media, our medical consultants at Ramsey have already met, and will continue to work on the development of a plan designed to provide maximum understanding of the problem, as well as one that will provide maximum protection to the health of both inmates and staff. He thought that might take about two weeks. I will urge them to complete it sooner than that, so that we can resume normal routine as soon as possible. . . .

On Monday, August 12, 1985, the grievant and several Union representatives met with Warden Erickson and several representatives of the Prison administration to discuss the grievant's status. Warden Erickson testified that he had not yet decided what discipline to administer. They reviewed the grievant's refusal to pat search inmates on the previous Friday. The grievant said that he feared for his life and that he did not accept the nurse's explanation about the risk of contracting the disease. He was concerned because he had cuts on his hands from work he did at home.

Warden Erickson asked the grievant if he was ready to return to work, and the grievant responded that he was ready to do so if he could wear gloves. Erickson said he was reluctant to permit the use of gloves because he thought their presence might increase fear in the institution and because his medical advisors had told him that wearing gloves was not necessary. The meeting ended without a decision about the discipline that would be administered, but the grievant's refusal to conduct pat searches without gloves continued.

Later the same day, Monday, August 12, 1985, Warden Erickson received a call from the Associate Warden and another call from an administrative assistant. Both of them said that they had received inquiries from guards about the use of gloves when pat searching inmates. Warden Erickson then decided to permit the use of gloves during pat searches. He testified that "quite a few" guards began to pat search while wearing the disposable gloves available from the Food Services Department of the Prison, but at the time of the hearing only one guard continued to use gloves for pat searches.

Warden Erickson consulted with members of his administrative staff and decided to discharge the grievant. On Wednesday, August 14, 1985, Erickson sent the following letter to the grievant informing him of that decision:

> I have completed my investigation of the August 9, 1985 incident in which you refused direct orders from your supervisor. Based upon this investigation you are advised that you will be terminated from your position as a Corrections Counselor III of this facility at the end of the regular business day, Friday, August 16, 1985. . . . This action has been taken as a result of your violation of institutional rules governing Standards of Conduct—Insubordination.

> Specifically, on Friday, August 9, 1985, while in the office of your supervisor, CCIV Marvin Merth, you stated that you would not pat search inmates. You were given a direct order from your supervisor to pat search inmates, which you refused to obey . . . [The letter describes the grievant's subsequent refusal to pat search on the same day, in Fink's office.]

> On August 12, 1985, . . . you reaffirmed that you refused direct orders from your supervisor to conduct pat searches on August 9, 1985. You again stated you were not satisfied with the explanation given by Health Services staff regarding AIDS and "feared for your life" regarding the danger of AIDS in the facility.

> Your refusal of direct orders constituted gross misconduct and clearly jeopardized the overall security and safety of the facility . . .

> Your action of disobeying direct orders jeopardized the continuity of proper supervision and chain-of-command procedures. You are a well experienced employee in this facility and know full well the nature and necessity of a paramilitary operation and requirement to "obey the order and question it later."

> In addition, being a lead-worker, your position carries the responsibility of providing direction to your fellow staff members. Your refusal of direct orders has the potential of disrupting the chain-of-command function as well

as security functions. By this action, the security of the facility and the safety and welfare of staff and inmates were endangered.

Your actions of insubordination will not be tolerated and, therefore, in the best interest of all involved, this termination is enacted. . . .

On Monday, August 19, 1985, Warden Erickson sent a memorandum to all staff and inmates, notifying them that the lock-up would end the next day. He also noted that Dr. Michael T. Osterholm, the State Epidemiologist, had met with the administrative staff on the previous Friday, August 16, 1985, and that he had prepared a video tape on AIDS for viewing by the staff and inmates.

Dr. Osterholm gave testimony, a summary of which follows, about the nature of AIDS and the ways in which it may be contracted. The disease is caused by a virus. Thus far, only about 10% to 20% of those who carry the virus experience fatal damage to the immune system—the symptoms that have come to be known as AIDS. An additional 30% of those who carry the virus experience the non-fatal symptoms of ARC, described above. The virus may be transmitted, however, by anyone who carries it—even those who have neither the symptoms of AIDS nor of ARC.

The number of people from whom the virus may be contracted, therefore, far exceeds the number who have actually developed symptoms. Fortunately, the virus is not easily passed by one who carries it. The virus passes with body fluids— blood, semen and the mucous fluids of the sexual organs. At one time, it appeared that the virus could be passed in saliva, but the latest knowledge indicates that if such passage is possible the quantity of saliva passed must be substantial and contact with it must be prolonged. The virus cannot be passed by mere touching of the kind that occurs when a pat search is conducted, even if the one searching has cuts on his hands.

DECISION

The Employer's brief emphasizes the usually reasonable requirement that an employee who questions a supervisor's order should, nevertheless, perform as directed and have the propriety of the order determined later by use of the grievance procedure. The Union argues that this case falls within the exception to the rule—that an order that presents immediate danger to the employee need not be followed before its propriety is determined.

The Union urges that, in the present case, the standard for measuring whether there was such danger should be, not an objective, scientific measure of the risk of contracting the virus, but the grievant's perception of that risk. The Union would use this subjective measure of risk because it alleges that the Employer was at least partly responsible for the grievant's exaggerated fear of the disease.

According to the Union, the Employer contributed to the grievant's fear in several ways. The Union alleges that the Employer did not respond to its September 15, 1983, request to develop policies designed to protect the guards—by furnishing protective equipment and by identifying prisoners who carried the disease. Further, the Union contends that the grievant's fear of the disease was increased by the Warden's August 8, 1985, memorandum to the inmates, which, contrary to the nurse's advice, implied that the disease could be contracted by casual contact; thus, the memorandum warned:

Do not share your personal items, i.e., toothbrushes, drags off cigarettes, etc. with anyone!

No one really knows all the ways AIDS is transmitted, so be careful. Wash your hands regularly and practice good hygiene.

The Union also argues that the Employer's decision to discharge the grievant is not consistent with previous discipline for similar cases of insubordination. The Union notes the short suspensions administered in the following two cases. The first such case occurred in September, 1984. The Employer suspended a guard for five days for disobedience described in the letter of suspension:

This action is taken as a result of your violation of institutional rules governing Standards of Conduct—Disobeying a Direct Order.

Specifically, on September 11, 1984, you were given orders by CCIII Gary Baggott to supervise PCU [Protective Custody Unit] inmates at Recreation. You initially accepted the assignment, but later called back to CCIII Baggott questioning the order and that the assignment should have been given to a lesser officer in a reserve status. You again were instructed to supervise PCU inmates at Recreation by CCIII Baggott. When you were to relieve a fellow officer, you refused to accept the keys to Recreation and a radio, and refused to escort PCU inmates to the Recreation area.

At that time, CCIII Mattoon ordered you to take PCU assignment, which you refused. He again ordered you to escort the inmates to PCU, and he also advised you to address any appeals regarding this complaint after completing the assignment. At this time, you again refused to accompany the PCU inmates to Recreation and another officer had to be assigned at that time.

The second suspension for disobedience noted by the Union was based on an occurrence in July, 1985. The Employer suspended a guard for two days for the following conduct, as described in the letter of suspension:

This action is taken as a result of your violation of institutional rules governing Standards of Conduct—Disobeying an Order.

Specifically, on July 11, 1985, you were given instructions from your supervisor to fill an armory ammunition order. You stated to your supervisor that you did not have time and would not fill the ammunition order. Your supervisor explained that the order would not take more than a few minutes; that you did not have to do it immediately; and that it could be done anytime between July 11, 1985, and July 14, 1985. You replied to your supervisor, "No, I'm not going to do it, you do it."

At that time your supervisor stated that she was your supervisor and that you were to obey her instructions. You again refused and began to walk out of the office. You were called back into the office and given a direct order to fill the ammunition request. You replied, "I don't care, I am not going to do it, you do it."

The Employer contends that the decision to suspend in these two cases was appropriate, because in neither case did the refusal to obey affect the security of the institution. The Employer views the grievant's refusal to pat search inmates as far more serious because searching inmates is essential to the security of the institution. The Employer compares the grievant's disobedience to another previous case in which it decided to discharge a guard who, when ordered to do so, refused to reveal the name of an inmate involved in a possible security breach within the Prison. Although an arbitrator reinstated that guard without back pay after eight and one-half months, the Employer argues correctly that its choice of discipline was consistent with its choice in the present case. In both cases, when it considered the disobedience of an order to be a threat to the security of the Prison, it selected discharge as the appropriate discipline.

I would agree with the Employer that discharge of the grievant was appropriate discipline for his refusal to pat search, except for two mitigating factors. *First,* I agree with the Union that the Employer was at least partly responsible for the grievant's exaggerated fear of contracting the disease. It is true that Nurse Bennett provided the grievant with correct information—that the disease could not be contracted easily and that it could not be contracted by casual contact. The grievant, however, had just read the Warden's memorandum, which recommended against the sharing of cigarettes and advised the washing of hands and the use of good hygiene. Further, the memorandum warned, "No one really knows all the ways AIDS is transmitted, so be careful."

These statements support the grievant's reluctance to believe what the nurses had told him. No doubt, Warden Erickson made these statements because he was uncertain, just as was the grievant, both about the manner by which the virus could pass and about the reliability of current medical knowledge. Although Warden Erickson quickly changed his uncertain opinion about both matters, the grievant did not. That the Warden thought more effort would be needed to provide accurate information is apparent from his continuation of the lock-up until August 20, and from his provision of Dr. Osterholm's educational video tape to inmates and staff on August 19.

The *second* factor that should mitigate the penalty for the grievant's refusal to pat search arises out of the meeting between the grievant and the Warden on August 12, 1985. Warden Erickson testified that at the time of that meeting he had not decided on the appropriate discipline. He asked the grievant if he was ready to go back to work, i.e., to pat search inmates in the usual routine. By that question, Warden Erickson indicated that the grievant would not be discharged for his refusal to pat search on the previous Friday if he would change his mind. More importantly, the question also indicated that on Monday Warden Erickson did not regard the Friday refusal to pat search as an offense requiring discharge.

The grievant's response to the Warden's question was that he would pat search inmates if he could wear gloves. The matter would have been concluded then, without the grievant's discharge, if his meeting with the Warden had taken place a few hours later, after the Warden decided to permit guards to wear gloves when pat searching. Presumably, that decision, made in response to requests from guards, was made, not to avoid the risk of their contamination, but as an accommodation to their fear.

Even though the meeting with the grievant had ended before the Warden decided to permit the use of gloves, the Employer's position in this matter would have suffered no detriment if the same permission had been extended to the grievant several hours after the meeting or even the next day. At the meeting, the Warden was willing to conclude the matter without discharge, indicating that he was willing to treat the grievant's actions on Friday as something less than a dischargeable threat to security. Moreover, the grievant did nothing at the meeting itself or during the time between the meeting and the decision to permit the use of gloves that could constitute a new threat to security. After the meeting, when the decision was made to permit the use of gloves, the grievant's unwarranted fears could have been accommodated, just as were the fears of the other guards.

I conclude that the two factors I have described mitigate the grievant's fault and justify reduction of his discharge to a lesser discipline. Of course, the grievant should have obeyed the order to pat search without condition, but the fear that caused his refusal of the order was at least reinforced by the inaccurate memorandum of August 8, 1985. He should be permitted reinstatement to his position—something he would have obtained if the August 12, 1985, meeting had occurred after the Warden decided to permit the use of gloves. I do not award back pay, because granting the grievant such relief would reward his misconduct.

AWARD

The grievance is sustained. The Employer shall reinstate the grievant to his position without loss of seniority and without back pay.

December 10, 1985   _____

                                         Thomas P. Gallagher, Arbitrator

Appendix E
Sources of Further Information Concerning AIDS

———

Sources for Information about AIDS

Federal Public Health Service   Centers for Disease Control
1-800-342-2437 or 1-800-443-0366   1-800-447-AIDS

Northern California
1-800-FOR-AIDS

Southern California
1-800-922-AIDS

To obtain the Surgeon General's Report on AIDS, write:
Inter-America Research
1200 E. North Henry Street
Alexandria, VA 22314

To obtain a pamphlet entitled "Answers about AIDS," write:
AIDS Report
American Council on Science and Health
47 Maple Street
Summit, New Jersey 07901

Inter-America Research also has the following pamphlets: Gay and Bi-Sexual
Men and AIDS; Caring for the AIDS Patient at Your Home; If Your Test for
Antibody to the AIDS Virus Is Positive . . . ; AIDS and Children; Information
for Parents of School Age Children; AIDS and Children: Information for
Teachers and School Officials; AIDS and Your Job—Are There Risks; and
Coping with AIDS.

Index

About the Author

W illiam F. Banta is a director and shareholder with the law firm of Kullman, Inman, Bee & Downing, a professional corporation based in New Orleans, Louisiana. Founded in 1946, the Kullman firm represents management in labor matters before the National Labor Relations Board, Equal Employment Opportunity Commission, Occupational Safety and Health Administration, and both state and federal courts.

Mr. Banta, who graduated from Northwestern University in 1965 and The George Washington University School of Law in 1968, has advised both private and public employers on employment and labor relations matters during his nineteen years of management practice. A significant portion of his work is on behalf of health care facilities, and he is currently a director of U.S. Health Corporation, a holding company for several hospitals, with headquarters in Columbus, Ohio. He is a member of the American and Louisiana State Bar Associations, the American Bar Association Forum Committee on Health Care, and the American Academy of Hospital Attorneys of the American Hospital Association.